Time to Shake Up the Primary Curriculum

Time to Shake Up the Primary Curriculum

A step-by-step guide to creating a global, diverse and inclusive school

Sarah Wordlaw

BLOOMSBURY EDUCATION
LONDON OXFORD NEW YORK NEW DELHI SYDNEY

BLOOMSBURY EDUCATION
Bloomsbury Publishing Plc
50 Bedford Square, London, WC1B 3DP, UK
29 Earlsfort Terrace, Dublin 2, Ireland

BLOOMSBURY, BLOOMSBURY EDUCATION and the Diana logo are
trademarks of Bloomsbury Publishing Plc

First published in Great Britain, 2023 by Bloomsbury Publishing Plc

Text copyright © Sarah Wordlaw, 2023

Sarah Wordlaw has asserted her right under the Copyright, Designs and Patents Act, 1988,
to be identified as Author of this work

Material from Department for Education and Ofsted reports used in this publication
are approved under an Open Government Licence: www.nationalarchives.gov.uk/doc/
open-government-licence/version/3/

Every effort has been made to trace copyright holders and to obtain their
permission for the use of copyright material. The publisher would be grateful to
be notified of any errors or omissions and corrections can be incorporated
into future reprints or editions of this book.

Bloomsbury Publishing Plc does not have any control over, or responsibility for, any
third-party websites referred to or in this book. All internet addresses given in this
book were correct at the time of going to press. The author and publisher regret any
inconvenience caused if addresses have changed or sites have ceased to exist,
but can accept no responsibility for any such changes

All rights reserved. No part of this publication may be reproduced or transmitted
in any form or by any means, electronic or mechanical, including photocopying,
recording, or any information storage or retrieval system, without prior
permission in writing from the publishers

A catalogue record for this book is available from the British Library

ISBN: PB: 978-1-8019-9119-3; ePDF: 978-1-8019-9121-6; ePub: 978-1-8019-9122-3

2 4 6 8 10 9 7 5 3 1 (paperback)

Typeset by Newgen KnowledgeWorks Pvt. Ltd., Chennai, India
Printed and bound in the UK by CPI Group (UK) Ltd, Croydon, CR0 4YY

MIX
Paper | Supporting
responsible forestry
FSC
www.fsc.org   FSC® C013604

To find out more about our authors and books visit www.bloomsbury.com
and sign up for our newsletters

This book is dedicated to my dad,
who taught me to rise up.

Contents

Acknowledgements ix
Foreword x
Introduction xii
How to use this book xviii

Part 1 Analysing the current curriculum 1

1 Where are you now? Auditing your current curriculum 3

2 Where do you want to be? Setting whole-school intent for new curriculum and key research 17

Part 2 Shaping the curriculum 27

3 Literacy: Book choices with different voices 29

4 History: Making the unseen seen 55

5 Geography: A global view, representative and varied 77

6 The arts: Art and design, music and drama 95

7 STEM: Science, maths and technology 119

8 Physical education 137

9 SMSC: Collective worship, assemblies and charity work 151

Part 3 Remapping the curriculum 169

10 Mapmaker, mapmaker, make me a map… A practical guide to mapping out curriculum 171

11 Learning environments: Inside, outside and dress code 181

12 Implementation and monitoring impact of your wonderful new curriculum 191

A final word 201
Appendices: Curriculum maps 203
Further reading 245
Bibliography 249
Index 257

Acknowledgements

I would like to thank all the people who supported and inspired me. My lovely mum, Cory, Lisa and the wonderful Francesca, for their kindness and patience. The amazing practitioners I have worked alongside and, of course, the incredible young people I have had the privilege of teaching.

Foreword

It was in 2011 when a fresh-faced Sarah Wordlaw first entered the school I was teaching in. Like most new teachers, she was full of ideas – an enthusiastic ball of energy ready to take on the world. The sparkle in her eye told me that she wanted to make a difference, wanted to be the teacher whom children reminisced about fondly in years to come. As leaders, we see this regularly. Each year a new batch of energised teachers enter our schools with that same sparkle. Unfortunately, what we also see is this energy and excitement fade as the weight of the task takes hold, and that sparkle starts to lose its shine. Teachers who wanted to make a difference become resigned to just getting through the day. Those who once dreamed of inspiring the next generation to greatness now dream only of finally finishing the never-ending list of tasks.

Thankfully, every so often we find an educator capable of keeping the dream alive – an educator who is unapologetically driven and believes that, as teachers, we are responsible for the next generation. Sarah is that leader. Not only has her sparkle remained intact but, as the years have passed, she has strengthened her conviction and relentless ambition to design and implement a curriculum that does more than just tick boxes. Sarah sees the diverse curriculum as non-negotiable and her schools have consistently wrestled with what many leaders put in the 'too hard' basket; this has led to transformative education for the young people she works with. Throughout her career she has pushed colleagues to have uncomfortable conversations, to unpick what diversity is in a modern world and to enrich the offer within their settings.

I've been an executive headteacher in London for the past five years, and I know all too well the challenge of designing a courageously diverse curriculum. Pressures on leaders to meet key performance indicators have resulted in narrowed curriculum offers, which has in turn led to dry, joyless lessons designed to jump statistically through metaphorical hoops and over public relations hurdles. Smart school leaders have learned that, to avoid the punitive and public criticism of poor league table performance, they need to lead their schools with a new focus, designed to deliver results that meet the publishable requirements of their political overlords. In order to keep up, schools have begun concentrating their efforts on getting students with Ds to become Cs, abandoning Es and neglecting Bs and As because they have already passed the required level. Even our youngest children in primary schools are being labelled and overlooked, as adults declare around them, 'They will never reach the required standard; just concentrate on those that might.' Booster classes proliferate to progress children newly described as 'on the cusp', whilst those who are more or less able are left to run out the time until the test. It would be almost impossible to design a system more efficiently ruthless in its ability to disengage learners, dismay and demotivate a generation of teachers or disempower a future workforce. And all of this had already begun before the added complication of the post-Covid world in which we find ourselves today.

So where does this leave our young people? We simply toss them out into a world full of long-held prejudice and injustice, for which they are grossly under-prepared, and hope that they find their way. The book you're about to read gives us hope that there is another way. For the past 11 years, Sarah has developed her skills in curriculum design and has a proven track record of success. She makes a compelling case for challenging ourselves to design a curriculum that is brave and bold. A curriculum that doesn't just pay lip service to creating a more enlightened generation, but does it by weaving exposure into the everyday lives of children. The book is more than just a viewpoint or collection of ideas; it's a toolkit, a step-by-step guide to creating a more diverse curriculum. Wherever you are on your journey, this book can provide the extra inspiration and guidance to take you to the next step.

Diversifying the curriculum is not progressive or innovative; it should not be viewed as something that schools do once the rest of the curriculum is set. It should, and must, be your starting point – the pillars on which you build your curriculum. I will be asking all my leaders to read this book and learn from the experience that Sarah brings to the page.

By following the guidance set out in the pages within, you can ensure that every single child in your school can not only see themselves within that curriculum but will be exposed to the beauty of difference, as they become the future that we all need.

Pia Longman,
executive headteacher

Introduction

The very fact that you, an educator, is reading this book brings hope for a better future for education. It means that you're interested in questioning and developing the curriculum that you deliver. Interested in continually pursuing inclusive education for young people. Interested in opening up avenues and thought processes that are yet to be explored and challenging current perspectives. Education is powerful; it is a chance to change life opportunities for young people, in particular those from marginalised communities. As educators, we too are on a learning journey with developing our understanding of the world, our subject knowledge and our own ability to critically think in order to deliver the absolute best for those whom we teach. Diversity, inclusion and visibility in the classroom is a constant journey; there is no end point where you wake up and excitedly exclaim, 'Hey, I'm fully diverse and inclusive now!'. We all have our own biases – known and unknown – based upon our own experiences of life and personal education. It is important to be able to become more self-aware, to question, discuss and respectfully challenge each other on thoughts, beliefs and understandings of the world, in order for us to grow as individuals and, furthermore, educators.

It's our responsibility (and privilege) to ensure that the next generation is more enlightened than we are currently, to teach young people that there are **no outsiders** in our society, irrespective of race, disability, sexuality, religion or gender identity. To fight for institutional change to both recognise and eradicate discriminatory beliefs. It is a fact that no child is born racist, homophobic or sexist. These are behaviours that children learn early on, from outside influences – another reason why diverse and inclusive teaching is imperative to both build and change our society for the better (Wordlaw, 2019).

Why is this needed?

In 2020, the death of George Floyd rallied a resurgence in the ferocity of the Black Lives Matter movement, sparking more conversations around the issue of institutionalised racism in our society – both globally and nationally.

As a mixed race person, in my own primary schooling I was one of very few non-White people (I use this particular term because this is how I personally identify *myself*) and I always felt outside of the 'norm'. I never saw myself represented in any learning that was taught, with the exception of a tokenistic Black History Month assembly once per year, which sparked other children asking whether my family came from a 'poor country in Africa' and whether they could touch my hair.

Twenty-five years later, as a senior leader and practitioner based in South London schools with majority Black cohorts, I have always found it patronising to celebrate Black culture tokenistically and have personally found a lack of *deliberate* diverse and inclusive teaching.

I was interested in whether other teachers from marginalised communities had similar experiences within their education – not just related to race, but also sexuality, gender, disability, religion and culture. Surveying other practitioners, it was fascinating (and quite upsetting) to read other experiences that mirrored my own: a sense of feeling 'othered' (whether deliberate or not) and a general frustration at currently not delivering as well-rounded a curriculum as could be taught now. One teacher reflected on being told that AIDS was 'given to the world by Black people' in a secondary science lesson. Perhaps the most shocking were some of the reflections on current practice and curricula, and some battles with adapting and developing more inclusive practice. Many schools – even though it is statutory to teach – won't even touch on discussing sexuality and the fact that different families exist. One teacher requested a book about Malala to be on the literacy long-term plan and was met with a 'How will the White children relate to this?' response, which is simply astounding. The bottom line is that racially literate teachers will teach in a racially literate way – will include lessons, discussions and opportunities for reflection in all subjects. Some subjects lend themselves to open discussions about race, disability and sexuality – like PSHE, literacy and citizenship – whereas others can be more challenging (for example, maths).

What is racial literacy?

'Biases are the stories we make up about people before we know who they actually are.' (Myers, 2014)

Racial literacy is having the awareness, knowledge, skills and dispositions to talk openly about racism and race. This includes having a rich vocabulary of appropriate and respectful terms like *race, racism, prejudice, upstander, ally* and so on. It means being able to notice racism or racist views when they occur and being equipped with strategies to cope with and challenge them. It is an understanding of the roles that race and racism hold in our society.

There are many – from both White communities and others – who may feel afraid or uncomfortable talking about race. Perhaps they feel that they 'don't see colour' – however, this is unhelpful. It is important to see colour – to accept and notice that we have both similarities and differences and that the White experience is vastly different from the experience of the global majority. Some may believe that if they teach in a place that is predominantly White, there is less need for discussions on race. However, this is incorrect! Racially homogeneous schools can and do benefit from increased racial literacy as much as culturally diverse schools. This is the time to step up and increase our racial literacy as a profession; students from all races need us to do so (Howard, 2020).

> 'Racial literacy and a commitment to anti-racism should be considered a key competency for entering the teaching profession.' (Joseph-Salisbury, 2020, p. 22)

Should diverse teaching only be taught in 'diverse' schools?

All schools, regardless of their cohort, should teach from actively anti-racist, anti-homophobic, anti-ableist and anti-xenophobic perspectives (to name a few!). This is whether you work in a school within predominantly White communities or predominantly more racially diverse communities. In addition, Dr Remi Joseph-Salisbury states that 'white teachers should engage with concepts of white privilege, white power, white complicity and white supremacy, in order to reflect on their own racialised positions' (2020, p. 22). School leaders must continually cultivate racially literate teaching to challenge such perspectives, as a whole-school approach. Teaching forces must also strive to be diverse in order for teams to be exposed to different perspectives, improve cultural engagement and open dialogues. These ultimately promote creativity and, with enhanced engagement from children and families, pupil performance also improves. Teaching a diverse curriculum benefits not only the children from within those categories, but *everyone*.

What the research says

The proof is in the facts. It is a fact that discrimination – both conscious and unconscious – is still extremely prevalent in our society. It is a barrier that many face, and is one that we as educators have a chance to do something about.

What the research says

'Exclusion rates for black Caribbean students in English schools are up to six times higher than those of their white peers in some local authorities…' (McIntyre et al., 2021)

'Gypsy, Roma and Traveller children were also excluded at much higher rates, with Roma children nine times more likely to be suspended in some areas. And exclusion rates for mixed-race white and black Caribbean students were more than four times higher than their white peers in several local authorities.' (McIntyre et al., 2021)

'Nearly half of lesbian, gay, bi and trans pupils (45 per cent) – including 64 per cent of trans pupils – are bullied for being LGBT at school.' (Stonewall, 2017, p. 6)

'The majority of LGBT pupils – 86 per cent – regularly hear phrases such as "that's so gay" or "you're so gay" in school.' (Stonewall, 2017, p. 6)

'Seven in ten LGBT pupils (68 per cent) report that teachers or school staff only "sometimes" or "never" challenge homophobic, biphobic and transphobic language when they hear it.' (Stonewall, 2017, p. 6)

'In the year ending March 2020, the Crime Survey for England and Wales estimated 1.6 million women aged 16 to 74 years in England and Wales experienced domestic abuse, around 7% of the female population.' (Office for National Statistics, 2021)

'Children with SEND from low-income families have poorer educational outcomes – whether in terms of academic achievement, wellbeing or exclusion rates – and these outcomes have a direct effect on their earning potential later in life.' (Shaw et al., 2016, p. 12)

'Gypsy/Traveller children, mostly either Gypsy/Roma or Travellers of Irish Heritage, have the lowest results of any minority ethnic group and are the group most at risk in the education system.' (Rashid and Tikly, 2010, p. 8)

'Black pupils and those from Pakistani and Bangladeshi backgrounds achieve poorer examination results than do other groups.' (Rashid and Tikly, 2010, p. 8)

'95% of young Black British people have witnessed racist language in education. More than half of males said they hear racist language in school "all the time".' (YMCA, 2020)

Personal experience

I have had two recent experiences that have highlighted for me the importance of writing this book. Firstly, I have been applying for my first headship and have been invited to many interviews (with varying levels of success!). In a recent interview, in a London school that was looking to develop its curriculum and deliver racial literacy training, I was given the feedback, upon being successful, that they felt that I brought 'colour and flavour' to the day but I simply was not experienced enough. Now there was no deliberate malice in this comment; however, in a school advertising for someone to champion diverse practice and racial literacy, I feel that this was clumsy and, quite frankly, inappropriate feedback. Feedback should support and develop someone's practice and approach to interviewing, not adjectives to describe that person. I also asked myself: did they/would they give the feedback of 'colour and flavour' to my White counterparts? Who knows.

The second experience was in the summer term of 2022 when I took my Year 6s away for their school journey to a well-known outdoor experience centre. One of the activities was a campfire, led by the instructors, involving storytelling and songs. When the instructors announced that the theme of the evening was 'A Journey to Africa', I had a shiver of nervousness and looked over to my colleagues to see whether it was just me. It wasn't. The instructors then went on to tell a story of a person from England taking a 'journey to Africa', via ship, and arriving at a 'banana plantation'. They then sang a song about this. Upon arriving at said 'banana plantation', the voyager came across 'a man who lived in a shack, who made medicines'. They then sang a song about this. My colleagues and I were incredulous about the content of this 'campfire singsong', but before we could muster any words to say to each other, one of the children had yelled out, 'Africa is actually a continent, what country specifically do you mean?'. I'm not sure that I have ever been prouder of an untimely call-out from a child. I felt horrified by the session but proud that a child had questioned it publicly. This is the impact of strong, anti-racist and anti-discriminatory teaching. The worst part of this experience was that, upon giving feedback to the company the morning afterwards, the response was that if my school were to come back, they would not timetable this session for them. The point is that this practice was reinforcing negative stereotypes that 'people from Africa' live in shacks, work on plantations and are witch doctors. The reaction from the company completely highlighted for me how entrenched ignorance is, the desperate need for racial literacy and the fact that many people do not know that they do not know how to spot or question deeply rooted racism.

Post-Covid is a chance to start again – developing new ways of working, shaking up the curriculum and being part of building a better global community through rich, inclusive and diverse education. Let's shake things up. Let's make sure that the next generation is more tolerant, empathetic and able to critically think and voice well-rounded views.

How to use this book

The purpose of this book is to create space to consider a) the quality of your current provision and b) how it can be further developed to include all. In a period of turbulence and fundamental shifts in how we understand race equality, diversity and inclusion, *Time to Shake Up the Primary Curriculum* is a significant practical guide for school leaders and those who aspire to leadership. This book provides a step-by-step toolkit for first analysing the curriculum currently being taught. From there, it provides a comprehensive guide to remapping the curriculum, establishing a whole-school strategic approach.

Before we take a (deep) dive in (excuse the Ofsted 'joke'), let's first define what is meant by 'diverse', 'inclusive' and 'visibility', plus other terms referenced in this book. Language evolves rapidly and the terminology relating to diversity and inclusion is complex and often contested; there are some differences in interpretation and meaning both within and between countries. For the sake of simplicity, the following terminology has been used, according to the Oxford Learner's Dictionaries (2022):

Diverse: very different from each other and of various kinds

Inclusive: deliberately including people, things, ideas, etc. from all sections of society, points of view, etc.

Visibility: the fact of attracting attention or being easy to see

Equity: This means enabling people to achieve the same outcomes, sometimes through different means.

Equality: The equality that we fight for is being equal in rights, status, advantages, etc. This also means everyone being treated the same regardless of their starting point (which doesn't always work!).

Neurodiverse: showing patterns of thought or behaviour that are different from those of most people, though still part of the normal range in humans – this term is often used as an alternative way to describe people who are on the autism spectrum

Disability: a physical or mental condition that makes it difficult for somebody to do some things that most other people can do

Race: one of the main groups that humans can be divided into according to their physical differences, for example the colour of their skin; the fact of belonging to one of these groups

Ethnicity: the fact of belonging to a particular ethnic group (a group of people that share a cultural tradition)

Please note that the concept of 'race' is socially constructed. Everyone has an ethnicity, but 'race' is something that we made up as a society, in the same way that gender is a social construct. The term 'race' has been used throughout history to put different groups in categories based on physical differences, and has undoubtedly been used to justify genocides.

Ethnicity and race are often mixed up and used interchangeably. Someone's ethnicity is more about *communities* with shared history and traditions. It refers to culture, family, literature and shared language and geographical origin.

Here are some further definitions that it is important to understand, in order to truly shake up the curriculum:

Orientalism: a stereotyped and colonist vision of 'the Far East' and Asian culture – 'the Orient' itself is a colonial creation and was put in place to draw binary distinctions between 'the West' and 'the East', i.e. civilised vs uncivilised, exotic and strange lands steeped in mysticism

Colourism: discrimination against darker skin tones, typically amongst people belonging to the same ethnic group

Fatphobia: discriminatory behaviour towards people who are seen as overweight and/or obese

Homophobia: discriminatory behaviour towards gay, lesbian and/or queer people

Transphobia: discriminatory behaviour towards transgender people

Ableism: discriminatory behaviour towards people with disabilities

Xenophobia: discriminatory behaviour towards people from other countries

The power of language: Appropriate terms

The language used around describing people's 'race' or ethnicity is important, and is ever-changing as we become more aware and challenge stereotypes as a society. In this book, I will mostly use the term 'Black' in its political sense. This has been used because the National Education Union (NEU) uses this term in the 'Framework for developing an anti-racist approach' (2021), where it states 'Black is used in its political sense to denote a solidarity between Asian, African and Caribbean and all people of colour who identify with political "Blackness". "Black" was first used by white people to describe colonised and enslaved Asian and African people as a derogatory comparison to White. This term was reclaimed in Britain as part of the struggle of working-class African Caribbean and Asian communities against racism in the 1970s.' (p. 22)

The term 'global majority' is 'a collective term that first and foremost speaks to and encourages those so-called to think of themselves as belonging to the global majority. It refers to people who are Black, Asian, Brown, dual-heritage, indigenous to the global south, and or have been racialised as "ethnic minorities"'. (Campbell-Stephens, 2020, p. 1)

With these definitions in mind, our curriculum should actively teach about, represent and *deliberately* include different races and ethnicities, people with disabilities, the LGBTQIA+ community, different religions, women's history and rights, and different cultures.

This includes ensuring a well-rounded British history curriculum, including Black British, British Asian, women's and queer history and associated role models. It includes learning about and from people with disabilities. It includes challenging European bias across the curriculum. It includes developing a richly diverse music, arts and PE curriculum. This book supports teachers to use these areas to teach social justice, sustainability and human rights and develop children's voices to articulately justify their thoughts. Developing voices raises awareness and empowerment, particularly in marginalised communities.

There are also links to places to develop teachers' subject knowledge within each of the subject chapters.

PART 1

Analysing the current curriculum

1 Where are you now? Auditing your current curriculum

As our understanding of matters grows and society evolves, so must our curriculum. Think about what you want to achieve with your curriculum: to foster learners who are more enlightened than the current generation. Ask yourself, what does your current curriculum offer? How truly inclusive is it?

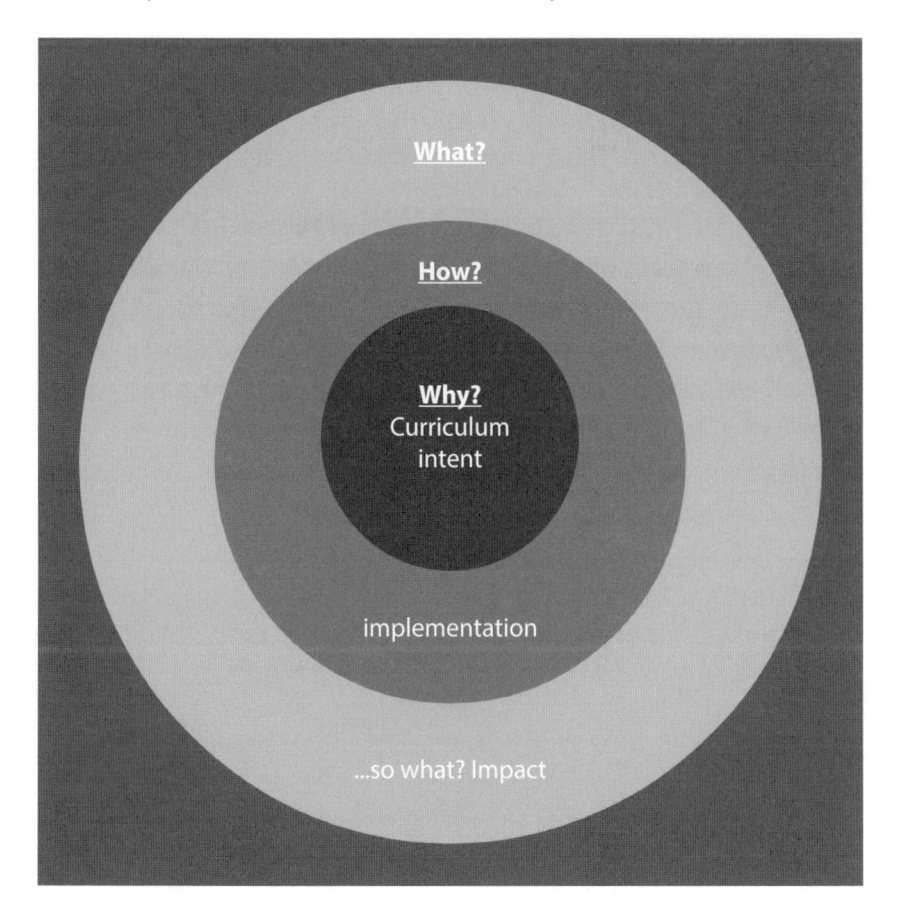

What?

How?

Why?
Curriculum intent

implementation

...so what? Impact

Before thinking about diversifying the curriculum, you must first understand where you are now. This comes through auditing the curriculum and subject knowledge. This cannot be done by one person, but must be a team effort.

> **Top tip!**
>
> Curriculum development needs to be part of the school's strategic plan, alongside rigorous professional development to support teaching and learning.
>
> Think about:
>
> 1. What are the curriculum's strengths and weaknesses?
> 2. How does professional development support teaching?
> 3. How do resources support learning and development?

Steps to auditing

1. Meet as a team to discuss and clarify the **school's vision.** This is the basis for everything really, as all subjects and areas of the school must be in line with this.

2. Everyone must be on the same page with the purpose of auditing, striving for more inclusivity and visibility, a willingness to improve subject knowledge and being open to having conversations challenging bias.

3. Agree the aim of the audit, i.e. to improve inclusion, diversity and visibility in the curriculum.

4. Each subject should be audited in light of anti-racism, LGBTQ inclusivity and disability inclusivity – there are some examples below of auditing resources and where to find more information.

Note!

Auditing takes time. It is the process of gathering evidence from curriculum mapping, children's work and pupil voice, teachers' subject knowledge, the parent community and governors. You need headspace and time to do this properly. Be sure to set aside – or request – time to do this. If you're requesting time out of class to do this, make sure that you have your intended impact in mind when you request it, i.e. 'I'm requesting time out to audit the curriculum so that it can be further developed in line with the school's vision, and ultimately positively affect outcomes for children.'

Diversity of thought matters

Whom you invite to the table to audit matters. Diversity of thought can only come about through a mix of people sharing ideas and thoughts. For example, if only the experienced teachers who have been teaching your current curriculum then audit it, I would wonder where is the room for growth? Think about how you can put together a diverse group: teachers of different lengths of teaching experience, male and female, leaders and non-leaders, teachers and non-teachers, different ethnicities and abilities, etc.

A fully rounded view

These audits are best carried out with a cross-curricular approach. This way there is a fully rounded view of the school's practice, rather than a subject-specific view. You may want to create working groups for each area. This could include subject leaders, phase leaders, the SENDCo and any other staff members who are interested in or passionate about improving diversity (they don't have to be teachers!). In fact, diversity of thought – from a mixed auditing working group – is vital in completing a great audit. This could be introduced in a staff meeting or, even better, an inset day, to gather support and excitement.

What to look at when auditing:

- curriculum maps
- long-, medium- and short-term plans
- a sample of lesson plans (just to get a feel of practice – you do not need to be looking at *every* individual lesson plan!)
- pupil book study – asking children about their learning alongside them showing you some book work
- trips and workshops
- assemblies/collective worship
- special events
- policies: teaching and learning, anti-bullying, behaviour, child protection, etc.
- school website.

There are many existing auditing resources that can be used to do this. Listed on the following pages are key questions to ask yourself when auditing, and where to find existing audits to support your evaluations.

Auditing the curriculum: Anti-racism

Unfortunately, we are facing growing intolerance and racism, despite existing anti-racist legislation such as the Universal Declaration of Human Rights and the Equality Act 2010. Challenging racism should not be the responsibility of solely Black staff or pupils, but the global majority have a unique perspective and particular understanding and expertise in relation to practices and policies that can often be exclusionary. If we are not actively anti-racist, we are complicit in racism. Experiences and viewpoints should be closely considered. It is important to take a step back to look at the curriculum in light of eliminating European bias and to ensure that there is a range of global cultures and histories taught. As educators, we have to become more racially literate so that we can aim to eliminate racism and cultural bias. An example of becoming more racially literate is thinking about the terms that we use when describing race, and being open to having them respectfully challenged. I personally don't use the acronym 'BAME' as I find it inaccurate and problematic to group 'minority ethnic' people together, which is an extremely broad brush with which to paint all 'people of colour'. This acronym puts 'Whiteness' as the norm within their respective local contexts, when often it is the opposite that is true. 'Global majority' is a more inclusive term, as it recognises a range of cultural and ethnic groups (Campbell-Stephens, 2020).

Before starting your audit on how racially and culturally diverse your curriculum is, have your aims in mind. A good example of aims for reviewing the curriculum in light of anti-racism is as follows:

Representation, reframing and anti-racism

1. 'Improving diversity and representation across the curriculum: this is about asking whose stories you tell and who tells these stories. It's also about making sure […] pupils see themselves reflected in your curriculum, all year round. For example, including Black Tudors in history lessons or talking about the Arabic origins of algebra in maths

2. Re-examining how certain subjects are taught through a western or colonial lens, and reframing this: also known as "decolonising the curriculum". This isn't necessarily changing what you teach, but how you teach it. For example, teaching the British Empire as "invading and exploiting" rather than "exploring and settling"

3. Teaching explicitly about racism and anti-racism (past and present) within your curriculum: it's important to teach this in a British context, and do this all year round. For example, teaching about the Bristol bus boycott, not just Rosa Parks'. (The Key, 2020)

There are fantastic auditing tools on The Key. Many schools already pay for access to The Key; ask your senior leadership team (SLT) whether the school already has access to this resource. If not, it is relatively inexpensive and an excellent set of resources. The audit for reviewing the curriculum for anti-racism is excellent, though it still uses the acronym 'BAME'. The section 'Anti-racism: how to review and reframe your curriculum' (The Key, 2020) includes a downloadable audit tool, separated into each subject. This includes questions/things to look for within the curriculum, space to indicate whether the school does or does not do this and evidence against each, followed by advice on next steps.

This audit includes questions like:

- 'Is the history of [...] people taught mainly during Black History Month? Do staff feel that this means [Black] history is "covered" and therefore less of a priority the rest of the year?'
- 'Where does the history of non-European people and cultures **begin** across your curriculum? For example, does the history of Africa begin with slavery? Or the point at which Britain abolished slavery? Does the history of India begin with the East India Company?'
- 'Where does the history of ethnic groups **within Britain** begin in your curriculum? Does it imply that there were no non-white people in Britain before the Windrush generation?' (The Key, 2020, pp. 1–2)

The National Education Union (2021) provides further suggestions:

- Where and when are the positive contributions of Black people throughout both history and in contemporary society learned?
- 'Is Black History Month in October the only part of the year/curriculum where there is a focus on the contributions of Black citizens/communities to British and global history or contemporary society? If so, how can Black perspectives in all subjects be reflected all year round?' (p. 15)
- 'Does the school… 's approach to wellbeing and belonging understand the psychological harms caused to Black pupils from racism and the way racism is internalised?' (p. 16)

Beyond the curriculum

Having considered the curriculum audit questions, now is the time to look beyond the curriculum at all the other jigsaw pieces that make up your practice and ethos as a whole.

- Does school leadership model a commitment to anti-racist values?
- Is training on offer to address racial equality?
- Is there a whole-school approach to racial equality and are all staff on board?
- Is the staff team diverse and do global majority staff members feel that their opinions are valued?
- What are the links between race and wellbeing?
- What are the links between race and 'behaviour'?
- How can you use your local community to frame discussions around protests, struggles or campaigns led by global majority communities in your area?
- All policies (including the anti-bullying policy, behaviour policy and child protection policy) should include a statement about zero tolerance for racism and actively promote racial equality.
- 'All behaviour policies must support positive behaviour for learning and support young people to take responsibility for their behaviour. However, there are huge racial disparities in exclusions: and zero tolerance behaviour policies are shown to disproportionately harm and segregate Black pupils, working class pupils and children with SEND. Your behaviour policy should empower you and your colleagues to make professional judgements. Staff must feel supported and part of a team – but behaviour policies must aim to support pupil wellbeing and understand what is causing or triggering challenging behaviour. Adverse childhood experiences (ACE) play a huge part in what contributes to children's behaviour.' (NEU, 2021, p. 8)
- How diverse are the toys/dolls around the school (particularly in EYFS)?

A note about decolonising education

What would the world look like now without colonialism? Colonialism is the practice of a powerful country taking control of less powerful countries, using the less powerful countries' people and resources to improve its own wealth and power.

'Decolonising is a way of thinking that interrogates how colonisation shapes the way we think, our education system and the curriculum. The legacy and ongoing impact of the ideas that shaped colonisation and the actions of the British empire contributes to contemporary racial inequalities. Discussions about decolonising education is one essential step to developing anti-racist educational spaces. Understanding the context for today's immigration debates is impossible without understanding that large numbers of people who came to the UK didn't actually come as migrants; they came from colonies and former colonies as citizens. A representative and relevant education system should reflect Black children's histories, achievements, culture and politics. All children deserve to see themselves reflected in their books, schools and communities and to achieve this we must rethink both curriculum and assessment.' (NEU, 2021, p. 16).

Black History Month

We couldn't think about auditing the curriculum without thinking about Black History Month. My opinion of Black History Month has swung back and forth over my time firstly as a learner in school and secondly as a teacher. I used to find it incredibly tokenistic and patronising. However, a great leader has strong opinions, but opinions that are easily changed upon evidence. I believe that I previously thought Black History Month was tokenistic because there was no other meaningful learning of and from Black people and Black cultures. However, I have come back around to the belief that Black History Month *is* extremely important and valuable, *when coupled with an all-round diverse curriculum.*

When planning out events for Black History Month, be sure to focus on Black role models who demonstrate excellence, and not just excellence in fighting against racism.

Auditing the curriculum: LGBTQ+ inclusive teaching

There should be LGBTQ+ inclusivity across the curriculum and not just in stand-alone RSE (relationships and sex education) lessons or during LGBT History Month. This is so that it reflects the diversity in gender and sexuality of modern British society. There may be children in your school who come from LGBT families, as well as staff members and governors (and perhaps some older children who have begun developing feelings about their own sexuality). It is imperative to teach that there are no outsiders in our society (Moffat, 2019). Only keeping topics and lessons about sexuality confined to a small number of assemblies, RSE or PSHE (personal, social, health and economic education) lessons is not likely to have the intended impact of truly LGBTQ+ inclusive practice.

Your staff must be on board to educate themselves on LGBTQ+ and gender issues – ensure that you actively work to improve the staff's knowledge and literacy surrounding this area. The more that staff know, the more impactful curriculum development and practice will be. You can do this through many ways: firstly, by providing space and time for open and honest conversations, where staff are able to speak freely about what they do and what confuses them and be willing and open for respectful challenge. Making various different sources of information available to staff can help in improving their knowledge surrounding these issues, such as books, articles, magazines, TV shows and documentaries, and podcasts.

There are brilliant resources on the Stonewall website about LGBTQ best practice and creating an LGBTQ inclusive learning environment (which you can learn more about in Chapter 3), but again I would visit The Key for the auditing tool. It is also important to take a wide view of how representative your LGBTQ teaching is – for example, are the representations taught of the LGBTQ community exclusively White, exclusively male or exclusively able-bodied?

The Key page 'Curriculum audit: gender and LGBTQ+ inclusivity' (2021) has information on where to start and also a downloadable audit tool, including questions such as:

- 'Do the books you study feature characters that conform to gender stereotypes (e.g. powerful, brave men and timid, caregiver women)?' (p. 3)
- 'Does your history curriculum cover the history of gay, trans and gender equality movements (e.g. Stonewall, the Suffragettes)?' (p. 4)
- 'When looking at different cultures around the world, do you highlight the different views held about gender and sexuality (e.g. different genders, different styles of dress)?' (p. 4)
- 'Do you tend to use men as the "default" for humans"?' (p. 10)
- 'Do the illustrations, images or diagrams of humans you use (e.g. in resources, on slides, or in textbooks) tend to be of men?' (p. 10)
- Do your images of families all look the same, i.e. a 'nuclear family'?
- 'Is your PSHE curriculum part of a whole-school approach, including a pastoral system that can deal with specific issues that arise (such as sexual harassment or other incidents)?' (p. 13)

Beyond the curriculum

For a school to be truly inclusive, the ethos and culture surrounding the curriculum should also be reviewed and audited for:

- the hiring of staff and training
- diversity in displays around the whole school environment and eliminating segregated areas like 'boys' library corner' or 'books for girls'
- all policies (most specifically anti-bullying policy, behaviour policy and child protection policy) including a statement about zero tolerance for:
  - homophobic language
  - sexist language
  - gendered or homophobic harassment
- the language surrounding gender and sexuality used across the school – Stonewall's primary curriculum has fantastic glossaries for staff and pupils (Stonewall, 2019)
- wider community – ensuring that you invite a range of people to run assemblies and career and whole-school events, actively including LGBTQ+ and female role models (Fowler, 2021)
- gender-neutral toilets.

Auditing the curriculum: neuro and physical diversity inclusive teaching

We are often told as educators not to 'reinvent the wheel', hence why I have given examples of existing audits for anti-racism and LGBTQ inclusive teaching. However, when auditing my curriculum, I could not find an existing audit for disability-inclusive teaching. I am not referring to including pupils with SEND within teaching; rather, to learning about and learning from disability. So I made one. Whether this is indicative of the possible segregation of **neuro and physically diverse people**/people with disabilities within society or simply my searching skills I don't know. The one that I made needs development but it is just a starting point.

It includes questions such as:

- Do the books that you study feature neuro and physically diverse people?
- Do you have books written by people with disabilities?

- Are there books in your library/book corners both about and by people with disabilities?
- Do you celebrate the Olympics and Paralympics?
- Do you describe people with disabilities as 'heroes' just for living their lives or finding diverse ways to do everyday tasks? This is extremely unhelpful!
- Do you ask children with disabilities to model great practice in PE lessons or only non-disabled children?
- Do you include images of people with disabilities in lessons? For example, in the Clip art that you use as part of your slides, do you have families with a parent with a disability?
- Do you have visitors to the school for assemblies who have disabilities, where visits/assemblies are not necessarily *about* their disability?
- Are there displays around the school with a variety of photos of people/role models with disabilities?
- Are people with disabilities overwhelmingly presented as victims of history or in need of help, rather than empowered?

It is important to note that ableism is defined as 'unfair treatment of **disabled** people by giving jobs or other advantages to **able-bodied** people' (Oxford Learners Dictionaries, 2022).

> **Top tip!**
>
> Watch Stella Young's Tedx Talk 'Inspiration porn' (2014). She talks openly and comedically about people with disabilities being 'inspiration' for non-disabled people simply for doing everyday tasks in a different way.

Beyond the curriculum

Now it is time to look at your general practice and language outside of the classroom. These lift your practice from tick-box exercises to true inclusion.

- As mentioned before, the language that we use is powerful; check your policies to ensure that appropriate up-to-date terms are used to refer the neuro and physically diverse students (and staff).

- Ensure that your school accessibility plan is up to date and purposeful.
- Check that your learning environments are accessible to all – including resources being in reach and visible.
- Ensure that the background colour of slides is accessible to dyslexic students – for example, dark text on a non-white background.
- Include pictorial labels/Makaton for all labels in the classroom.
- Provide books that all children can access, e.g. tactile books with audio description for visually impaired children.

Auditing the curriculum: Religion (both explicit and discrete teaching)

The teaching of RE (religious education) in primary school is imperative to children developing mutual respect and tolerance of others, helping children to develop values and beliefs. It promotes empathy and active understanding of others, which is essential to living happily within a diverse society. It also equips young people with the critical thinking needed to tackle the sometimes polarised views of religion that they can come across over social media (for example TikTok videos). It develops understanding of reasoned debate and provides fantastic opportunities for reflection.

Great religious education teaching should encompass theology (beliefs), philosophy (thinking) and human and social sciences (living). Here are some auditing questions as suggested by Chipperton et al. (2018):

- Is there a shared understanding of the purpose of RE across the whole school community?
- Which factors influence the planning of your RE curriculum?

Theology (belief)

Where do beliefs come from? For example, does your RE curriculum enable pupils to examine:

- sacred texts – stories from sacred texts and narratives from a range of religious traditions such as the Bible, Quran, Torah and Bhagavad Gita? Do you consider the author, context and target audience?

- texts produced by people who have reasoned and written about beliefs – key theologians and thinkers from a range of religious traditions, such as Ghandi, Martin Luther King, Dalai Lama, Aung San Suu Kyi and Dietrich Bonhoeffer?
- how people's experiences have impacted their beliefs – for example, the story of Bilal, Saul's conversion on the road to Damascus, the Hanukkah narrative of the oil lasting eight days, the impact of scientific discoveries on belief and vice versa, or an account of a miracle at Lourdes?
- how reliable sources of information and belief are – for example, looking at authorship, bias and historical accuracy?

Are there opportunities to reflect and discuss:

- how beliefs have changed over time?
- how events in history and society have influenced beliefs and the impact that persecution or prejudice has had?
- how different beliefs are related to each other?
- the similarities and differences between beliefs from within, between and beyond belief systems?
- how beliefs shape the way in which believers see the world and each other?
- the ways in which believers see the world through the lens of their beliefs?

Philosophy (thinking)

Does your RE curriculum include opportunities to reflect on:

- the nature of knowledge, meaning and existence?
    - How do we know?
    - What is happiness, hope, truth or knowledge?
- how and whether things make sense?
    - Learning to construct a response that makes sense
    - Discussion of big questions
- the issues of morals: right and wrong, good and bad?
    - What influences people when they make moral decisions?

- Ethical and moral issues: religious/worldwide responses to a range of issues (such as peace and conflict, justice and injustice, discrimination and prejudice, poverty).

Human and social sciences (living)

Does your RE curriculum include opportunities to reflect on:

- the diverse nature of religion?
- the diverse ways in which people practice and express their beliefs?
  - Symbolism, festivals, expression of faith through music and art, rural and urban faith communities
  - Diversity of thought within religions, for example Jehovah's Witness, Protestants and Catholics, Sunni and Shia
- the ways in which beliefs shape individual identity or identity shapes beliefs?
  - Issues of self-identity
- the ways in which beliefs contribute to and impact on communities and vice versa?
    Family life
  - Faith communities
  - School community
  - Wider local communities
- the ways in which beliefs contribute to and impact on society and vice versa?
  - Influence of culture on beliefs and vice versa
  - Influence of politics on beliefs and vice versa
  - Influence of social norms like laws and traditions on beliefs

Beyond the curriculum

- Are there opportunities for children to reflect upon ideas and discuss thoughts and beliefs across the curriculum?
- Are there books about and by authors from a wide range of religions?
- Are you storing sacred texts in the correct way, e.g. is the Quran kept on the highest shelf in your class/school library?

To sum up

The tools in this chapter provide a method of reviewing where you are currently with your curriculum, and will hopefully give you an idea of what needs to be developed. You can complete these audits in whatever way suits you and your position within the school. They could be completed in a staff meeting as discussion points, or completed as a fact/evidence-finding task. However it is done, the purpose is to help to reshape and restructure the direction of your subject.

You might find particular strengths in one area and another area that needs development. Share your results with the team and discuss how to move forward, and what specifically to focus on. Once you have an idea of where you currently are, you can think about the school vision and priorities moving forward.

Key takeaways

- **Audits can be carried out on the curriculum, long- and medium-term planning and learning environments.**
- **Audit beyond the curriculum too – look at staffing, policies and practice.**
- **Ensure that the group of people who are part of the audit are diverse.**
- **Create time and space to discuss findings, and use this to shape the school's vision and priorities for the year.**

2 Where do you want to be? Setting whole-school intent for new curriculum and key research

So… you have audited the curriculum at your school, and now you're ready and raring to go. In order to move forward, you need to shape your curriculum intent clearly, so that the work that comes next has a clear direction. Curriculum intent simply means the why, what and how of your curriculum. What exactly are you intending to do with your curriculum, why do you intend to do that and how do you plan to get there?

You must first consider the purpose of your curriculum:

- What strong educational principles do we, the school and leaders, believe in/practice?
- What do we want our curriculum to achieve?
- How would we like children to leave our school?
- What skills will a child who starts in Reception and leaves in Year 6 have?
- How do we prepare children for life beyond primary school?
- What values do we hold?
- What do we believe is right for the children?
- What pedagogical approaches and evidence-based research should we follow?
- What should the curriculum *not* be?

Examples of educational principles are:

- a language-rich curriculum
- a 21st-century skill-rich curriculum
- a knowledge-based curriculum

- a skills-based curriculum
- … or both?
- a human rights and activist curriculum (my personal favourite!).

The answers to these questions guide deep discussions surrounding your aims. Once you have your educational principle, you can build a curriculum statement around this. Don't just follow trends – they go out of date. Think about the true educational principles and evidence that guide your practice.

Here's an example from one of my schools:

Small school, big heart.

At XXXX we deliver a Global Citizenship Curriculum; entrenched in social justice, equality, diversity, inclusion and sustainability. We weave this with our school values of:

Community, Pride, Empathy, Happiness, Individuality, Creativity

Here's another great example:

Learning Together for a Better Future.

RESPECTFUL CITIZENS in a WORLD OF POSSIBILITIES.

> **Top tip!**
>
> If you are relaunching your school values, the only way to make them meaningful is to have all stakeholders involved (children, staff, parents and governors). At my school we asked people: What words come to mind when you think of our school? We then grouped all words that were similar and got the staff team to vote for one word per group that represented that group. For example, we grouped together joy, happiness, smiles and joyful, and happiness was voted to be the most representative word. We then gave all stakeholders a list of the words (by way of a Google Form) and came up with our most popular six values – as listed in our curriculum statement.

What will you offer your pupils?

Once you have a clear intent, you need to think of what experiences you will offer your pupils. This is where networking with your local community helps; really get to know what is around you: museums, local businesses, charities, outdoor spaces, workshops, arts centres, sports centres, etc. Think about a child entering in Reception and leaving in Year 6 – what will they experience over their career at your school and how do they develop from one year to another?

Programmes of study

Of course, the National Curriculum sets out objectives and a broad structure of skills per subject. But building upon that, you'll need to think of your schemes of work, which deliver your intent. These must be broken down, showing clear progression and thinking about long-term planning.

- How do you intend to cover the fundamental aspects and concepts of the National Curriculum subjects?
- How will each skill build over time and year group?
- How will knowledge build over time?
- How will you ensure depth of understanding?
- How do you allow for full coverage?
- How do you communicate this with staff, children, parents and governors?
- How will learning be adapted for children with SEND?
- Do projects actively include and represent a variety of people from different ethnicities, races, religions, genders, neurodiversities, physical disabilities, sexualities, etc.?

You could buy in schemes of work – some are great, some are less great. Or you could use existing schemes as a base on which to build.

I mapped out the long-term plans with topics building upon skills year upon year, and found various different schemes of work for each topic, put them together and created something bespoke. There are lots of resources out there!

Case study: Curriculum intent rooted in global citizenship

A great place to start I found was looking at the United Nations (UN) 17 Sustainability Goals. This is what is in place to make our world a better place, led by the United Nations Development Programme. The UN 17 Sustainability Goals replace the Millennium Development Goals (MDGs), which started a collective effort globally to tackle poverty and development priorities. Coming from a place of determination to improve the lives of all is a fantastic place to base your curriculum intent.

You can link each of your projects, subjects, assemblies, school events, staff training, fundraising events and much more to one (or more) of the goals. This gives you the 'why' of your curriculum. What you then need to work out is the 'how'. What schemes of work and pedagogies will you use to be the vessel of delivering this intent? Will you use cooperative learning as a whole-school pedagogy because it provides a quality education (Goal 4) for all through communication and language? What PSHE scheme will you use to ensure good health and wellbeing (Goal 3)?

For example, summer term 1's whole-school focus is sustainable development. All classes complete cross-curricular projects rooted in this goal, such as:

- Reception: Growing
- Year 1: Farm to plate
- Year 2: Climate change
- Year 3: Bees!
- Year 4: Renewable energy
- Year 5: Poaching
- Year 6: Human rights

Within these projects, knowledge and skills are built on from year to year, so that a child leaving my school would have a rich understanding of the elements of sustainable development.

SUSTAINABLE DEVELOPMENT GOALS

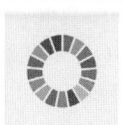

1 NO POVERTY	2 ZERO HUNGER	3 GOOD HEALTH AND WELL-BEING	4 QUALITY EDUCATION	5 GENDER EQUALITY	6 CLEAN WATER AND SANITATION
7 AFFORDABLE AND CLEAN ENERGY	8 DECENT WORK AND ECONOMIC GROWTH	9 INDUSTRY, INNOVATION AND INFRASTRUCTURE	10 REDUCED INEQUALITIES	11 SUSTAINABLE CITIES AND COMMUNITIES	12 RESPONSIBLE CONSUMPTION AND PRODUCTION
13 CLIMATE ACTION	14 LIFE BELOW WATER	15 LIFE ON LAND	16 PEACE, JUSTICE AND STRONG INSTITUTIONS	17 PARTNERSHIPS FOR THE GOALS	

The above image is the Sustainable Development Goals, created by the United Nations found https://www.un.org/sustainabledevelopment/. The content of this publication has not been approved by the United Nations and does not reflect the views of the United Nations or its officials or Member States.

What does the research say?

The NEU 'Framework for developing an anti-racist approach' (2021) states:

'How can the concept of global citizenship be helpful to engage your students? Global citizenship education provides a chance for young people to reflect on their roles and responsibilities regarding issues of equality and justice in human development – individually, locally and globally. This is not an additional subject area but rather an overarching approach to classroom practice that is best embedded across the curriculum (core, extra and hidden) and life of the whole school and its community. The UNESCO framework for Global Citizenship Education (2018) has three dimensions: -

a) *Cognitive: supporting pupils to acquire knowledge, understand and develop critical thinking skills to analyse and assess global issues and the interconnectedness and interdependency of countries and different populations*
b) *Socio-emotional: supporting pupils to have a sense of belonging to a common humanity; sharing values and responsibilities, sharing empathy, solidarity and respect for differences and diversity*
c) *Behavioural: supporting pupils to act responsibly for a more peaceful and sustainable world.' (p. 14)*

In this same report, Daniel Kebede (2021/22 President of NEU) explains:

'the concept of "decolonising education". In practice, decolonising education means rebuilding a school system that supports all students, staff and teachers. A system that is responsive to the particular needs of each and every child. Decolonising education involves examining the limitations and biases of the current curriculum; the omissions in initial teacher education and training; and examining the political and societal legacies of colonialism and how they have influenced education policies. Collectively, we must also challenge the political environment (globally and nationally) that is emboldening an anti-immigrant, "blame foreigners" populist narrative. I know most teachers absolutely want to ensure that education is free from any form of discrimination or bullying but many need support to do this. I hope every school or college will find this framework helpful in the quest for racism-free education.' (NEU, 2021, p. 3)

Diversity of thought: The importance of inclusive recruitment

It is important to say that the best, most innovative results come from having diverse teams. A homogenous team of leaders and teachers is only going to get so far with shaking up the curriculum. I read some astonishing statistics in the NFER 'Racial equality in the teacher workforce' report (2022) that:

- The **overwhelming majority** (96 per cent) of headteachers are from White ethnic backgrounds, compared to 83 per cent of people in the wider population.
- Eighty-six per cent of publicly funded schools in England have all-White senior leadership teams.
- Sixty per cent of schools in England have an all-White teaching staff.

- Children entering school today have a high probability of rarely or never being taught by a teacher from an Asian, Black, mixed or other ethnic minority group.

The recommendations from the report are to make a more equitable workforce by equalising opportunities for progression for people from different ethnic groups.

How to ensure that your recruitment process attracts a wide range of applicants

Here is a list of things to think about when recruiting, to ensure that the process is inclusive:

- Think about where you advertise. If you only advertise on TES, for example, you will only get people who look there. Consider advertising on different platforms too, such as the Young Black Teachers Network (@ybtn_uk) or BAME Ed Network (@BAMEednetwork).
- Think about your application form and job advert – are you expecting people to write in prose in their personal statement? Or could they write in bullet points? This would be more inclusive to teachers for whom English is not their first language, for example.
- Consider blind shortlisting. I am on the fence with blind shortlisting; however, some people swear by it. This is where you only look at the application without looking at the person's name, age or where they went to school.
- Make the mentality of recruitment that of adding to the team rather than fitting in with the current team.
- Consider your language – words matter. Ensure that your adverts do not contain gendered language or bias.
- Consider giving the interview questions out before the interview. Ask yourself, what is the purpose of the interview? Is it to test under pressure (which it may be!) or is it to dig deeper into someone's motivations, ability and passion? You could give candidates the questions upon arrival. This would make the difference for some candidates; personally, I know that I can absolutely smash a presentation and lesson observation but I have previously struggled with the interview part – this would have really helped me.

- Consider your interview and shortlisting panel – is it a range of people/job roles/gender, etc.? Ensure that a conversation is had beforehand as to what the panel would like to add to the team and agree on this.

Research, research, research!

So… you've audited your current curriculum offer. You've put together your intent for redesigning your curriculum. Now it's time to research! This is a step-by-step guide of where to start researching for developing the curriculum. It is extremely important to know the children, families and local community, because this helps you to design the most impactful curriculum. A truly diverse curriculum represents both the local and also national and global community. For example, it is as important for a school in Brixton, South London to learn about the *Windrush* as it is for a school in the Outer Hebrides.

Here are some questions to research in relation to your cohort:

Pillars of the local community

First, it is important to look at the pillars of the local community:

- What is the history of the area?
- What is the ethnic breakdown of the local community?
- What key figures are there within the community?
- What key features are there within the community? For example, are you near a historical park, museum, coastal region, football stadium or area of national beauty?
- What religions/faiths are represented in the local community?
- What places of worship are there?
- What is the housing like?
- What languages are predominantly spoken in the local area?

School cohort

Next, have a look at your school cohort. You'll be able to find answers to the following questions based upon the information collated on your MIS (management information system).

- What is the ethnic breakdown of your school?
- How many and which languages are spoken?
- What religions are represented in your school?
- What disabilities are there in your school?
- What family structures are there (i.e. two-parent, single-parent, children in foster care, LGBT+ families, etc.)?

School staff

Diversity and inclusion are important in both the curriculum that is taught and also *who* is teaching said curriculum. School teams should be diverse: a range of people from different walks of life and with differing life experiences.

- How diverse is your school staff?
- Are the heritages and backgrounds of the local community represented through the staff that work at the school?
- What languages are represented in the school staff? Is there a staff member that can speak each language represented by the children and families?

Once you have got this information, use this to map out the curriculum for each subject. For example, if you have a large British Somali cohort, ensure that you have some study of British Somali history. If you have autistic children, ensure that you have books about autism in each book corner in the school.

You should be able to identify some gaps in your staff team, and so whatever your gap is could be used as a priority upon your next round of recruitment, i.e. thinking about where you can advertise roles in order to attract candidates to add to your team.

To sum up, it is important to know your cohort and the wonderful threads that make up the tapestry of your school. This not only allows you to develop meaningful relations with your school community, but also helps with planning a truly inclusive curriculum.

Key takeaways

- Get together and think carefully to consider the purpose of your curriculum.
- Build your aim into a statement.
- Map out your long-term plans in line with your curriculum statement.
- Ensure that there is progression from year to year and that children have opportunities to meet the National Curriculum objectives with a depth of learning through your programmes of study.
- Get buy-in from all stakeholders by articulating your intent clearly and with purpose.
- Don't reinvent the wheel. Maybe it's got a few dents over the years – so just reshape it!
- Getting to know your local community helps to shape your curriculum offer, as you can ensure that there is representation and visibility for all.
- Shape your recruitment priorities in response to the gaps in your staff team.
- Curriculum also needs to provide opportunities to learn about groups from our national community and global community.
- If your cohort is predominantly homogenous, it is important to learn about other groups too. For example, you don't only learn about British Indian history if there are British Indian children in your school.

PART 2

Shaping the curriculum

3 Literacy: Book choices with different voices

This chapter looks at developing inclusive and diverse practice in delivering National Curriculum English, through considering diverse reading spaces and methods of teaching, and makes suggestions as to how to expose children to a wide range of people through literature. It gives direction on whole-school events and how to raise the profile of reading. Furthermore, it discusses using diverse texts as a basis for teaching high-quality reading and writing, with a comprehensive list of books across the key stages.

Know what you're aiming for

Be sure to have a clear idea in your mind of what you are aiming for with your literacy curriculum, and that it is set out in your literacy teaching and learning policy. This should be in line with your curriculum intent, and should include all aspects of literacy: phonics, reading, writing, spelling, speaking and listening, etc.

Here's an example:

> At XXXX School, we believe that the exposure of children's literature within the primary school setting is vital to a rich context for learning – not only within English as a subject but also to support building a reading culture throughout the school.
>
> We aim to use high-quality books that offer opportunities for empathy and can aid philosophical inquiry, as a means of developing the spoken language requirements through debate, drama and discussion, using the issues raised through, and within, the text.
>
> We use a variety of diverse books to teach inclusivity, teaching that there are no outsiders in our society.

When mapping your year, first map out the genre of writing (to ensure full coverage) and then match books/planning to the genre.

Genres of writing with examples:

- narrative, such as ballad, poetry, short story, myth, legend, science fiction, fantasy, fable, anecdote and information narrative
- recount, such as journal, diary, newspaper article, historical recount, biography, autobiography and memoir
- information reports, such as descriptive report, scientific report, classifying report and historical report
- procedure, such as instructions, procedural recount, recipe, directions and manual
- persuasion, such as discussion, advertisement, letter to the editor, speech and newspaper article
- explanation, such as scientific writing and spoken presentation.

The Literary Curriculum (www.literarycurriculum.co.uk) is a great resource of planning sequences for reading, writing and spelling, which includes up-to-date texts from a diverse range of authors and about a wide range of topics.

What does the research say?

Did you know that a study carried out in 2019 revealed that in the UK only one per cent of children's books published contained a Black main character (Maxwell, 2019)?

Representation within literature is extremely important when engaging young readers in reading. If children are able to see themselves, in some way or another, they are more interested and invested in stories. This is particularly the case for children from disadvantaged backgrounds, who we know have been disproportionately affected post-Covid. The reading spaces in your school need to have books that represent your school community. For example, if you have a largely Muslim community at your school, are there books (both fiction and non-fiction) about and written by this community?

> 'Literature is a curator of our imaginations, and schools are the caretakers of our young people's education.
>
> They are currently being denied access to the glorious, outstanding and often ground-breaking narratives coming out of Britain's Black and Asian communities.'
>
> (Bernardine Evaristo, author, cited in Elliott et al., 2020)

Runnymede commissioned a report, published by Penguin, entitled 'Lit in colour' (Elliott et al., 2020), which explores diversity in literature in English schools. It found that:

> 'in Key Stage 2, as well as texts taught directly through the curriculum such as the class reader topic book, or supporting texts to a topic, the major source of access to literature is independent reading. Independent reading includes levelled reading schemes by the major publishers as well as commercial children's fiction. This provides plenty of opportunities for a wide range of book encounters… Primary interviewees reflected on the need for greater representation in the classroom, and better understanding of how to talk about and mediate these texts for students. Malorie Blackman was the most popular author for primary, mentioned 14 times with a spread of texts; Benjamin Zephaniah was mentioned 12 times, two of which were in the context of Refugee Boy, six in the context of his poetry and a further four where only his name was mentioned. Onjali Q. Raúf's The Boy at the Back of the Classroom is taught by seven teachers, and Sharna Jackson's High Rise Mystery by five. The most popular fiction texts are therefore by two of the most famous Black British writers writing for children today, and two novels which are very recent and which have won awards. Fiction texts were by far the most commonly mentioned by primary respondents, with 55 separate books mentioned. Handa's Surprise was mentioned by three teachers, only one of whom appeared aware that it was written by a White woman. A classic of British children's books, it represents a very stereotypical view of Africa, which can provide an unbalanced view if not mediated by the teacher or counterpointed by other texts. Aside from Benjamin Zephaniah, Shel Silverstein's 'The Giving Tree' was the most popular poem and only nine poets were mentioned in total. A few non-fiction texts were mentioned: Hidden Figures by Margot Lee Shetterly was mentioned by three respondents, as was Vashti Harrison's Little Leaders. The use of the "Little People, Big Dreams" series and Little Leaders demonstrates the value and impact a well-curated themed series can have in providing a route into showcasing Black, Asian and minority ethnic people in the primary classroom. There is, however, a risk that the use of such texts suggests only extraordinary Black, Asian and minority ethnic people can be valued by society, rather than celebrating the full range of experience. One of the interviewees who works as a teacher educator spoke in her capacity as the mother of mixed-race children to note that for young children appearance tends to be the first marker through which they recognise difference. She argued that primary schools needed "to account for this in a celebratory way, not just intervene on this when problems with racism have already taken place" and that this required "good texts written by and featuring people of colour." Another interviewee suggested that Key Stage 2 provided a good opportunity to consider heritage texts in the context of race and empire,

beginning to explore texts in context in a way which would support their transition to secondary school. Forty of the primary respondents to the survey said that either before or in the wake of the Black Lives Matter protests of 2020 their schools were making changes to increase the diversity of their curriculum, although several said that they did not feel these changes went far enough.' (Elliot et al., 2020, pp. 11–12)

It also found that:

'one of the main themes identified in our research was teachers' perceptions of their own lack of knowledge, which prevents them from adding more diverse texts to the curriculum. This fell into two categories: first, where to start finding the books and choosing ones which were appropriate for teaching; and, second, the secure knowledge of how to teach them.' (Elliot et al., 2020, p. 19)

This is where CPD is imperative: training on racial literacy, LGBT-inclusive teaching, disability-inclusive teaching, etc.

Staff CPD

Building on the previous section, here are some suggested sources for training:

Racial literacy teacher training

The Black Curriculum (www.theblackcurriculum.com) provides training, both in person and virtual, on:

- Black British history
- racial literacy
- decolonising pedagogy and curriculum
- language use and more.

LGBT-inclusive teacher training

Stonewall (www.stonewall.org.uk) provides training, both in person and virtual, on:

- tackling homophobic, biphobic and transphobic bullying and language
- creating a trans-inclusive setting
- gender in the classroom.

Disability-inclusive teacher training

The Sightsavers charity (www.sightsavers.org) offers a great education pack for teachers.

Disability Matters (www.disabilitymatters.org.uk) offers free CPD, such as:

- hidden disabilities
- disability in the classroom.

The teaching of literacy

The first step to teaching diverse and inclusive literacy is ensuring that your reading spaces are full of a wide selection of books showcasing different races, religions, abilities, neurodiversity, genders and sexualities. These don't necessarily need to be books *about* these topics, just books that show both protagonists *and* authors from all walks of life. Later on in this chapter, there is guidance on:

a) fundraising to buy new books

b) suggested books lists.

Once you have got a wide range of books in your reading spaces and on your taught curriculum, your teaching of literacy needs to be actively anti-racist, anti-homophobic, anti-ableist and anti-sexist.

When reading a new book or a new text, introduce the author and their background. The intent of this is simply is simply information sharing for children, and, in the particular case of LGBT authors, normalises language such as 'gay' and 'lesbian'. If they are a gay author, tell the children that! If they have a disability, talk about the disability, etc.

Facilitate open conversations with children, asking them to discuss things like:

- What's special about this author?
- What might be their strengths?
- What challenges might they have faced?
- Do they remind us of any other authors or characters we know? How?
- What might we have in common with them?
- How are they different from us?

The most important thing that we can do as teachers is to **give children appropriate language** to discuss issues around diversity and to **challenge any inappropriate language or opinions respectfully, discussing why it's inappropriate and giving a relevant example**.

As an example of this, let's say that you introduced an author as being gay and there were some sniggers around the room. Instead of 'shhhing' children and moving on (as I have observed before!), stop them and say, 'Hmmm, I noticed that you made a funny noise then… Why?'. Allow children space and safety to discuss thoughts, and redirect them to a path of anti-discrimination. Follow up with a PSHE lesson/assembly. Write key words on the board. Talk to children about *why* we do not discriminate against *anyone*. Link this to British values: tolerance, individual liberty and mutual respect. Ask children to empathise: 'Has anyone ever made you feel bad about something? How did it feel?'

Diverse images

Ensure that when you are planning displays, PowerPoints, Word documents and the like, you use pictures and photos of a diverse range of people. We often don't think twice about searching Google Images for a background picture or side-image to go onto our presentations, but children are looking at these images for a large period of each day – they matter! Annoyingly, you often have to actively search for 'Black boy' on Google to find an image of a Black boy, whereas if you search for 'boy', what tends to come up is predominantly White people.

Think about images of families that you have displayed. Ensure that you include different family make-ups, people with disabilities, different religions, etc.

Top tip!

There are many websites or desktop publishing programs that provide symbol-supported resources (for example, Communicate: In Print or Widget), which enable all learners to access content. These are often just used for SEND children's resources, but they are invaluable and great practice would be to include these on all your PowerPoints. They help all learners to understand lessons through image, and not just SEND children. You can also edit symbols' skin colours and gender so that they are diverse and representative.

Symbols help to communicate ideas and information.

Symbols © Widgit Software Ltd 2002 – 2022

Modelling writing

When planning a writing sequence, be sure to think carefully about the protagonists of your narratives. For example, do you have an equal amount of stories written from a female character's perspective as well as a male? Have you written a story from the perspective of a person with a disability? Does the main voice of the story/writing have a 'nuclear family' or something different? This is a great opportunity for building diversity and inclusion!

These learning experiences facilitate building empathy with others, whilst also providing visibility for marginalised children.

English as an additional language

It is your responsibility as a teacher to make sure that all children, irrespective of their language skills, are actively engaged in learning. Research has found that multilingual and bilingual students often have stronger working memories and longer attention spans. In fact, more of the world's population is bilingual or multilingual than only speaking one language (Marian and Shook, 2012). Therefore, having EAL students could encourage the whole class to focus even more! Research has also found that pupils in diverse schools have an enhanced ability to use higher-order cognitive thinking skills and think creatively. Using images and visuals supports the learning of EAL pupils.

Here are some further strategies:

- Teach the 'word of the day' with kinaesthetic actions, and make sure that the word is linked to the learning of the day. The actions help all learners to understand the context of learning.
- Give children a vocabulary book, like their own personal dictionary, labelled with pages A to Z. They can add in new words with sketches or pictures, or labels in their first language. These books move with the children through every class and every year of school.

- Scaffold responses with talk frames for how to respond, including key vocabulary with images (like Communicate: In Print, as mentioned earlier).
- Include first language words on slides too! If you have a child whose first language is Polish, can you include some key words in Polish on your slides? This is also educational for non-Polish children in the classroom and creates a wonderfully inclusive atmosphere where all children are exposed to new language!

Raising the profile of reading

Take a look at your reading spaces: your school library (if you're lucky enough to have one) and the reading corners. Take stock of which books are there and what representation you need. Do you have a range of races represented through the books? Are there books from authors from different backgrounds? Are there a range of life experiences demonstrated through fiction? Are there books that challenge the role of women? Are there books that explore stereotypes of masculinity and femininity? Are there books in the home languages of the children in your class? Are there books about and by people with disabilities? Are there books challenging the 'helpless' stereotype of people with disabilities?

The following are some suggestions for how to raise the profile of reading in your school/classroom.

Author of the week

Highlight an author a week, showing a photo of the author and a blurb about their life. Ensure that you choose different types of authors each week, from a range of races and genders and including people with disabilities.

Book fairs

Get on Twitter and find out whether there are any diverse bookshops/sellers nearby. Check out your local newspapers and festival events – you'll be sure to find someone. If there isn't one, you could start your own book sale. This would be more to raise the profile of reading diverse books rather than working as a fundraising event, but it would be fun if you got parent volunteers and children involved. In London – where my school is – we got in touch with @RubyReads, a diverse bookseller, who now comes at the end of every half-term to sell beautiful books.

This picture shows the Ruby's Reads book stall, selling books on the last day of term. Check out Ruby's Reads @rubyreads_uk on Instagram for details.

First Page Friday

First Page Friday aims to introduce the school community to new books, generating excitement and intrigue. It's a fun, super-simple way to bring modern voices into your curriculum each week and to encourage your students in their independent reading. It works by getting a child, staff member or parent to read the first chapter to an audience. You then make the book available for them to access (either in your school library, book corners or online). This can be facilitated in different ways: it could be a child reading it in assembly or, at my school, we record the child reading it and it's posted on our School Story on ClassDojo for the whole school community to see. It is also a great way of engaging reluctant readers, by choosing them to facilitate reading the first page. In my school, we struggled with boys' engagement in reading, and so we choose predominantly boys to read First Page Friday books, ensuring that the books are diverse books that the children have *chosen*, and this has exponentially improved boys' engagement in reading.

Pupil voice

Get buy-in from the children. Ask them which kind of stories they like. Diversity in the *type* of book is also necessary to engage all readers. For example, are there picture books as well as textbooks in a Year 6 classroom? Are there graphic novels? Are there recipe books? Are there magazines? Are there books in different languages? Are the languages of the class represented in the texts in the book corner?

Once you have an idea of:

a) what the children are interested in
b) the context of the class
c) the context of the local community

… you can get ordering!

From personal experience, the impact of having new books, representing a vast group of different types of people, transformed reading and reading culture within my school. Children who had been disinterested in reading were suddenly asking to take books home and to read to the class.

LGBT+ inclusive teaching

Battling ignorance and push-back can sometimes be experienced when diversifying practice. Unfortunately, one of the areas in which this has happened is LGBT-inclusive teaching. I have found from experience that battling this head-on, fully understanding your expectations as a practitioner, and addressing your policy and ethos assist in meeting prejudice and moving forward together.

Case study: LGBT+ inclusive teaching and challenging prejudice

It is important to say that there is sometimes parent push-back in relation to LGBTQ-inclusive teaching. This is something that I personally experienced at my school in 2022. My Year 4/5 class were reading *Pride: The Story of Harvey Milk* as part of a project on activism and non-fiction writing. Despite informing parents at the start of the term of the books that we were reading over the coming weeks, when it came round to reading it in class later in the term, there was an influx of parent complaints. These complaints came in thick and fast, over our school messaging system and also on the playground. There were parents audibly talking about it outside the school gates too. The complaint was over learning about a gay man (Harvey Milk) and celebrating his activism.

The main complaint that I received was that parents felt that it was against their religion to discuss gay people and they didn't believe that it was a 'right way to live'. One parent even described it as 'an illness'. Parents asked for their children to be withdrawn from the lessons.

This in itself I found difficult to challenge. As a queer person myself, I felt personally upset by it and also sad that there was a battle against learning that people *actually exist*. It is not a question of right and wrong, and it is also not a question of beliefs. It is discriminatory to campaign against the teaching that a group of people exist.

It had to be tackled head-on; otherwise, it was going to get out of hand. I have previously had individual parents complain here and there about celebrating LGBT History Month, but never had I experienced a large group of parents campaigning against the teaching.

Firstly, I invited the parents in as a group to discuss concerns. I wrote to them before and explained the structure of the meeting, which was:

- Teacher (me) to explain what was being taught and the language that was being used and to show the parents the book itself, plus the work that had been completed by children.
- Teacher (me) to explain the expectation of LGBT-inclusive teaching, as set out by the Department for Education (DfE). Parents cannot withdraw their children from LGBT-inclusive teaching.
- Parents to be given a chance to respectfully voice their concerns.

What came out of the meeting were several things: mainly a lack of understanding from parents as to what schools were required to teach but also, more prominently, a lack of LGBT literacy from the parents. Many of the parents openly discussed how no one had ever spoken to them about the LGBT community, and that they did not know anyone who was gay. Many also said that because no one had spoken to them about it, and within their community it wasn't spoken about, they didn't have the language to speak about it with their children. They felt unconfident themselves, and this was behind part of their reaction. Many of them said, 'I am not homophobic but I don't want my children learning about gay people.' In the meeting, whilst it was challenging, I was able to respectfully challenge this sentence. In fact, it is homophobic to not want children to learn that gay people exist. I likened it to learning about race and asked whether it would be OK if someone said, 'I am not racist but I don't want my children learning about Black people'. When put that way, parents began to change their way of thinking.

Another misconception around primary school LGBT-inclusive teaching is that it is teaching about *sex* rather than *relationships*. We explained to parents that we teach that different family structures exist: some children have one parent, some children have two different-gendered parents, some children have two parents of the same gender and some children live with their family members or in foster care. We explained that there are children in our school and people in our community who have lots of different family structures, and they must be protected from discrimination and be made to feel accepted and normal.

I'm not going to lie; it was certainly a challenging meeting, but I am so pleased that it happened because it has made a huge impact on the engagement of parents in learning. Most of the parents thanked me personally for the meeting.

As a result of the meeting, I did several things. To be honest, I had never really thought about parents not having the language themselves to discuss LGBT+ issues with their children. So I made a 'Parents' Guide to LGBT-Inclusive Teaching' (see p.43).

Also, following the meeting, I:

1) worked with the parent community to shape the RSE policy
2) continued to invite parents in to discuss any concerns and make it clear what the intentions of the curriculum are and how it is in line with national DfE policy
3) worked with the staff team so that everyone was clear on appropriate language to use and how to address concerns from parents – through coaching, staff meetings and planning support.

It is important to say that I am a member of SLT. If you are in a similar situation as I was in the case study discussed, but as a class teacher, ask a member of SLT to support you in a meeting. I also had the chair of governors in my meeting, plus my two parent governors, so it was a group of people together having a professional conversation, and it was understood by the parents that it was a school decision to teach this unit and was part of a bigger vision of actively teaching against all forms of discrimination.

What does the DfE say about LGBT-inclusive teaching?

The DfE gives guidance on the teaching being 'sensitive and age appropriate in approach and content' and states that it should be 'fully integrated into their programmes of study for this area of the curriculum rather than delivered as a standalone unit or lesson. Schools are free to determine how they do this, and we expect all pupils to have been taught LGBT content at a timely point as part of this area of the curriculum.' (DfE, 2019, p. 15)

The guidance also states that children should be taught 'that others' families, either in school or in the wider world, sometimes look different from their family, but that they should respect those differences and know that other children's families are also characterised by love and care' (p. 20), and 'about different types of bullying (including cyberbullying), the impact of bullying, responsibilities of bystanders (primarily reporting bullying to an adult) and how to get help… what a stereotype is, and how stereotypes can be unfair, negative or destructive' (p. 22).

Developing an RSE policy?

Stonewall has a fantastic guide to developing great LGBT-inclusive practice, which can be found on their website at: www.stonewall.org.uk/ten-steps-implementing-lgbt-inclusive-rshe. It gives advice on understanding the needs of LGBT pupils and/or families, equipping staff with training and support, and monitoring and assessing your current provision.

Parent guide to LGBT-inclusive teaching

After meeting with the parents, I designed a 'Parents' Guide to LGBT-Inclusive Teaching', which reframed all the concerns that were brought up during the meeting, plus supported parents/carers to have well-informed conversations at home.

Here is my guide as an example:

LGBT-Inclusive Teaching

The importance of talking to your children about discrimination

At [INSERT SCHOOL NAME], we actively challenge and fight against all forms of discrimination. Just like Black history, we learn about and celebrate diversity in all its forms throughout our school year and throughout the curriculum; we teach equality and social justice for all races, genders, sexualities, religion, abilities and more. We are required to do so by the Department for Education. We are proud of the curriculum we teach and its impact upon developing well-rounded citizens in our young people.

The rainbow flag is a symbol of hope. Many people throughout history have used this flag, from LGBT to NHS Clap for Carers to its use in religious history. This flag is a symbol of hope and promotes inclusion and equality and most of all... happiness.

The purpose of this newsletter is to give you some information to discuss at home with your family.

Tackling homophobia

Homophobia is dislike of or prejudice against gay people. It is important to understand that in our society, lots of different people exist. We actively teach understanding, social justice and equality. We teach these through our varied curriculum, where we challenge phobic views of groups of people within our society (and community). We challenge stereotypes and learn how to think critically about issues. We tackle discriminatory language and have zero tolerance for bullying in all its forms. We educate against discriminatory language and teach acceptance.

The lesbian, gay, bisexual and transgender community have been through many struggles throughout history, and it is important to learn about this struggle, the fight for change and the continued journey towards equality, in the same way in which we learn about fights for race equality and much more. This is always done in an age-appropriate way.

We teach that love is love. Families come in all different shapes and sizes: two-parent families, single-parent families, two mums, two dads, living with grandparents, living in foster care and many more. The glue that keeps families together is love.

Definitions

Lesbian: A woman who is attracted to other women.

Gay: A man who is attracted to other men.

Bisexual: A person who is attracted to men or women.

Transgender: A person who does not identify with the gender that they were assigned at birth. This includes people who identify outside the gender binary, for example non-binary and gender-fluid people.

Queer: can be used to refer to a person's gender identity and/or sexual orientation. It is sometimes used as an umbrella term for LGBT+ identities.

Gender: Often expressed in terms of masculinity and femininity, gender is largely culturally determined and is assumed from the sex assigned at birth.

Why do we learn about different families, including LGBT?

In September 2020, the Department for Education made it statutory for schools to discuss different families' relationships, including having families with two mums or two dads. This is because much research (Stonewall, 2019) was done into young people's experiences of school and it was found across the UK that many young people in LGBT families or older teenagers who identified as LGBT themselves had experienced significant bullying due to this fact.

We include the teaching that different family relationships exist, explore role models during LGBT History Month and discuss how the London Pride protest is a way for people to express themselves, like the Black Lives Matter protests.

The overall aim of these teachings is to 'promote equality and diversity for the benefit of the public', because if we can accept others for who they are, then we are more likely to be accepted for who we are.

Talking about LGBT families is always age-appropriate, not related to sex and NOT about trying to influence anyone's sexuality, in the same way that teaching the history of the Holocaust is not about promoting the views of the Third Reich.

However, it IS about:

- normalising language used when talking about LGBT matters
- not being afraid to mention that people in current life and history – for example, Oscar Wilde – were gay, and this influenced much of their work
- challenging homophobia or bullying of LGBT people
- promoting tolerance and acceptance of all people as human beings, regardless of their sexuality.

Our values

Here are five British Values that educational establishments are obliged to teach:

- democracy
- the rule of law
- individual liberty
- mutual respect
- tolerance of those of different faiths and beliefs.

These values underpin our very society and are used to protect British citizens by creating a 'code of conduct' that we aim to adhere to. The last three values are vital in accepting, promoting and celebrating our diversity, so that people of all creeds, races and sexualities can feel safe and valued.

Alongside this, we have our **school values**, which underpin everything that we do:

- pride
- individuality
- creativity
- happiness
- empathy
- community.

I'm struggling – how do I talk to my child about this?

Just like with any topic, children may have questions about families. They may ask why a family has two dads or two mums. It is important firstly when speaking about families to centre it around 'love' and the fact that the key component of any family is love.

The focus in primary schools surrounding this issue is teaching the fundamental building blocks and characteristics of positive relationships, with particular reference to friendships, family relationships and relationships with other children and with adults.

Address any hateful or discriminatory statements immediately – for example, using the work 'gay' as an insult. You could compare it to someone using the work 'Black' as an insult and how that would be considered racist. Using the word 'gay' as an insult is considered homophobic.

Key statements to share with your child:

- Families are about love, no matter who the parent/s are.
- Families look after each other.
- We are all equal and everyone deserves respect.

Use current events or TV shows as a way to inspire a conversation. You might see a gay couple on TV and prompt a conversation into what makes a family a family, i.e. people who love each other.

It may be that you find this matter challenging to discuss because perhaps you were not taught about different family relationships in your own schooling. We all must work together to educate ourselves, to enable us to have open and honest conversations and create a better, more inclusive future for our children.

Want to find out more?

Visit: www.lgbtplushistorymonth.co.uk

Stocking your reading spaces and mapping out topics

The books that you have in all your reading spaces – classrooms, corridors, library, staff room, school office, window ledges – are incredibly powerful tools with which to include, actively teach and expose children to a wide range of people.
Make sure that you:

- Have books that represent your **school community** (refer back to your audit of your school cohort, including staff). For example, if you have a child with autism, ensure that you have books across your reading spaces that are both *about* autism and also *feature* characters with autism.
- Have books that represent the wider national community. If your cohort is predominantly White, ensure that you have books with main characters who are Black, for example.
- Have books that show a variety of different family units and that are LGBT-inclusive.

It's a good idea to keep a record of which classrooms contain which books, so that you have a clear understanding of how you are meeting the needs of the children.
Here's an example that I made of book coverage in my current school:

<u>Inclusive books per classroom July 2020</u>

<u>Themes</u>
Celebrating global majority cultures/challenging racial stereotypes
Celebrating LGBTQA+ communities/ challenging gender stereotypes
Inclusive of disability/challenging stereotypes about disability

Classroom	Book	Quantity
Nursery	*Not My* - Anastacia Higginbotham *Lovely* - Jess Hong *The Skin I'm In* - Pat Thomas *All Are Welcome* - Alexandra Penfold	1
Reception	*Lubna and the Pebble* - Wendy Meddour *It's OK to be Different* - Sharon Purtill	1

	Mixed - Arree Chung *Baby Goes To Market* - Atinuke	
Year 1	*Amazing* - Steve Antony *All Are Welcome* - Alexandra Penfold *He's Got The Whole World In His Hand* - Kadir Nelson *Cool Cuts* - Mechal Renee Roe *I Can Still Do Everything with One Arm* - Katie Laurel Wells	1
Year 2	*I Love My Hair* – Natasha Anatasia Tarpley *Max and The Tag Along Moon* – Floyd Cooper *It's Ok to Be Different* – Sharon Purtil *And Tango Makes Three* – Juston Richardson *The Great Big Book Of Families* – Mary Hoffman	1
Year 3	*The Great Big Book Of Families* – Mary Hoffman *Crown: An Ode To the Fresh Cut* – Derrick Barnes *Jabari Jumps* - Gaia Cornwall *Little Leaders: Bold Women in Black History* – Vashti Harrison	1
Year 4	*Knock Knock* – Daniel Beaty *Pansy Boy* – Paul Harfleet *Emmanuel's Dream* – Laurie Thompson *Black Heroes* – Arlisha Norwood	2
Year 5 and 6	*The Undefeated* – Kwarme Alexander *Rainbow Revolutionaries* – Sarah Prager *The Red Tree* – Shaun Tan *Black Heroes* – Arlisha Norwood *Sulwe* – Lupita Nyong'o	3
Other Areas		
School Library	*The Undefeated* – Kwarme Alexander *Black Heroes* – Arlisha Norwood *Sulwe* – Lupita Nyong'o *Little Leaders: Bold Women in Black History* – Vashti Harrison	1

	Knock Knock – Daniel Beaty *I Love My Hair* – Natasha Anatasia Tarpley *Rainbow Revolutionaries* – Sarah Prager *The Great Big Book Of Families* – Mary Hoffman *I Can Still Do Everything with One Arm* – Katie Laurel Wells *Emmanuel's Dream* – Laurie Thompson *Amazing* – Steve Anthony	
School Office	*Young, gifted and black* – Jamia Wilson *Queer heroes* – Arabelle Sicardi *Emmanuel's Dream* – Laurie Thompson	1

On the following pages you'll find a selection of books, separated by area of inclusivity. These books are both for your reading spaces and also for you to plan writing or reading sequences around.

> **Top tip!**
>
> Choose one book from each section and add to each year group's long-term plan. Plan either a sequence of reading (comprehension questions per chapter) or writing around the texts. For some of the books mentioned, there are already high-quality writing sequences planned and I've provided direction for where to find the planning.

Suggested titles

Personal favourites

Sulwe by Lupita Nyong'o, illustrated by Vashti Harrison
This powerful picture book is written by actress Lupita Nyong'o about colourism, self-confidence and finding true beauty within. Lupita celebrates her Kenyan culture within this book.

Under My Hijab (hardcover) by MS Hena Khan, illustrated by Aaliya Jaleel
This book's intention is for readers to appreciate and understand the hijab and the women who choose to wear it. Beautifully illustrated!

The Arrival by Shaun Tan
This stunning picture book explores migration and refugees through evocative images. It explores leaving your hometown because of war, violence or fear and arriving somewhere new. It delves into being faced with new ways of life, new languages and new people. A brilliant provocation for extended writing for upper Key Stage 2: narrative, newspaper and poetry. You can find planning sequences for this book on The Literary Curriculum website at www.literarycurriculum.co.uk. Shaun Tan was also the first global majority author to win a Kate Greenaway Medal in 2020.

The Other Side of Truth by Beverley Naidoo
This is the story of Femi and Sade, two children who are political refugees from Nigeria, who are sent to London and abandoned. It is the story of how they navigate coping with the police, social services and bullies at school. The book explores prejudice and racism, and overcoming barriers. It's also fantastic for upper Key Stage 2 writing – writing sequences can be found on the TES website.

This Book is Anti-Racist by Tiffany Jewell, illustrated by Aurelia Durand
This Book is Anti-Racist explores what racism is, where it comes from and self-identity. It teaches children to be ANTI-racist rather than non-racist. It is full of activities and challenges to do.

Black and British: A short, essential history by David Olusoga (suitable for Year 6+) and *Black and British: A forgotten history* by David Olusoga (suitable for younger children)
David Olusoga is an award-winning historian and broadcaster. The 'Black and British' collection is a fascinating and detailed introduction to 1,800 years of Black British history, ranging from the Roman Africans to the Black Georgians to the present day.

LGBT and challenging gender stereotypes

Pride: The Story of Harvey Milk and the Rainbow Flag by Rob Sanders, illustrated by Steven Salerno
This wonderful book captures the remarkable story of how the rainbow flag came to exist, the inspiring work of social activist Harvey Milk and flag designer Gilbert

Baker, and how the flag went worldwide. A story of hope, love, equality and pride. The Literary Curriculum does a fabulous writing unit on this book for Year 4.

Rainbow Revolutionaries: 50 LGBT people who made history by Sarah Prager, illustrated by Sarah Papworth
This non-fiction text, which is beautifully illustrated, explores LGBT+ people both past and present, and the impact that they have had upon the world. One of the favourites in my classroom!

Suffragettes: The battle for equality by David Roberts
This book was published in 2018 to mark the anniversary of women receiving the vote. It is an illustrated information book that works chronologically through the history of suffrage. A fantastic writing sequence can be found on The Literary Curriculum.

Gender Swapped Fairy Tales by Karrie Fransman and Jonathan Plackett
A truly 'girl power' text, this book has classic fairytales, rewritten where females are the heroes and not the helpless girls in need of saving – where princesses rescue princes and the queens are valiant and brave. A wonderful book and, quite frankly, one of my favourite books as an adult too!

People with disabilities

Sometimes by Rebecca Elliott

This is a great book for anyone who has a sibling in hospital. A story of love and bravery, Toby's big sister Clemmie has to go to hospital sometimes but still somehow manages to have fun. Sometimes they play games and sometimes Clemmie just wants to lie still and hold her sibling's hand.

Just Ask: Be different, be brave, be you by Sonial Sotomayor and Rafael López

This fabulous book gives many different examples of disabilities and was authored by Supreme Court Judge Sotomayor, who has lived with diabetes since childhood. Each character shares their disabilities and asks questions that both able-bodied and non-able-bodied children can relate to.

Wonder by R.J. Palacio

Wonder is a story about friendship, bullying and self-confidence. It is the story of Auggie, who has a facial deformity/difference, and him navigating his way to a new school. This is a wonderful transitional text for Year 6s moving into secondary school. R.J. Palacio actually wrote this book in response to her own son crying after noticing a girl with a facial deformity. Heart-warming and beautifully written.

Just Like Me: 40 neurologically and physically diverse people who broke stereotypes by Louise Gooding, illustrated by Melissa Iwai, Caterina Delli Carri, Cathy Hookey and Angel Chang

A collection of 40 role models from around the world who are all neuro or physically diverse. Beautifully illustrated and expertly written. A must-have for all libraries!

Top tip!

You will find a comprehensive list of books on the companion website, alongside other resources to point you in the right direction. Think about the wonderful understanding of a child who starts in Reception and leaves in Year 6 having read and studied in depth the books above. That is why we do what we do. Remember to give children opportunities to publish

> writing: this could be creating a class writing book, photocopying work to be sent home or for display, or posting on Twitter or a class blog/school website. This gives real purpose to writing, and ideas are shared and celebrated on a whole-school basis.

Budget and fundraising

Let's face it – buying new books is expensive and not all schools have the budget to simply restock all book corners. In a previous school, we were in a deficit for some time, so all books were bought through fundraising. If your school has a struggling budget, there are some simple ways in which to fundraise to restock your libraries:

- **Go Fund Me:** start a Go Fund Me campaign, explaining the exact amount that you need and what you are using it for. The more detail that you give about what specifically you plan to buy and, most importantly, the desired impact upon children, the more funds that you will be able to raise. In my school, which is situated in the middle of an estate in Camberwell, we raised £850 in one week, from Tweeting our campaign to local businesses. You can also send the campaign out to families to share amongst their networks too.

- **Amazon Wish List:** Create a Wish List on Amazon of all the books that you are hoping to buy. Once this is done, you can share your Wish List online: Twitter, Facebook groups, text to parents/carers, etc. People are able to buy books from the Wish List and get them sent directly to your school; they can do this anonymously or share their names. We filled up our library doing this last summer!

- **Birthday book:** Another way to begin to fill classroom book corners is to ask children to bring a 'birthday book' instead of cake when it's their birthday. This is so that they can share a story, which is much sweeter! If every child did this on their birthday, not only would the school be full of books to which children have a personal link, but it also brings a wonderful sense of community to reading and books.

- **Local newspapers:** Get in contact with your local newspapers and ask whether they want to help you to fundraise and share your campaigns. Generally speaking, local newspapers always want to get involved with helping out with children's learning, so you'll find that they'll be happy to oblige!

To sum up, books are a wonderful way in which to represent and hear different voices, viewpoints and perspectives, providing children with a platform to explore difference and build empathy and understanding.

Key takeaways

- Look at your reading spaces and books, and stock them up with diverse texts, showing a wide range of representation.
- Keep a school-wide record of the books that you have used in each year group, so that there are no repeats.
- When mapping out your English curriculum, first map out the genre of writing across the year, and then use diverse and inclusive books as a basis for your planning.
- Use a range of images on your teaching slides.
- Train up your staff team so that they are confident to address any discriminatory language head-on, and inform children of appropriate language.

4 History: Making the unseen seen

This chapter looks at the different areas of the history National Curriculum for Key Stage 1 and Key Stage 2, and how you can link your findings about your school and national community from your audit in Chapter 2 under each. It then gives direction for how and where to research relevant and interesting topics and how to link them to curriculum objectives. Furthermore, it discusses which topics are suitable for which key stage and how you can plan for progression across the curriculum.

In terms of history, you must have a commitment to researching and reading to develop your own subject knowledge, because unfortunately history has pretty much always been taught in the UK from a colonial, White-centric perspective. An absolute must read is David Olusoga's *Black and British*. There are three versions: an adult version (which is dense and fascinating), an older child's version (which I have used in reading lessons for upper Key Stage 2) and a beautiful illustrated history book.

> 'The refusal to accept that the black presence in Britain has a long and deep history is not just a symptom of racism, it is a form of racism. It is part of a rearguard and increasingly unsustainable defence of a fantasy monochrome version of British history.'
> (Olusoga, 2017)

In *Black and British*, Olusoga comprehensively explains Britain's troubled history with the Caribbean and Africa, mapping out the slave trade; it includes fascinating historical evidence and even childhood memories. He describes Black British history as woven into the threads of the economic and cultural history of the nation. There is also a brilliant documentary series on BBC iPlayer called *Black and British: A Forgotten History*, which is a good place for subject knowledge development.

Another must-read is The Black Curriculum website and resources (www.theblackcurriculum.com). The Black Curriculum is a social enterprise aiming to support the teaching of Black history all year round and to ensure that all children feel seen and included. There are brilliant resources, lesson packs and informative videos on the website, plus links to where teachers can further develop their subject knowledge. The content of this website is for teachers of eight- to 16-year-olds.

History curriculum – where to start?

Know what you're aiming for

Before you map out your history topics, make sure that you have a history teaching and learning policy in place, with a clear statement of what you are aiming to achieve in history.

An example is:

> **At XXXX School, we are proud of the diverse history curriculum, entrenched in inquiry and critical thinking.**
>
> **Our history curriculum ensures that children learn about a broad range of history, covering perspectives from: different races, ethnicities, women's voices, disabilities, LGBTQIA+ voices and different religions. There is a whole-school theme each term, related to the United Nations' 17 Sustainability Goals – ways to make our world even better.**

Staring at a blank whole-school curriculum map can be equal parts exciting and unnerving. It is not a quick job; it takes time to map out progression and coverage. Have the National Curriculum for history printed ready, get your highlighter pens out and take it step by step. Here's a few tips on where and how to start, taken from an article that I wrote for UKEDChat Magazine (Wordlaw, 2022):

Local history

Look at your cohort and local community: ethnic breakdown, different religions, abilities and cultures. Ensure that there are history projects and themes reflecting the cultures and backgrounds in your cohort. Use your local community for expertise! Get parents, carers, faith leaders, charities, local services and businesses in to speak to and inspire the children. Get out and about and involved in community issues and events.

National history

Irrespective of your cohort, we are a diverse nation and the best way to improve empathy and reduce discrimination in all its forms is through education. A rich study of national history cannot be crammed into one year, but ensure that by the time a child leaves your school, they've had access to an inclusive national history.

> **Top tip!**
>
> Some suggested study areas for British history that extend pupils' chronological knowledge beyond 1066: the *Windrush*, migration to Britain through time, Emmeline Pankhurst, women's suffrage, London Olympics and Paralympics, Olive Morris, Mary Seacole and women in Parliament.

International history

Obviously it is impossible to encompass the world's history within a primary school curriculum, but ensure that your studies of a non-European society contrasting with British history are varied across the year groups. Even though ancient Benin and Baghdad are suggested in the National Curriculum, I've rarely seen them appear on curriculum maps. When studying the World Wars, look at the Black soldiers who fought both for Britain and in Britain. Be sure to include freedom fighters from all walks of life when studying historical role models – for example, Harvey Milk fighting for gay rights or Emmanuel Ofosu Yeboah, who brought the world's attention to the fact that disability does not mean inability (Wordlaw, 2022).

On page 58 you can find an example of a whole-school curriculum map for history.

Key Stage 1 history

In this section, each heading is taken from the history National Curriculum, and then underneath is a list of topics that you could include to meet this objective. There are also tips on where to find further information or existing schemes of work.

Changes within living memory; where appropriate, these should be used to reveal aspects of change in national life

Food

This is a chance to look at how food has changed over the last 100 years and an opportunity to look at different types of food from different cultures and

History whole-school curriculum map

	Autumn 1	Autumn 2	Spring 1	Spring 2	Summer 1	Summer 2
School global curriculum theme	**Power and governance**	**Social justice and equality**	**Identity and diversity**	**Human rights**	**Sustainable development**	**Peace and conflict**
Year 1	Gunpowder plot	Sarah Forbes Bonetta Nelson Mandela (significant individuals)	Emily Davison and women's suffrage	Food technology – changes in living history	Nurturing nurses – Florence Nightingale and Marie Curie	Walter Tull and World War 1
Year 2	Queen Victoria What was London like then?	Elizabeth Fry and social activism	Ibn Battuta the explorer	The school day – changes in living memory	Mary Seacole and healthcare	Great Fire of London
Year 3	Iron Age	Martin Luther King and Jesse Owens	Ancient Egypt		Anglo Saxons and Settlements	Julius Cesar
Year 4/5	Shang Dynasty	History of British Civil Rights: LGBT, Race, Disability	A local history study: Camberwell's Black History		The Roman Empire World War 1	

understand where they come from. You can also look at the availability of food for different groups of people.

This gives children an opportunity to talk to their parents or carers, grandparents and family members about food, meals and popular foods through the ages. This also provides crossovers with geography, where children can map out where different food originated from.

> **Top tip!**
>
> This is a fantastic opportunity to organise a **whole-school event**. The amazing thing about food is that it is something that everyone – irrespective of their background, socio-economic status, first language, nationality, etc. – has experience of and can share. Create a space where families can bring in food from their home or food representing their heritage. This is a wonderful way to include and celebrate a wide range of cultures from families and staff members. Having an international food festival or family feast is a great way to include sometimes hard-to-reach families and build relationships between school and home.

Music

How has music changed and what different types of music are there? This is an opportunity to explore the music of different cultures: reggae, folk and tribal. Again, it is also another opportunity to include the parent community and local community. Get in touch with local musicians and ask them to come in. Survey the parent/carer community and see whether there are any musicians or friends of musicians. The chances are that someone in your school community will have links with musicians of sorts. This allows for a real rooted experience of music and a celebration of the link between music and culture.

A day in the life

Study how school life has changed. Look at different groups of people within this.

Lord Alf Morris

Look at his work, which led to the Chronically Sick and Disabled Persons Act in 1970.

Events beyond living memory that are significant nationally or globally (for example, the Great Fire of London, the first aeroplane flight or events commemorated through festivals or anniversaries)

National days

Canada Day, National Day of Poland, Indian Republic Day, Peru Day, Hamilton Trust Remembrance Day

The Bristol Bus Boycott of 1963

In 1963, a Black man named Guy Bailey was refused a job as a bus conductor in Bristol, because of the colour of his skin. After this, a boycott of the Omnibus Bus Company followed, and on 28 August, this racist rule was changed. The Bristol Bus Boycott was part of paving the way for the 1965 Race Relations Act in Britain, which banned racial discrimination in public places and made an offence of promoting hatred on the grounds of 'colour, race, or ethnic or national origins'.

The lives of significant individuals in the past who have contributed to national and international achievements; some should be used to compare aspects of life in different periods

- **Princess Sophia Duleep Singh:** a suffragette and campaigner for women's rights who fought for gender equality in the early twentieth century. She was also the goddaughter of Queen Victoria!
- **Emily Davison** and women's suffrage: an English suffragette who fought for women to have the vote in the early twentieth century.
- **Rosa May Billinghurst:** a suffragette who attended all her rallies in her wheelchair. She even chained it to the railings at Buckingham Palace.
- **Elizabeth Fry** and social activism: Fry helped people in need and was a very religious woman. She is particularly known for her work in prison and she fervently believed that all people, including prisoners, should be treated with kindness and respect. There's some good information on her on the BBC Bitesize website.

- **Mary Seacole:** a British–Jamaican nurse and business woman who cared for soldiers during the Crimean War.
- **Mary Anne Galton:** one of many women who decided to abstain from buying and eating sugar, to protest against the slave trade. Women who ran households took the lead on abstaining from sugar. In 1806, Mary Anne Galton moved to Bristol.
- **Louis Braille:** a French educator and inventor who created braille, a system to be used by blind people to read and write using raised dots on a paper.
- **Helen Keller:** a blind and deaf educator and activist who advocated for people with disabilities.
- **Bayard Rustin:** a gay, Black activist who was a part of the civil rights movement in America, fighting against violence, homophobia and racism. Watch the video 'Black & LGBT+ History Month' by Pop'n'Olly/Olly Pike at www.youtube.com/watch?v=5OYY-hykYjw as a provocation to draw links between Rustin and Martin Luther King. This is great for discussions around fairness and how we should treat each other.

The Historical Association has excellent schemes of work on the following:

- **Sarah Forbes Bonetta:** the West African Yoruba orphan who became a protégée of Queen Victoria, spending her lifetime between the British royal household and her homeland in West Africa.
- **Ibn Battuta the Explorer:** an Arab-Berber Maghrebi explorer and scholar who travelled 75,000 miles across and beyond the Islamic world.
- **Walter Tull and World War I:** a soldier in World War I and a professional football player. He is recognised as the first ever Black officer to lead White British soldiers in battle.
- **Grace O'Malley:** known as the Pirate Queen of Ireland, she was considered a fierce leader and she defended the independence of her territory when large parts of Ireland were coming under British rule.
- **Isambard Kingdom Brunel:** considered one of the best civil engineers in history, he was an English civil engineer who worked on the design and construction of the Thames Tunnel.

Significant historical events, people and places in their own locality

This section will require research into your local area. Delving into the history of your nearest high street tends to be a lovely project for children and an opportunity to develop historical skills. This is a great chance to speak with the parents/carers of your cohort, invite local people in to discuss the local history and create a bespoke medium-term plan fitting for your school. Invite a range of people, including, for example, religious leaders to lead assemblies or speak with classes about their beliefs and practices.

Key Stage 2 history

The National Curriculum states that:

> 'Pupils should continue to develop a chronologically secure knowledge and understanding of British, local and world history, establishing clear narratives within and across the periods they study. They should note connections, contrasts and trends over time and develop the appropriate use of historical terms. They should regularly address and sometimes devise historically valid questions about change, cause, similarity and difference, and significance. They should construct informed responses that involve thoughtful selection and organisation of relevant historical information. They should understand how our knowledge of the past is constructed from a range of sources.' (DfE, 2013a, p. 3)

There is less wiggle room in the Key Stage 2 history curriculum, as many of the topics are inherently Eurocentric and White-centric, so you will need to work hard on finding examples of Black people/culture within British history. For example, there were many Black Victorians; we just don't often see them in textbooks. When planning/designing your curriculum, be sure to be actively inclusive of Black people, women and people with disabilities. Likewise, the Key Stage 2 curriculum pre-1066 periods may make the inclusion of the history of people with disabilities more challenging, due to lack of recorded evidence.

Below are some suggestions to research and add into your plans, with suggestions for further reading at the end of the book on page 245.

Changes in Britain from the Stone Age to the Iron Age

There is a great opportunity to explore gender roles in society whilst learning about the Stone Age and Iron Age. For years, there has been the assumption of men as 'hunter-gatherers' and women as 'nurturers'. However, in 2018, an archaeologist from the University of California made an interesting discovery, which blew thinking about gender roles during this era out of the water.

On a dig in Peru, remains were found, including human bones and a vast stone toolkit. Initially, the team thought, 'Oh, *he* must have been a great hunter', based upon the tools. However, it was soon found out that the human bones were actually those of a woman; they were biologically female. This smashed the stereotype of men being hunter-gatherers and women looking after the babies. Furthermore, this discovery led them to find out that between 30 and 50 per cent of big game hunters were indeed female.

Within the stone tool set was found tools for killing animals, tools for cracking bones and tools for tearing flesh. This find would make a fantastic basis for historical enquiry for Key Stage 2.

For example, give children photos of Stone Age tools and ask:

- What are these?
- What are these used for?
- Who would use them?
- What are they made from?
- Who made them?

Based upon their answers, this would facilitate a great conversation into gender roles. You could then give them the report about the 2018 discovery and discuss their reaction to this.

The full report of the 2018 discovery can be found on the National Geographic website, by searching for 'prehistoric female hunter discovery upends gender role assumptions', or at the following link:

www.nationalgeographic.com/science/article/prehistoric-female-hunter-discovery-upends-gender-role-assumptions

The Red Lady of Paviland

The Red Lady of Paviland was, in fact, not a lady at all; they were a man, sporting a necklace of shells. The skeleton was discovered by a vicar in 1823, in Gower,

Wales. On this archaeological dig, they had believed the remains to be the bones of a woman; however, upon recent carbon-dating, the sex was found to be male, providing an interesting opportunity for questions:

* What could this tell us about life at the time?
* How reliable is evidence?

The Roman Empire and its impact on Britain

The Roman Empire was vast and spanned from 750 BC, when the city of Rome was founded, to 467 AD, when the Roman Empire fell. There were many African people who were part of the Roman Empire. Some African people came to Britain as soldiers, and there is some evidence of African soldiers stationed at Hadrian's Wall in Cumbria. They were thought to have guarded the fort walls.

Ivory Bangle Lady

In 1901, skeleton remains of who is known as the 'Ivory Bangle Lady' were found in York. The remains were dated back to the fourth century and she was believed to have come from a wealthy family and was of mixed North African heritage. Amongst her remains were found elephant ivory bracelets (hence the name 'Ivory Bangle Lady'), beads, a blue glass jug and pendants. During the Roman times, blue was considered protection from evil during the afterlife. Her skeleton and artefacts are on display in Yorkshire Museum, so if that's in your neck of the woods, go and visit!

Learning about the Ivory Bangle Lady can be a provocation for much historical enquiry:

* Why might women and children have migrated during the Roman Empire?
* What can this tell us about Romans in Britain?
* Is she wealthy or poor? How can we tell?

Beachy Head Lady

In 1953, the skeleton of a Roman woman was found near Beachy Head, in East Dean, East Sussex. She was of sub-Saharan African origin and lived in England whilst under the rule of the Romans. Historians were unsure about whether she was born in Britain or in Africa, but they know that she was around 30 when she died. This discovery was actually quite unusual because she was sub-Saharan

African – not North African, like Ivory Bangle Lady, which was part of the Roman Empire – and sub-Saharan Africa was beyond the Roman Empire, to the south.

This finding can be a great tool for getting children thinking about asking historical questions.

Give them the images of Beachy Head Lady and ask them to think about what they could ask as historians to find out more, and what this tells us about that period of time.

The role of women in Roman times

An interesting example to look at with regard to women's roles in Roman Britain is to discuss the Roman gladiator. Archaeologists in London found what some historians believe is the grave of a female gladiator in 1996. Historians know that women did fight in amphitheatres, but this was the first actual grave found (so far). This example can be used to stir up questions about gender roles.

Britain's settlement by Anglo-Saxons and Scots

Abbess Hilda of Whitby

Abbess Hilda of Whitby was a Christian saint and the founding abbess of the monastery at Whitby, which was chosen as the venue for the Synod of Whitby. She is an important figure in the Christianisation of Anglo-Saxon England, and many kings throughout Europe sought her advice on matters as she was very wise. In Oxford, St Hilda's College is named after her.

The Viking and Anglo-Saxon struggle for the Kingdom of England to the time of Edward the Confessor

Ivar the Boneless

Ivar was born around 794 AD and was nicknamed 'Ivar the Boneless' as he was born with a physical disability that meant he couldn't walk. Historians believe that he may have had brittle bone disease (or osteogenesis imperfecta). He was the son of the famous Viking warrior Ragnar Lodbrok and the Princess Aslaug Sigurdsdottir, which, luckily for him, meant that he wasn't killed because of his disability, as he was a Viking prince. An incredibly gifted warrior, Ivar was one of the most feared Vikings of the time. He invaded and occupied England.

'Ivarr grew up to be very clever and found ways to become a great Viking leader despite his disabilities. He solved the problem of not being able to walk by being carried into battle on the back of his shield. He was a fearless type of warrior called a "Berserker". Berserkers completely lost control in battle as if they were in a trance. Nowadays, when we talk about people going into a frenzy, especially if they're angry, we might say they're "going berserk". The Berserker fighting style is where this phrase comes from.'
(Skybadger, 2022)

A local history

Obviously, local history is specific to your area and individual school, but there are a few ways to learn a bit more about it if you are unsure. Speak with the school community, parents and carers. The likelihood is that some of them will have lived in that area their whole lives and they'll be able to give you some information and spoken history about the area. Speak to the pillars of the community, religious institutions, local businesses, the library, etc. Build up a picture of the local history and its journey through time.

A study of an aspect or theme in British history that extends pupils' chronological knowledge beyond 1066

The Paralympics and the history of sport

In 1948, the Paralympics were born from a wheelchair archery competition being held on the lawns of a hospital. Now, the Paralympics are one of the biggest sporting events on the planet, encompassing elite disabled athletes and sporting icons.

Campaigns for equal rights

Here you could look at and draw similarities between various different campaigns for equality, such as:

- Marsha P. Johnson, LGBT+ and trans activist, and the Stonewall riots
- Harvey Milk and gay rights
- Olive Morris and the campaign for race equality
- Votes for women
- Phyll Opoku-Gyimah, otherwise known as Lady Phyll, a British LGBT+ rights activist, anti-racism campaigner and also the co-founder of UK Black Pride.

History of Gay Rights in UK

Pride parade take place in many areas, both urban and rural, each year. Pride is a global movement aimed at fighting for equal rights for LGBTQ+ (lesbian, gay, bi, trans and queer) people all over the world, raising awareness and a celebration of diversity.

In 2017, it was the 50-year anniversary since it stopped being illegal for two men to be in a relationship in England and Wales, otherwise known as the 'decriminalisation of homosexuality'. There are still places in the world where it is illegal to be gay.

Throughout history, LGBTQ+ people have struggled to be accepted and treated the same as people who are not gay.

'Homosexuality was often treated as an illness by doctors and psychiatrists, who thought they could "heal" people by treating them. Lesbian, gay, bisexual and transgender people were often forced to hide their identities from their families, friends, colleagues and in public to avoid the risk of being singled out, harassed or becoming a victim of violence.' (Professor Brian Heaphy from the University of Manchester, cited on BBC Newsround, 2022)

Timeline of events

- 1969: The Stonewall riots (BBC Newsround, 2019) started after the police raided a gay bar called the Stonewall Inn, which was a popular place for gay people to hang out, starting the gay rights movement.
- 1972: The first Pride festival in London, where 2,000 people took part in marching to raise awareness for gay rights.
- 1988: A law called Section 28 was introduced, meaning that teachers were banned from 'promoting' gay relationships in schools or even talking about them. This was changed in 2003.
- 2000: Gay and bisexual people were legally allowed be in the armed forces.
- 2002: Gay people were legally allowed to adopt children.
- 2003: Section 28 was overturned.
- 2004: Civil partnerships became legal for gay people, meaning that gay couples had similar rights to married couples.
- 2008: Encouraging homophobic hatred became illegal.
- 2013: Gay marriage was made legal in England and Wales, and later in Scotland.

The study of gay rights in the UK is a study of basic human rights and a fascinating one at that.

Women and Space

There is a fantastic resource on women and space on the Historical Association website, written by Karen Doull. In the resource it describes how in the 1960s women began to be part of space exploration, for example Ludmila Tereshkova (who was a Russian astronaut) being the first women in space in 1963 and American Sally Ride in 1983.

Exploring spices

Since the ancient times, spices have been highly valued, and they provide a wonderful window into different societies and their cultural traditions. Spices have been used to season food but also as medicines to heal ailments and diseases. From being traded on the Silk Road to the spice trade routes that were blocked by the Ottoman Empire, spice provides a wonderfully diverse historical project, which everyone can relate to. There are also opportunities to link with cooking and nutrition in DT (design technology) and to run parent events.

Female migration to Australia

There is an interesting history of female migration to Australia: that of women arriving at the Hyde Park Barracks, which was an immigration depot for unaccompanied women. Many women came from Ireland in the late 1840s, as Ireland was going through famine at the time. Sydney Living Museums website has a great primary school information page about female migration to Australia, and lots of learning resources to draw from.

Alan Turing

Turing was a gay man who made one of the first computers. He was instrumental in decoding during the Second World War but was treated very unfairly because he was gay.

- If Alan Turing were alive now, would he have been treated differently?
- Can you imagine life without coding and technology?

Tudors (1485–1603)

John Blanke

John Blanke was the royal trumpeter to Henry VII and Henry VIII. In the early sixteenth century, John Blanke, or 'the Black Trumpeter', was a highly respected musician. There is historical evidence of John through an image on a tournament scroll (see p.69). When Henry VIII and his wife Catherine of Aragon gave birth to a son (on 1 January 1511), a large celebration was ordered by the royal family. This was a two-day Tournament of Westminster, where there is an account of a Black musician assumed to be Blanke. Twice he appears on the Westminster Tournament Roll manuscript, and a 'blacke trumpeter' is also mentioned in the Treasurer's accounts (Zick, 2008).

The Black Curriculum website explains: 'Not much is known about John Blanke due to the poorly documented material of him living, and the fact that he lived so long ago. However, it has been researched that he came to England in 1501 as one of Catherine of Aragon's attendants, when she married Prince Arthur, Henry VIII's older brother.' (2021)

Jacques Francis: The salvage diver

Jacques Francis was born off the West coast of Africa in the 1520s. When he came to England, he settled in Southampton, where he worked for another man. Henry VIII's great warship, the *Mary Rose*, was built as a result of England and France fighting, beginning in 1545. Unfortunately, the *Mary Rose* sank in Portsmouth Harbour before actually doing any fighting! As you can imagine, there were lots of guns and weapons aboard the sunken ship, which Henry wanted to retrieve, as they were worth a lot of money. A study of the bones and belongings of the crew (found in 1982, when the ship was raised from the seabed) revealed bones of men originating from different parts of the world, including North Africa.

Jacques Francis was amongst the divers who were tasked with retrieving these weapons. He was one of the best divers at the time. Of course, this was before what we now know as scuba diving gear, which meant that Jacques would have had to hold his breath whilst diving for extended periods of time, bringing the objects back up to the surface from the seabed.

Provocation questions:

* Why might many West Africans have been good swimmers at the time?
* What might it have been like swimming to the bottom of the ocean and bringing objects up?
* How did Jacques Francis help Henry VIII?

This picture shows John Blanke, The Black Trumpeter, at Henry VIII's Tournament. By Anonymous - https://manyheadedmonster.wordpress.com/2015/07/27/john-blanke-henry-viiis-black-trumpeter-petitions-for-a-back-dated-pay-increase-2/, Public Domain, https://commons.wikimedia.org/w/index.php?curid=91397289

Mary Fillis: The Moroccan convert

Mary Fillis was born in 1577 in Morocco. She came to England when she was six or seven and was raised as a Muslim. In London, where she lived, she was considered a servant rather than a slave, with a wealthy family. She then went to work for Millicent Porter, a seamstress. At 20, she was baptised and converted to Christianity. This was considered a big deal, as it meant that Mary now had godparent guardians: Millicent Porter, William Benton and Margery Barrack. Mary went on to become a seamstress herself.

Provocation questions:

* How do you think Mary came to Britain from Morocco in North Africa?
* What might her journey have been like?
* What was life like in Tudor England for Mary?

Dr Jason Todd and Chris Lewis (n.d.), in their report 'Bringing the untold stories of Black Tudors into the classroom', explores the following Black Tudors – research their lives and add to your planning!

> **Dederi Jaquoah, the prince of River Cestos** – the son of King Caddi-biah, who was the ruler of a kingdom which is now modern-day Liberia.
> **John Anthony, mariner of Dover** – a sailor, thought to have come to England alongside the pirate Sir Henry Mainwaring.
> **Cattelena of Almondsbury, independent single woman** – living in Bristol until she died in 1625, she was not *owned* rather she owned possessed property herself, the most prized of which was a cow.

Victorians (1837–1901)

Pablo Fanque

Pablo Fanque was a Black British equestrian performer and, in addition, was a circus proprietor – in fact, the first recorded non-White British circus owner in Britain. His circus was extremely popular in Victorian Britain for many years, a period of time that many people regarded as the golden age of the circus. Since the 1960s, Fanque is best known for his mention in the song 'Being for the benefit of Mr Kite!' by the Beatles, from *Sgt. Pepper's Lonely Hearts Club Band* (1967). The image on the next page is a drawing from Illustrated London News March 20, 1847 found at https://upload.wikimedia.org/wikipedia/en/0/08/Fanque_at_Astley%27s.jpg

Arthur Wharton

Arthur Wharton was the first Black professional football player, born in Ghana in 1865, and moving to England in 1883. He was a fantastic all-round sportsman. Not only was he the first Black professional football player but he was also, at the time, the first official fastest man. He was also a keen and talented rugby player and cricketer. Check out the Arthur Wharton Foundation for more information on him and his life: www.arthurwhartonfoundation.org

The achievements of the earliest civilizations

Strong women in ancient civilisations

Take a look at the following female leaders in ancient civilisations and use evidence to prompt children to think about what artefacts can tell us about life at the time.

Nefertiti (Egyptian queen)

Queen Nefertiti was a powerful woman who reigned as queen of Egypt alongside the Pharaoh Akhenaten from 1353 to 1336 BC.

This picture shows Wharton (seated second from left on front row) while playing for Darlington F.C., in 1887. By unknown author, https://commons.wikimedia.org/w/index.php?curid=42394473

Cleopatra (queen of Egypt)
Cleopatra VII Thea Philopator was born around 69 BC and ruled for roughly 21 years in the Egyptian city of Alexandria. She ruled Egypt before it was taken over by the Roman Empire. She wasn't Egyptian at all; she was Greek. She was extremely intelligent and spoke both ancient Egyptian and Greek. She would often read scrolls from the library of Alexandria, and many historians believe that she brought peace to Egypt during one of its most challenging times.

Fu Hao (Shang dynasty)
Fu Hao was an army leader and powerful ruler, whose grave was excavated in 1976. In her grave was found many artefacts, which guide what we currently know about the Shang dynasty. This finding was important because it is the only royal tomb from the Shang dynasty that was undamaged, thus still containing her many precious items, meaning that historians could learn a lot from it. In her tomb were the remains of six dogs and 16 humans, more than 450 bronze objects (such as 130 weapons, bells, knives and mirrors), jade and stone objects, more than 550 bone objects (like bone hairpins and arrowheads), lots of pottery objects and Shang money (known as cowry shells).

Show children photos of the artefacts found in her tomb:

- How can we use these artefacts to learn about Shang times?
- What do these tell us about how she lived?
- What do these tell us about how people lived?
- What don't these tell us about how people lived?

Ancient Greece – a study of Greek life and achievements and their influence on the Western world

Ancient Greeks with disabilities

The Spartans did not recognise a physical disability as a reason not to join the military or fight. Amongst the famous 300 who stood with Leonidas was Eurytus. Eurytus had an eye condition, but he fought and died with the 300, as a brave soldier.

There were no wheelchairs in Ancient Greece; prosthetic arms and leg were crafted out of wood. An example of this is Hegesistratus, who was imprisoned by the Spartans. In order to escape, he had to cut off his own foot, and he then went on to make his own prosthetic foot from wood. Ancient Greeks also made corrective boots for those who struggled with walking.

- How might life have been different for people with disabilities during the Ancient Greek times?
- What similarities might there have been for people with disabilities during the Ancient Greek times?
- What skills might a doctor in the Ancient Greek times need?

Agnodice of Athens

In the fourth century, Agnodice of Athens was the first female doctor, and had to dress as a man so that she could train. Women were legally barred from training as doctors at the time, but this did not stop her. She had to cut off her hair and wear 'men's clothes' in order to pass.

- Why was it so difficult for Agnodice to become a doctor?
- How does her experience contrast with now? Is this the same for all places?

A non-European society that provides contrasts with British history – one study chosen from: early Islamic civilisation, including a study of Baghdad c. AD 900; Mayan civilisation c. AD 900; Benin (West Africa) c. AD 900–1300

Zubayda bint Ja'far al-Mansur

Zubayda, from Bahdad, was said to be the most powerful and richest woman in the world. She was famous mainly due to actively making the pilgrimage to Mecca safer, through funding waystations and wells between Baghdad and Mecca. She also is remembered for the reservoirs and artificial pools and wells that were built on this path.

Provocation questions.

- What do you think it was like to go on a Hajj during the time at which Zubayda lived?
- How did she impact the pilgrimage?
- What might the Hajj be like if she hadn't done the work she did?

Lady K'abel

Lady K'abel, or 'supreme warrior', was a Mayan military ruler and queen. As the warrior queen, her role was more important than the king's. Much like Fu Hao, when her tomb was discovered in 2012 in Guatemala, she was found with lots of artefacts, which taught historians much about the seventh-century Maya.

I've really gained a love of history myself from developing my subject knowledge through curriculum mapping, and I hope that you do too!

Key takeaways

- When mapping out your history curriculum, first map out topics for the long-term plan and then, once you have mapped out your topics relating to the National Curriculum, you can add in diverse and inclusive learning within these topics.
- Think about how to build on prior knowledge from one year group to the next – for example, think about what you would like a child leaving Key Stage 1 to know and understand when they move into Key Stage 2.
- There are lots of existing resources, so use them and build upon the content.

5 Geography: A global view, representative and varied

'A high quality geography education should inspire in pupils a curiosity and fascination about the world that will remain with them for the rest of their lives.' **(DfE, 2013b)**

This chapter looks at the different areas of the geography National Curriculum for Key Stage 1 and Key Stage 2, giving direction as to how and where to research relevant and interesting topics and how to link them to curriculum objectives. Furthermore, it discusses which topics are suitable for which key stage and how you can plan for progression across the curriculum.

Geography is all about the world and helps us to understand its people, places and wider environments, and how these three things interact. It is enquiry-led and supports us to understand change – how and why people, places and environments change – and think about our future. It celebrates the importance of location and how places are connected and what they are like. With this in mind, geography plays a critical role in challenging issues of prejudice, inequality, racism and stereotyping the 'other'. Geography must value different cultures, rather than simply look at festivals and folklore seen through the lens of a more 'dominant society' towards minority groups.

Teaching children to be geographers supports them to both ask and answer fundamental questions like:

- Where is this place and what is it like?
- Why is this place like this?
- What might it be like in the future and why?
- How has it changed? Why has it changed?
- What can we do to influence change?
- How is this place connected to its people/environment/other places?
- Why is this place connected to its people/environment/other places?

A richly diverse geography curriculum looks to understand how diverse and different perspectives and values can change and/or influence places and their environments. Stepping back and looking at how places and people are interconnected and, through this, studying inequality helps children to understand the world better and think critically. Geography is not to be studied in isolation; it is entwined with other curriculum subjects, like history, to serve as a vehicle for children to develop well-rounded perspectives and make sense of the world around them.

Subject knowledge of maps

In terms of decolonising the curriculum, it is important to recognise how many of the maps used today were designed from a Eurocentric perspective, making Africa, for example, appear much smaller than in reality. The Mercator map (on page 79) does not accurately portray the sizes of countries; for example, Greenland is actually much smaller and Europe is actually half the size of South America. Throughout history, those who had the maps ruled and conquered (and, most often, colonised). There are many maps that are also full of prejudice – for example, depicting Asia as the 'dangerous East' – and there have been maps designed with different centre points, such as an Islamic Mecca-centred map found in Isfahan. There are other projections of the world, such as Peters, which shows:

> *'an equal-area projection which became the centrepiece of a controversy surrounding the political implications of map design. The argument goes something like this: Mercator inflates the sizes of regions as they gain distance from the equator. Since much of the developing world lies near the equator, these countries appear smaller and less significant. On Peter's projection, by contrast, areas of equal size on the globe are also equally sized on the map so poorer, less powerful nations could be restored to their rightful proportions.' (Guardian, 2009)*

Top tip!

Add maps to your classroom displays, even if they are not about geography. If you have a literacy working wall, for example, add a map of where the book is set. This exposure to maps, place and direction builds up a wider understanding of place.

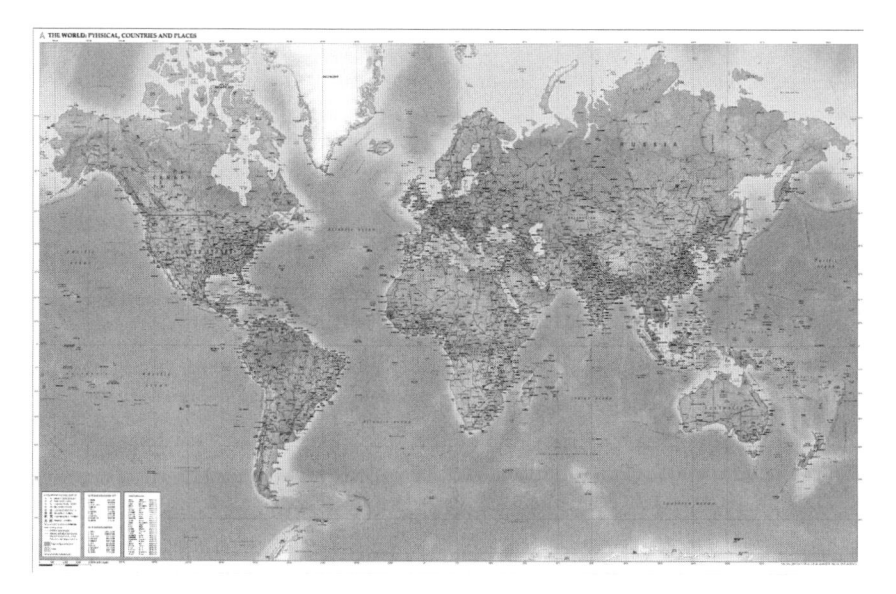

Combined map of the world in Pseudo Mercator projection showing physical, political and population characteristics, as per 2018. Image taken from: https://commons.wikimedia.org/wiki/File:Mercator_world_map_(physical,_political,_population).jpg

Geography curriculum – where to start?

Know what you're aiming for

Before you map out your geography topics, make sure that you have a geography teaching and learning policy in place, with a clear statement of what you are aiming to achieve in geography.

An example is:

> At XXXX School, we are proud of the diverse geography curriculum, entrenched in current issues and critical thinking.
>
> Our geography curriculum ensures that children learn about a broad range of geography, covering perspectives from: different races, ethnicities, women's voices, disabilities, LGBTQIA+ voices and different religions. There is a whole-school theme each term, related to the UN's 17 Sustainability Goals – ways to make our world even better.

As mentioned in Chapter 2, the United Nations 17 Sustainability Goals is a great place to start when thinking about projects for children to develop their geography skills. The purpose of the goals is to make the world a better and more sustainable place – what better starting point around which to base learning? It's real and helps children to make sense of the world and their place in it.

The goals are:

- no poverty
- zero hunger
- good health and wellbeing
- quality education
- gender equality
- clean water and sanitation
- affordable and clean energy
- decent work and economic growth
- industry, innovation and infrastructure
- reducing inequality
- sustainable cities and communities
- responsible consumption and production
- climate action
- life below water
- life on land
- peace, justice and strong institutions
- partnerships for the goals.

The Sustainability Goals provide a fabulous resource for teaching children relevant geography, deep-rooted in activism for a better world. They are also a great place to start when thinking about how to map out relevant and inclusive geography, rooted in real-life contexts. On the UN website, you can find a child-friendly booklet, 'The world we want: A future for all', explaining each of the goals in detail: www.un.org/sustainabledevelopment/wp-content/uploads/2015/03/SDGs-child-friendly.pdf

Challenging bias

As educators, we have a huge role to play in shaping how children look at the world. We must make sure that images we use and information that is shared about places are well-rounded and provide opportunities to challenge bias. This is to make sure that we give the 'whole picture' when learning about a place.

An example of how to do this is to learn about a new place by giving children six images of this place (e.g. tourism, urban areas, food, local life, agriculture and natural landscapes, etc.), without telling them what the location is. Ask children to discuss their impression of the place; this could be done with Year 1 right up to Year 6. But here's the clincher! Give another group of children six contrasting photos of the *same place* relating to each of the areas above. Each group will have a different impression of the place based upon the images that they have been given. See what happens when you reveal to the children at the end of the session that all images come from the same place. Ask children to think about what questions they would like to ask as a result and get them to discuss the findings! The bottom line here is that all the images given were 'real', but a photo alone cannot give you the 'whole picture' of what a place is like.

Subject content from National Curriculum and linked projects

On the following pages are areas of the National Curriculum, with ideas for projects that are diverse and inclusive, along with the areas of the UN 17 Sustainability Goals to which they link.

Locational knowledge

Sustainability Goals links: 15. Life on land; 14. Life below water
Children should be taught to:

Key Stage 1

- name and locate the world's seven continents and five oceans
- name, locate and identify characteristics of the four countries and capital cities of the United Kingdom and its surrounding seas.

Key Stage 2

- locate the world's countries, using maps to focus on Europe (including the location of Russia) and North and South America, concentrating on their

environmental regions, key physical and human characteristics, countries and major cities
- name and locate counties and cities of the United Kingdom, geographical regions and their identifying human and physical characteristics, key topographical features (including hills, mountains, coasts and rivers) and land-use patterns; and understand how some of these aspects have changed over time
- identify the position and significance of latitude, longitude, equator, Northern Hemisphere, Southern Hemisphere, the Tropics of Cancer and Capricorn, Arctic and Antarctic Circle, the Prime/Greenwich Meridian and time zones (including day and night).

Locational knowledge means to be able to know and recall where places are and to know what is there. The aim of this is for children to be able to develop their own mental maps and be able to talk about what is in each of the places. They must be exposed to maps, globes, atlases and aerial photos regularly to develop a really strong locational knowledge – across the curriculum, and not just in geography. You must make sure that the maps you have are up to date; ensure that you audit your atlases and globes to make sure they show the world as it is now! I recently found Czechoslovakia in an atlas in my school library!

Use school trips as a provocation to map out journeys. It doesn't have to be a geography trip; any and every trip provides a great opportunity for children to understand their location. Before the trip, ask children:

- Where are we going?
- How are we going to get there? Is there more than one option?
- What landmarks will we pass?

It is also a great opportunity for problem-solving. Ask: What if there are no buses? What if the road is closed? What if we get lost – which landmark would we look for to find our way? For older children, you could even print off a map for children to have with them on the journey or, even better, get children to draw a map. When I take out Year 5 and 6 on trips, I always print off one map between two and sometimes deliberately take wrong turns – there are always children who notice and correct me, which is a great learning opportunity for them.

Barnaby Bear

Barnaby Bear is a cuddly toy that children can take home over the weekend and take photos of where he/she has been. This is a great way to get children thinking about places. This tends to be used mainly in Key Stage 1, but it is equally effective in Key Stage 2 (though you may need to get buy-in by choosing a different toy that the older children like!). There is a wealth of free Barnaby Bear teaching resources online (including TES and Twinkl).

> **Top tip!**
>
> The first time that you write to your new class's parents and carers (perhaps you send a curriculum letter at the start of the year), ask them to take photos of any places, landmarks and countries that they visit and send them to you. Tell them that it helps to build children's sense of place and it also makes a fabulous working geography display in your classrooms/ corridors.

Children can develop their locational knowledge both through explicit lessons and also as part of a wider project. There are opportunities for developing locational knowledge through the teaching of PE and orienteering too. The British Orienteering website has a great free resource for primary orienteering that you could use: www.britishorienteering.org.uk/images/uploaded/downloads/schools_tri_o_resources.pdf

Place knowledge

Sustainability Goals links: 15. Life on land; 14. Life below water
Children should be taught to:

Key Stage 1

- understand geographical similarities and differences through studying the human and physical geography of a small area of the United Kingdom, and of a small area in a contrasting non-European country.

Key Stage 2

- understand geographical similarities and differences through the study of human and physical geography of a region of the United Kingdom, a region in a European country and a region within North or South America.

There is a wonderful opportunity with geography to link lessons with art, to allow children to explore the beauty of the world, ask questions and think critically. Kandinsky and Mondrian are both artists who use shape and colour to explore landscapes. Use these as provocation! First show children some examples of their art. Ask them:

- What can you see?
- What do you notice?
- What is this place like?
- Why might this place be like this?

Then, following this, take children out on a field trip: a walk around the school building or a walk around the local area or a park. Allow opportunities for children to stop, notice, draw and take photos. There is beauty in stopping, looking and listening to the space around us. Depending on the key stage, older children could jot down questions that they want to ask about the environment and write lists of natural and human features that they notice. Younger children might point out features that they see.

This learning opportunity feeds in nicely for children to then go on and:

- Draw a map of the area that they have visited.
- Paint their own picture, using colour and shape to show the human and natural features.
- Create a 3D map.

Building on this in Key Stage 2, and looking at regions in Europe and/or North/South America, satellite images are great to use. You could start by showing children a zoomed-in satellite image of a place. Get children to comment on the texture, shape and colour that they see. Prompt them to ask or note down questions. Then zoom out and do the same. This is a wonderful opportunity to look at the link between art and architecture too.

Human and physical geography

Human and physical geography is the meatiest part of the geography curriculum, and the one in which there are so many opportunities to develop critical thinking. This is the study of the natural and human features of our environment.

Key Stage 1

Sustainability Goals links: 1. No poverty; 2. Zero hunger; 3. Good health and wellbeing; 12. Responsible consumption; 13. Climate action

Children should be taught to:

- identify seasonal and daily weather patterns in the United Kingdom and the location of hot and cold areas of the world in relation to the equator and the North and South Poles
- use basic geographical vocabulary to refer to:
  - key physical features, including: beach, cliff, coast, forest, hill, mountain, sea, ocean, river, soil, valley, vegetation, season and weather
  - key human features, including: city, town, village, factory, farm, house, office, port, harbour and shop.

Here are a list of wonderful projects to add into your long-term plans, along with where you can find planning sequences to make your own:

Focus on frozen worlds (www.wwf.org.uk/sites/default/files/2020-05/LTLN_Frozen_Worlds_Web.pdf)
There is a great resource made by the World Wildlife Fund entitled 'Focus on frozen worlds', which explores the effect of climate change on the world's ice and goes into detail about how this affects the world and, specifically, animals such as penguins, polar bears and humpback whales. This resource is also linked to the Netflix documentary *Our Planet*, which is a great resource to pair it with.

Our changing world (PlanBee: https://planbee.com)
This project explores climate change for Key Stage 1, and develops the education of social responsibility. It looks at climates across the world and how they are changing – for example, ice, deserts and forests. It also explores flood and drought. This resource isn't free, but it is relatively cheap and is a whole term's set of lessons.

You can also download a progression of geography skills document for free from PlanBee, which I have found useful.

Exploring weather through story

The Geographical Association (2018) suggests using stories as a provocation to learn about and explore the weather. Here are some of their suggestions:

- *A Friend Like You* by Julia Hubery and Caroline Pedler
- *After the Storm* by Nick Butterworth
- *Alfie Weather* by Shirley Hughes
- *At the Beach* by Roland Harvey
- *Baby Rhino's Escape* by Adrienne Kennaway
- *Barnaby Bear at the Seaside* by Elaine Jackson
- *Blizzard!* by Jim Murphy
- *Bringing the Rain to Kapiti Plain* by Verna Aardema
- *Cloudland* by John Burningham
- *Cloudy with a Chance of Meatballs* by Judi Barrett
- *Down by the Pond: A surprise farmyard book* by Margrit Cruickshank
- *Five Little Fiends* by Sarah Dyer
- *Freddy the Frogcaster* by Janice Dean
- *Granny's Jungle Garden* by Colin West
- *Grandad's Prayers of the Earth* by Douglas Wood
- *Ice Bear's Cave* by Mark Haddon and David Axtell
- *If Frogs Made Weather* by Marion Dane Bauer

Key Stage 2

Sustainability Goals Links: 1. No poverty; 2. Zero hunger; 3. Good health and wellbeing; 4. Quality education; 5. Gender equality; 6. Clean water and sanitation; 7. Affordable clean energy; 8. Decent work; 9. Industry, innovation and infrastructure; 10. Reduced inequalities; 11. Sustainable cities; 12. Responsible consumption; 13. Climate action

Children should be taught to:

- describe and understand key aspects of:
    - physical geography, including: climate zones, biomes and vegetation belts, rivers, mountains, volcanoes and earthquakes, and the water cycle

- human geography, including: types of settlement and land use, economic activity including trade links, and the distribution of natural resources including energy, food, minerals and water.

Projects

Shaping our future: The climate challenge (WWF: www.wwf.org.uk/sites/default/files/2019-12/WWF_ClimateChallenge_Overview.pdf)

This is a wonderful set of climate-themed lessons to help children to develop their understanding of:

- what climate change is
- why it is happening
- what we can do about it.

It explores how many of the largest problems in our world, like poverty, extreme weather and animal extinction, are being caused by climate change. This project provides an opportunity for children to ask questions, think critically and develop an understanding of what needs to be done to protect what matters most to them: protecting animals, places and people whom they love.

There is also a set of resources on Oxfam's website called 'The human impact of climate change' (www.oxfam.org.uk/education/classroom-resources/human-impact-climate-change), which is great.

> **Top tip!**
>
> If you have the resources, take children out on a climate action march, or start your own in-school one!

The water fight (www.wateraid.org/uk/will-you-join-the-water-fight)

There are fantastic free teaching resources on the Water Aid website, this being one of them. This lesson pack is about clean water and sanitation. There are some quite visceral videos to watch as part of this project, so be sure to watch them first before showing them to your class (although they are age-appropriate). It starts with the provocation of asking children, 'What can't you live without?'. It looks at access to clean toilets and how some people do not have this. It prompts children to think about:

- the importance that water has in our lives
- what happens if people do not have clean water
- what happens if people do not have proper sanitation.

This project explores many of the Sustainability Goals, such as poverty, clean water and sanitation, and reduced inequalities. It is also cross-curricular and children have opportunities to develop literacy and PSHE too.

Land for life (www.wwf.org.uk/aid-match)
This project was designed by WWF, who collaborated with communities in both northern Tanzania and southern Kenya, with the aim of looking at how people and wildlife exist together and thrive. It explores keeping landscapes and wildlife healthy and the natural systems surrounding this. It also looks at some of the damage that humans have done to the natural area and what to do to improve it.

> **Top tip!**
>
> You may have families, teachers or people in your school community who come from areas that you study (e.g. Kenya, Tanzania, etc.). Invite them in to talk about their home or bring photos in; they may even have photos from their childhood. Hearing real-life experiences enhances children's engagement and connection to the topic.

Our planet: Biomes (WWF: www.wwf.org.uk/get-involved/schools/our-planet)
This is a great set of resources looking in detail at various different biomes, such as:

- seas
- frozen world
- freshwater
- grasslands
- jungles and forests.

It gives detailed and interesting information about all of the above, including beautiful images. These can be used as provocations for delving into these different areas of the planet.

> **Top tip!**
>
> Once children have learned *about* these biomes, ask them to demonstrate their learning by choosing how they want to show you. You could give them a choice of a piece of writing, a poem, a booklet, a painting, etc. Allow children the opportunity to talk through their final piece in pairs, asking a few children to share in front of the class. This is a wonderful assessment opportunity for you to walk around and listen in to the children as they talk, and gauge their understanding of the topic.

Animal ambassadors: Speak up for animals threatened by poaching (Tale 2 Tail: https://static1.squarespace.com/static/5c5d84cd90f9040c32c0031b/t/5c6e92324785d3665ffa5e1a/1550750395109/t2t-animal-ambassadors_lesson-guides-v3.pdf)

This is a fantastic free scheme of work surrounding the issue of illegal poaching of animals. Children often feel very deeply about the protection of animals, and this is a great project for developing critical thinking around moral questions, also building upon their citizenship and PSHE skills. This project in particular looks at the illegal ivory and wildlife trade. It allows children to understand which animals are endangered and why and to reflect on the beauty of wildlife through photography and illustration. It also provides a framework for children to express their views and know how to take action.

International Women's Day (Oxfam: www.oxfam.org.uk/education/classroom-resources/international-womens-day-assembly-and-activity-ideas/?pscid=ps_ggl_dsa&gclid=Cj0KCQjw-fmZBhDtARIsAH6H8qimcpIZJrR9zbexIZCbOBjOUkGyL8zvsVmJGOqXuwevGJMJzyM6oTUaAotgEALw_wcB&gclsrc=aw.ds)

This is a fascinating delve into issues surrounding gender inequalities around the world, exploring why there is a need for International Women's Day. It has facts and figures to highlight the global issues and develops children's understanding of gender stereotypes and how to challenge them. It also gives children language and opportunities to reflect upon discrimination and inequality and how we can make a positive change in the world.

Go bananas: Discover where food comes from (Oxfam: www.oxfam.org.uk/education/classroom-resources/go-bananas-help-learners-aged-7-11-disco ver-where-their-food-comes/#:~:text=Discover%20where%20our%20food%20comes,countries%20where%20bananas%20are%20grown.)

This project allows children to make connections between local and global areas by exploring the journey of bananas and how they get to our homes in the UK. It explores fairness and inequalities and provides a platform for children to think critically around these issues. There is learning about Fairtrade and a wealth of high-quality resources and photos to support teaching. There are great opportunities for cross-curricular work, including literacy and PSHE.

Stand with refugees (Oxfam: www.oxfam.org.uk/education/classroom-resources/stand-refugees/?pscid=ps_ggl_dsa&gclid=Cj0KCQjw-fmZBhDtARIsAH6H8qiCHwWkjGELYA4XUWqyAZwELVFFhYrq4tGnSYfIrsYrPqAhewauhfMaAjl2EALw_wcB&gclsrc=aw.ds)

This project looks at the push and pull factors of a person leaving their home, and looks at people who have been forcibly displaced from their homes. It allows for critical and reflective thinking about people who have had to leave their lives, families, livelihoods and communities behind because of conflict or disaster.

> **Top tip!**
>
> Remember that you may have pupils in your class who are refugees. Be sensitive to possible traumas that children may have; you may have children who are keen to share experiences and talk to the class, or you may have the reverse – children who go very quiet when learning about it. Preface your lessons with a chat around feeling safe and what to do if they learn or are shown something that worries them or reminds them of a memory, along with who they can talk to.

Geographical skills and fieldwork

Children should be taught to:

Key Stage 1

- use world maps, atlases and globes to identify the United Kingdom and its countries, as well as the countries, continents and oceans studied at this key stage

- use simple compass directions (north, south, east and west) and locational and directional language (for example, near and far; left and right), to describe the location of features and routes on a map
- use aerial photographs and plan perspectives to recognise landmarks and basic human and physical features; devise a simple map; and use and construct basic symbols in a key
- use simple fieldwork and observational skills to study the geography of their school and its grounds and the key human and physical features of its surrounding environment.

Key Stage 2

- use maps, atlases, globes and digital/computer mapping to locate countries and describe features studied
- use the eight points of a compass, four- and six-figure grid references, symbols and keys (including the use of Ordnance Survey maps) to build their knowledge of the United Kingdom and the wider world
- use fieldwork to observe, measure, record and present the human and physical features in the local area using a range of methods, including sketch maps, plans and graphs, and digital technologies.

Fieldwork is essential and must be planned into all projects. Allowing children to connect with places and environments is imperative in their development as geographers. Use your school locality to the max to build in opportunities for children to touch, feel, see, smell and hear real places. Get children using maps, both paper (Ordnance Survey) and digital (Google Maps). Maps, and using them to find your way around, are all about two key elements: direction and distance. These are the unchanging elements of map work, from EYFS right to the end of Year 6 (although the vocabulary around it will, of course, develop throughout the key stages to be age-appropriate). Put maps in your libraries and book corners! Every time you go somewhere, pick up a map. This could be a local train station, bus routes, museum, tube map, any maps you pick up on holiday, etc.

There is a wealth of great lessons on map skills on the Royal Geographical Society website (www.rgs.org/schools/teaching-resources), with PowerPoints, lesson plans and PDF resources, all free to use. There is also a vast amount of fieldwork resources to be found, including resources for:

- colour-blind-friendly mapping – inclusive teaching
- sustainability – looking after our world
- soundscapes – immersing in the acoustic environment
- geotagging – geotagging photos to share field trips with the world
- investigating opinions – interview surveys and questionnaires
- geography and core maths resources – important opportunities to develop mathematical, quantitative and statistical techniques
- rural investigations – investigating land use, function and issues in rural areas, and their changing identity and character
- urban studies – popular locations for fieldwork, since 70 per cent of us live in built-up areas
- ecosystems – geared towards a range of different ecosystem settings, ranging from coastal sand dunes to woodlands and inland waters
- stay-home stories – rethinking the domestic during the Covid-19 pandemic
- transport – fieldwork techniques using transport
- microclimate – microclimate data can be collected in any location, including the school grounds
- tourism and recreation – investigating the impact of tourism and recreation.

Case study: Climate change protests

One of the most successful projects that I have done recently was about climate change. The driving question of the project was: How can we use our voice to change the world?

We took a group of children to the climate change protests in central London, inspired by Greta Thunberg and her activism. We learned about her and how she used her voice to raise awareness through the book *Greta's Story: The schoolgirl who went on strike to save the planet* (Camerini, 2019). I must admit, the protest was busy and I found myself counting the children more than I normally would on a school trip – I was glad that they were in hi vis vests, so we could see them! One of the children said to me afterwards, 'I was glad to be wearing our school hi vis so people could see what our school believes in', which I thought was really sweet and made my day.

With the protest as a provocation, we then learned about climate change, the damage that has been done to the earth and what we could do to make things better. Children then showcased their learning at the end of the project, and were given freedom to choose how they wanted to demonstrate what they had learned.

The outcomes were amazing! Some children created their own placard boards, with slogans such as 'There's no planet B' and 'Save our world'. On the back, they did reflective pieces of writing about the reality of climate change. Some children chose to design T-shirts to spread awareness about how we can protect our earth, and one group even wrote a play (which they performed!). Planning a field trip to the protest, coupled with detailed geographical lessons and high-quality key texts, created a brilliant project where children were keen and engaged and made excellent progress.

To sum up, a high-quality and rich geography education is key in teaching global views and breaking down unconscious biases and colonial views of the world. Learning about and from different cultures, places and ways of life is imperative for children… and fun!

Key takeaways

- When mapping out your geography curriculum, first map out topics for the long-term plan and then, once you have planned your topics relating to the National Curriculum, you can add in diverse and inclusive learning within these topics.
- Be sure to plan fieldwork into every term's project – it doesn't have to be expensive or take time away from other subjects. It can simply be going outside and giving children real-life contexts to enhance their learning.
- Build up your collection of maps in your classroom and schools – ask teachers, parents and children to bring in any free maps that they see when they are out and about. Make sure your projects are varied and that the structure of the lessons allows for children to think and question.
- Lastly, there is a free teacher CPD resource for teaching outstanding geography on the Royal Geographical Society website here: www.rgs.org/schools/teaching-resources/from-good-to-outstanding-teaching.

6 The arts: Art and design, music and drama

This chapter looks at the arts across the curriculum and how to develop more inclusive and diverse practice. The arts are a wonderfully expressive platform to use to engage children in issues and get them talking about diversity. A rich arts curriculum allows children to grow skills, confidence and engagement, developing pride in their achievements as well as enabling the whole school to value creativity and expression. Excellent teaching of the creative arts is proven to improve students' wellbeing. In the report, 'Art works: Using arts to promote emotional health and wellbeing in schools' (City Arts, 2013), Kate Duncan notes that:

> *'art has long been known to have therapeutic properties. In creating visual images, people "draw" on the right side of their brains. This same side is used before spoken language develops and is where visual memories are stored. Creativity is also well recognised for its potential to heal people, express hidden emotions, reduce stress, fear and anxiety, and promote a sense of autonomy. Engaging young people in the arts can inspire and motivate, opening up new possibilities for creative expression and imagination. It can stimulate a young person's ability to question and connect with the world around them, and nurture positive aspirations, confidence and the capacity for autonomous critical thought. It can also help young people to develop the resilience to manage challenging life circumstances.' (p. 3)*

Visits to art galleries, heritage sites and theatres have an extremely significant impact on pupils' learning. In the most effective practice, teachers plan and prepare carefully for the visits so that the pupils get the most from the experience, and they follow up pupils' learning quickly once back at school. Be sure to enable *all pupils* to take part in trips and visits by reducing or waiving costs, especially for disadvantaged pupils. Trips also allow wonderful opportunities for children to work from observation and to capture multi-sensory experiences. Some examples are:

- Art galleries: Check out what is nearby to you. You may live near a large art gallery, like the Tate Gallery, or perhaps near a university where students

display their work in smaller exhibitions. Or if you live in a rural area, you may have artists in your local community who would love to show off their work to young people.
- Heritage sites: These could be anything from Roman forts to Victorian halls; check out the English Heritage Website for places to visit near you.
- Theatre: This could be musical theatre, concerts, local choirs and performances, plays, etc.

What is wonderful about the arts is that these subjects are cross-curricular and a brilliant vehicle for teaching about social justice and human rights.

What does the research say?

A report was published in 2016 after research into 'Equality and diversity in arts and culture with, by and for children and young people' by the Arts Council England found that studies suggested that young people have different, broader definitions of arts and culture to those of policymakers and funders; engagement in the arts is suggested by some studies as contributing to reducing the effects of disadvantage on educational attainment, and engagement in one aspect of arts, culture or sport tends to boost engagement in other aspects (Blood et al., 2016). In relation to gender, it found that employment data showed that women outnumber men across the cultural sector workforce as a whole, although they are underrepresented at senior and board levels. Girls were found to be more likely than boys to engage in almost all arts activities, both inside and outside of school. This pattern became clearer as young people got older and was reflected in GCSE choices. Interviewees tended to feel that targeting of content and artform, as well as using male role models, can be useful in encouraging boys to engage in arts and culture. They also felt that broader definitions of arts and culture for the purposes of activity and projects, such as gaming and popular music, also made a difference in engagement.

In relation to disability, the report found disparities between disabled and non-disabled children and young people, which seem to be driven largely by in-school rather than out-of-school factors. Disabled children had visited museums and cultural venues much less than their non-disabled peers. In addition, it found that having a clear leadership focus on inclusion, targeted funding and partnership with specialists were felt by interviewees to be positive steps towards better inclusion (Blood et al., 2016).

In relation to race, ethnicity and religion, it found that Black and minority ethnic people were less likely to have been taken to arts events whilst growing up, but there were differences between different ethnic groups and different artforms. It found that understanding the social and cultural context for different ethnic groups was key to delivering inclusive artistic activity and programming, acknowledging the increasingly blended and diverse nature of ethnic identity, and the importance of avoiding tokenism or 'labelling' (Blood et al., 2016).

Socio-economic status plays a huge role in engagement, or rather ability to engage with the arts. Adults who as children did not or could not engage in the arts become part of a cycle of fostering children who do not engage with the arts.

To combat this, schools must provide the experiences that those families who are under-served by our communities are not able to provide. Dedicate part of your pupil premium spend towards this. If a child cannot afford a trip due to money, let them go for free. Invite parents and carers to come along (for free!). You may introduce a parent to an experience that they too have never had and spark a new love of art.

Champions needed!

In order to teach outstanding, inclusive and diverse arts, you need a champion staff member to lead it – someone who is genuinely passionate about the role that the arts plays in the lives of children and young people. For some schools, you may be able to afford an 'art teacher'; for others, it may be one of your teachers or support staff who is passionate and able! You need a dedicated arts champion or lead – a person who is responsible for ensuring high-quality arts experiences for all children. Furthermore, best practice would be to have a link governor who also champions this.

Art curriculum – where to start?

The National Curriculum states that

> 'Art, craft and design embody some of the highest forms of human creativity. A high-quality art and design education should engage, inspire and challenge pupils, equipping them with the knowledge and skills to experiment, invent and create their own works of art, craft and design. As pupils progress, they should be able to think critically and develop a more rigorous understanding of art and design. They should

also know how art and design both reflect and shape our history, and contribute to the culture, creativity and wealth of our nation.' (DfE, 2013c, p. 1)

The aims of this are for pupils to:

- produce creative work, exploring their ideas and recording their experiences
- become proficient in drawing, painting, sculpture and other art, craft and design techniques
- evaluate and analyse creative works using the language of art, craft and design
- know about great artists, craft makers and designers, and understand the historical and cultural development of their art forms.

Know what you're aiming for

Before you map out your art topics, be sure to write your art teaching and learning policy, ensuring that you have a clear statement of what you are aiming to achieve in art.

For example:

At [insert school name], we are committed to ensuring that children see themselves and the community they live in reflected in the people they learn about and the images they see. We understand that children are exposed to stereotypes from an early age and that one role of school is to counter those experiences. We know that stereotyping leads to unconscious bias and as a school we have a duty to challenge those preconceived biases.

The area in which you can achieve the biggest impact of diverse and inclusive teaching is evaluating and analysing artwork and learning about artists and their craft. Art is also a way in which to explore different cultures but also, more importantly, explore different perspectives through a variety of lenses.

Ask yourself:

- How many artists of colour are included in your art curriculum – not tokenistically looking at African Art and African artists, but what about British artists of colour whose art is not necessarily *about* their heritage?
- How many artists with disabilities do you study?
- How many LGBT artists do you study?
- How many female artists do you study?

On the following pages, you will find suggested artists to learn about and include in your artists study. Make sure that you have enough timetable time dedicated to the teaching of quality art, and think about how it is distributed across the week/term/year. Great art teaching is taught discretely as well as being integrated into the teaching of other subjects. See how you can link it to your whole-school termly theme – for example, in my school we study Frida Kahlo as part of our 'Identity and Diversity' termly theme, which is also during LGBT History Month.

> **Top tip!**
>
> For every artist that you study, ensure that there is a book about their life (if one exists) displayed in your classroom. If one doesn't exist, this is a great opportunity for some cross-curricular work – get your class to write a book about them! Each child/group (depending on your age group) can write about a different aspect of the artist's life and work, creating a beautiful biographical book to display in your classroom. Over the year and across the school, you will begin to collect a wealth of both bought and school-written literature about a range of artists.

- **Clementine Hunter (1887–1988):** Clementine Hunter was an early-twentieth-century self-taught Black folk artist, who became a household name in Louisiana for her brightly coloured and whimsical depictions of plantation life.

- **Marlow Moss (1889–1958):** Marlow Moss was a British artist, born in London, and from an early age was curious about many different art forms, such as music, ballet, writing, art and architecture! Marlow's sex was unknown. They wore outfits that were considered 'masculine' at the time, such as suits. There is a famous piece of artwork by Marlow, to which they did not give a title – perhaps demonstrating that labels are not always needed in society?

- **Claude Cahun (1894–1954):** Claude Cahun was born in France and was a photographer who explored femininity and masculinity – and all the beauty in between. They were gender fluid. Cahun created self-portraits that aimed to ask the viewer to think about what it means to be feminine or masculine. Unfortunately, much of their work was lost during the Second World War. Find out more about Claude Cahun on the Tate website.

- **Frida Kahlo (1907–1954):** Frida Kahlo was a bisexual Mexican artist who developed a physical disability after a bus accident. She was most known for her brightly coloured self-portraits dealing with themes of identity and the human body. There is a great scheme of work on Frida on PlanBee.

- **Andy Warhol (1928–1987):** Andy Warhol was an openly gay American artist (even though being gay was illegal at the time), most known for his pop art movement. His work was eye-catching, colourful and extremely popular, and challenged society to think differently about things!

- **Zaha Hadid (1950–2016):** Zaha Hadid was the first woman to receive the Pritzker Architecture Prize and she also received the Stirling Prize (which is a highly prestigious architecture award). She was made a dame in 2021 by Elizabeth II, for her outstanding services to architecture.

- **Yayoi Kusama (1929–):** Yayoi Kusama is a Japanese artist who is sometimes referred to as the princess of polka dots. She creates paintings, sculptures, installations and performances… which all include dots!

- **Frank Bowling (1934–):** Frank Bowling was born in 1934 in Guyana, and grew up in New Amsterdam. His paintings are abstract expressionism, lyrical abstraction and colour field parking. In 2005, he became the first Black British artist to be elected as a Royal Academician, and was also awarded the Order of the British Empire in 2008 for his services to art. There are some fantastic resources and information about his work and life on the Tate Kids website.

- **David Hockney (1937–):** David Hockney is a gay British artist who was one of the big artists involved in the pop art movement. Some of his work depicts relationships between two men. He also paints seasons and landscapes and experiments with lots of different painting.

- **Sir Anish Kapoor (1954–):** Anish Kapoor is a British Indian sculptor who specialises in conceptual art and installation art. He has worked with a range of materials such as stone, wax and mirrors. He also uses negative space a lot! There are some great projects about Anish on TES.

- **Jessy Park (1958–):** Jessy Park is a self-taught artist with autism, who grew up in Massachusetts. She is passionate about Victorian architecture and astronomy, and much of her work includes detailed depictions of bridges, buildings, churches and houses. Her work is brightly coloured and distinctive!

- **Keith Salmon (1959–):** Keith Salmon is a British fine artist who is visually impaired. He paints mainly Scottish landscapes, specifically Munros (a type of Scottish mountain), and in 2009 he won the Jolomo Award for his amazing work.

- **Grayson Perry (1960–):** Grayson Perry is an English contemporary artist, writer and broadcaster and is widely known for his ceramic vases, tapestries and cross-dressing (as his alter-ego, 'Claire'). He won the Turner Prize and accepted the award dressed as Little Bo Peep. Grayson is not transgender, but his attitude towards gender shows us how we can explore different ways in which to present ourselves to the world. The British Council have created a great education pack called 'Grayson Perry: The Vanity of Small Differences'.
- **Peter Longstaff (1961–):** Peter Longstaff is a foot painter artist, who paints all his work using just his feet, as he has no arms. He paints beautiful and colourful landscapes and is from Norfolk.
- **Hurbin Anderson (1965–):** Birmingham-born to Jamaican parents, Hurbin Anderson paints vibrant pieces of still-life, landscapes and portraits on the themes of identity and heritage. There is great information on him and his work on the Tate website.
- **Stephen Wiltshire (1974–):** Stephen Wiltshire is an autistic artist, born in 1974 to West Indian parents. He is a world-famous architectural artist and he began drawing detailed sketches of London landmarks at just ten years old! He amazingly drew an eighteen-foot-wide panoramic landscape of the skyline of New York City after viewing it once during a 20-minute helicopter ride.
- **Makoto Azuma (1976–):** Makoto Azuma is a Japanese flower artist and botanical sculptor whose work is inspired by traditions of culture and exploring the idea of time. There are many fantastic YouTube videos capturing the work, especially fabulous time-lapse videos.
- **Lynette Yiadom-Boatye (1977–):** Lynette Yiadom-Boatye is a British artist who is best known for her portraits painted in muted colours. Her paintings are of fictitious people and raise questions of representation and identity.

The art environment

Children's artwork should be displayed widely in school foyers, corridors, classrooms and shared areas, accompanied by a blurb about the skills used and the meaning behind it. Work should be derived from your diverse range of classroom topics and large-scale projects, which benefit from trips, theme weeks or artist residencies. The prominence and quality of the artwork on display serves to create a stimulating ethos within the school, asking children to explore and question how art represents elements of society and both sets and reflects high standards in artistic work and a diverse range of topics.

Case study: Inspired by Frida!

This year I taught a scheme of work on Frida Kahlo. We looked at her work and her life and we discussed her ability to paint from her bed after she broke her back in a bus accident. This project coincided with LGBT History Month, so we discussed how Frida was bisexual and what that meant. The children were fascinated by her work and her story. We recreated pieces of her work and then created our own paintings inspired by her work. At the end of term, we held a parent showcase. The children were asked to demonstrate their learning on Frida Kahlo, given the choice to display it however they saw fit. The results were great! One child wanted to make a huge model of Frida's face (the same height as the child!). Another child made a clay model of Frida's painting from her bed, which was really sweet and creative – and skilful. Lastly, another group of children baked a cake and decorated it as Frida's face. The showcase was brilliant; children were able to show their work and use it as a platform to describe what they had learned about and from Frida. One child in particular, who is generally quite disengaged with learning, was especially engaged. She said that she didn't realise other mixed race people could look like her – she loved the fact that Frida was half German and half Mexican, and that she looked similar to her. She was actually the child who made the Frida cake and she even came to school the next day with a book about Frida that she'd begged her mum to buy her!

Music

The National Curriculum states that:

> 'Music is a universal language that embodies one of the highest forms of creativity. A high quality music education should engage and inspire pupils to develop a love of music and their talent as musicians, and so increase their self-confidence, creativity and sense of achievement. As pupils progress, they should develop a critical engagement with music, allowing them to compose, and to listen with discrimination to the best in the musical canon.' (DfE, 2013d, p. 1)

The aims of this are to enable children to:

- perform, listen to, review and evaluate music across a range of historical periods, genres, styles and traditions, including the works of the great composers and musicians
- learn to sing and to use their voices, to create and compose music on their own and with others, have the opportunity to learn a musical instrument, use technology appropriately and have the opportunity to progress to the next level of musical excellence
- understand and explore how music is created, produced and communicated, including through the inter-related dimensions: pitch, duration, dynamics, tempo, timbre, texture, structure and appropriate musical notations.

This is essentially learning about and from music, learning the structure of music and learning to create and perform music. There are wonderful opportunities in music to celebrate and explore diverse topics.

Know what you're aiming for

When writing your music teaching and learning policy, be sure to think about the following:

- a variety of cultures, religions and traditions being studied, reflecting the school cohort and also the international community
- a variety of teaching methods and different learning styles to meet the needs of all

- accessible teaching resources for all learners
- non-discriminatory and appropriate language
- actively tackling prejudice and stereotyping through the teaching of music
- avoiding stereotypes in examples and resources
- multicultural themes, instruments and resources promoting the celebration of diversity, representation and inclusion.

One way in which to achieve this when mapping out the year is to explore different musical styles, such as blues, rock and roll, hip hop, calypso, reggae, folk, opera, K-pop, rap, etc., study musicians from different backgrounds and traditions, and learn about the history of these genres. Music is a wonderful way to explore personal identity, social problems, justice and other issues.

It may take some time to develop your own subject knowledge, so you will find some places to start on the following pages.

> **Top tip!**
>
> A fantastic resource to buy into is Charanga (https://charanga.com/site). This has excellent and diverse resources as well as whole-school plans – both long-term and short-term – knowledge organisers, progression of skills documents, music sheet print-outs and how-to videos. It's not free, but it's not too expensive and is worth every penny, particularly if you have teachers who are unsure about how to plan and teach music to an excellent standard.

Genres of music

Across a child's primary school career, they must be exposed to a wide range of music, from popular, traditional and orchestral to jazz/improvised.

Here are some examples of genres of music to include in your whole-school map:

Popular	Orchestral	Traditional	Jazz/improvised
Pop	Classical	Religious	Jazz
Rap	Opera	Folk	Big band
Punk	Medieval	Flamenco	Latin
Hip hop	Indian classical	Samba	Dixieland
Heavy metal	Choral	Spiritual	Swing
House	Waltz	Gospel	Motown
Electronic	Baroque	Rumba	Gypsy jazz
Dance	Romantic	Gamelan	Blues
	Twentieth-century	West African drumming	Ragtime

On pages 106-107 there is an example of a music curriculum map.

Singing assemblies

Assemblies are a wonderful time to teach music, the history of genres and about musical legends and their backgrounds. In my school, I have linked the songs that I teach in the singing assembly (which is my favourite time of the week) to the whole-school theme, and used songs to engage and excite children about learning.

There are many different structures to a singing assembly. Here are some tips on delivering a powerful singing/music assembly:

- First, play children a song. Don't show them the video or a photo of the artist – simply listen. You might like to ask children to close their eyes whilst listening. After listening to the song (or an extract from the song), ask them:
  - Can you describe this song?
  - What do you think this song is about? How do you know?
  - What might the artist have been thinking about when writing this song?
  - What do we know about the artist from this song?
  - What genre of music do you think this is?
  - When do you think this song was written? What makes you think that?
- Another strategy is to show the children an extract of the lyrics without the music, e.g. the lyrics to the chorus. Again, ask them to reflect on the above questions.

Music curriculum map

	Autumn 1	Autumn 2	Spring 1	Spring 2	Summer 1	Summer 2
School global curriculum theme	Power and governance	Social justice and equality	Identity and diversity	Human rights	Sustainable development	Peace and conflict
Singing assembly theme	Explore power through song 'Something Inside So Strong' 'Power in Me' 'Power to the People' 'We are the Champions'	Gospel music 'This Little Light of Mine' 'Break Every Chain' 'Say Yes'	Around the world in music 'Touch the Sky' 'Shosholoza' 'Che Che Kule' 'Jambo Bwana' 'Kusimama' 'Born This Way'	Race and racial discrimination through music 'A Change Gonna Come Blowin' in the Wind' Female empowerment through music 'Respect'	Exploring the earth through music 'Big Yellow Taxi' 'Earth Song' 'Mercy Mercy Me'	Exploring peace through music 'All you need is love' 'Where is the love?' 'One love' 'Imagine'
Charanga Music Programme resources						
Year 1	How pulse, rhythm and pitch work together	Pulse, rhythm and pitch, rapping, dancing and singing	How to be in the groove with different styles of music	Pulse, rhythm and pitch in different styles of music	Using your imagination	The history of music

Music curriculum map

	Autumn 1	Autumn 2	Spring 1	Spring 2	Summer 1	Summer 2
Year 2	South African music	Festivals and Christmas	Playing together in a band	Reggae and animals	A song about being friends	The history of music
Year 3	R&B and other styles	Exploring and developing playing skills	Reggae and animals	Music from around the world, celebrating our differences and being kind to one another	Disco, friendship and hope	The history of music
Year 4/5	Rock anthems	Jazz and improvisation	Pop ballads	Old school hip hop	Motown	Classical
Year 6	Being happy!	Jazz and improvisation and composition	Benjamin Britten's music and cover versions	The music of Carole King	Create your own music inspired by your identity and women in the music industry	Classical

- The other way to introduce a song is to show only the video but with no sound. Ask the children what kind of music they think it is. You get all kinds of weird and wonderful ideas from this – it is a creative way to explore the different elements of music and its history.
- Once I have introduced a song, I teach about the singer/group – some background information about their life:
  - what genre of music it is, and how this links to other songs that children may know or have learned about
  - where they grew up and what was happening in the world at that time
  - information about their family, struggles and successes
  - how they link into the whole-school topic or theme.
- Then we move onto learning how to sing the song, breaking it down into parts.
- Then, we perform!

I like to start each assembly with a pop quiz about the song/artist learned about in the previous assembly, and use the previous week's song as a warm-up. At the end of the term, we have a good singsong and sing all the songs learned in that term!

Check the companion website for a list of child-friendly songs to sing in assembly, and some of the wider topics that they cover.

Some of my favourites include:

- 'Kusimama' – Swahili song meaning 'Stand Tall'
- 'Touch the Sky' from *Brave*
- 'Wonder' by Emeli Sandé
- 'True Colours' by Justin Timberlake and Anna Kendrick

The teaching of music

When teaching music and using songs and genres from across the world, be sure to study the elements of music as well as the context. These are the different things that we hear when we listen to music – what differentiates one piece from another.

The main elements of music are: timbre, texture, rhythm, melody, beat, harmony, structure, tempo, pitch and dynamics.

Being able to recognise, hear and describe these different elements allows us to understand music theory better and, coupled with an understanding of historical and social context, allows us to improve children's musical development.

Exploring history through music

We can tell a huge amount about a culture's struggle and evolution through music. It is a cultural practice passed on through generations, present from ancient civilisations until now. Music is powerful and, furthermore, can reach through all language barriers as something that we all have in common.

It is possible to trace modern-day hip hop to West Africa in 1800. Many West Africans who were traded into slavery and shipped across the Atlantic told stories of their memories and hopes through music, and some used instruments such as the banjo and tambourine. Some sang about hope through religion – for example, Christianity – and throughout time those Christian songs evolved into what we now call Gospel (which means 'good news'). In many modern-day rap songs, there are remnants of repeating verses and alternating singers prevalent in songs sung by slaves. This music, with a sadder, more downbeat tone, we call blues, and the more upbeat sounds grew to become jazz. Gospel music, over time, evolved to soul, and soul to R&B and hip hop.

One of the best music lessons that I taught was exploring the relationship between the following songs and how they demonstrate the evolution of music and the historical context in which each was created:

- 'We Shall Overcome' – a protest song, with the lyrics first published in 1901
- 'Georgia on my Mind' by Ray Charles
- 'Higher Ground' by Stevie Wonder
- 'What's Going On' by Marvin Gaye
- 'Jesus Walks' by Kanye West (clean version!).

Music as a source of education in communities

Throughout history, and in some places still today, music has been used as a key vessel to share information and educate communities about issues. Here are some examples of groups that have written songs to educate communities:

- **Kano Boys (Nigeria)** – songs to educate about health issues such as HIV
- **Dobet Gnahoré (Ivory Coast)** – songs to educate about gender equality

- **Lucky Dube (South Africa)** – songs to educate about peace between races ('Together as One' (www.youtube.com/watch?v=LIReRYHd1cU) was the first ever song by a Black artist played on a White radio station in South Africa)
- **Staff Benda Bilili (Democratic Republic of the Congo)** – songs to educate about health issues such as getting vaccinated for polio, which is especially powerful because all four band members are in tricycle-cum-wheelchairs as victims of polio.

Key artists from across the continents

Of course, world music is vast! But here is a guide to some artists/songs that you might like to map out or learn about, either as part of discreet music lessons or as part of wider curriculum projects. Much of the information below came from www.developmenteducation.ie, which is a fantastic free online resource that **focuses on the 'unequal and unjust shape of the world today'.**

Africa

- **Youssou N'Dour (Senegal):** With a musical style known as mbalax, Youssou is one of Senegal's most famous singers, singing a type of fusion music of traditional Senegalese sabar drumming and some Western musical styles such as soul and jazz. His music has lots of percussion and heavy rhythms.
- **Amadou and Mariam (Mali):** Amadou and Mariam are a blind couple who met in an institute for the blind in the 1970s. Their genre of music is Afro-blues, which blends blues guitar and Malian roots music (with a hint of Western pop!). Songs to look up are: 'Je Pense a Toi' (www.youtube.com/watch?v=iju1_DhH2Qs), 'A Radio Mogo' and 'Sibali' (www.youtube.com/watch?v=3KhFv1qJcao).
- **Fela Kuti (Nigeria):** Fela Kuti pioneered Afrobeats music and has also contributed greatly to the genres of psychedelic funk and traditional West African singing.
- **Mulatu Astatke (Ethiopia):** Considered one of the greatest Ethiopian musicians of the twentieth century, and the father of Ethio-jazz, Mulatu Astatke fused guitars, percussion and saxophones to create beautiful sounds.

Asia

- **Qawwali (Pakistan):** From the Punjab region of Pakistan and Northern Indian, Qawwali (meaning 'utterance of the Prophet') music is a form of Sufi devotional music.
- **Tuvan overtone singing (Mongolia):** Originating from southern Siberia, overtone throat singing is a technique that means that singers can essentially sing more than one note at a time. It is richly linked to culture and often sounds like the landscape or natural sounds that it is describing. An artist called Yat-Kha mixes traditional Tuvan folklore with Western rock influences, and does some really interesting covers of 'Love Will Tear Us Apart' (you can search for this on YouTube).
- **C-Pop (China):** The term 'C-Pop' refers to all forms of popular or mainstream music from China, such as Chinese pop, rock and R&B. Some resistance from the Communist Party has meant that C-Pop has moved to solely Taiwan and Hong Kong (despite being very popular in other areas of China!).

Europe

- **Taraf de Haïdouks (Romania):** Taraf de Haïdouks (www.youtube.com/watch?v=xnNCidccbG8) are a group of Romanian musicians; Johnny Depp famously invited them to play at the Viper Room club in Los Angeles because of their amazing and energetic performances. Their act is likened to more of a circus-like performance, and their name translated actually means 'band of outlaws'.
- **Ojos de Brujo (Barcelona):** Ojos de Brujo are a band from Barcelona who perform a mix of traditional flamenco sounds with hip hop and Catalan rumba. Many of their songs are about social issues and problems: 'Na En La Nevera' ('Nothing in the Fridge': www.youtube.com/watch?v=CDo1TzO1TuY) is about poverty, 'Piedras vs Tanques' ('Stones vs Tanks': www.youtube.com/watch?v=ZwKldTy8Q50) talks about war and 'Naita' deals with inequality.

Latin America

- **Samba (Brazil):** Samba (www.youtube.com/watch?v=bqao21cZ5nM) is syncopated rhythm and up-tempo beats and probably the most well known of the many genres of music from Brazil. It is associated with Rio de Janeiro's carnival and brings a party vibe! Samba dates back to the beginning of the twentieth century, when the music was slightly slower and more romantic compared to its funky rhythms today.

- **Cumbia (Columbia):** Cumbia (www.youtube.com/watch?v=xAe7V9Csd84) is from Colombia and lends its adapted versions of cumbia to other Latin American countries like Mexico, Panama and Peru. Cumbia's roots are from the time of Spanish colonisation, when Spain 'imported' many slaves from Western Africa, bringing with them music and beats that influenced the Colombian population. Amerindian flutes and percussion instruments were added to drums and claves to create the genre.

> ### Case study: Exploring human rights through song
>
> Music is powerful. As my school has a curriculum entrenched in human rights, I planned in assembly songs linking to different aspects of human rights. You could use these to teach as songs to sing or as music to listen to, as a provocation to prompt thinking or discussion surrounding an issue.
>
> I introduced learning about Pride at a previous school at which I worked; this was a church school and, to be honest, I felt a little nervous about introducing it in assembly, for fear of children making unkind comments or laughing, or it creating a situation that I couldn't control as a fairly young teacher (I'd been teaching for three or four years). I had decided that the route I would take would be talking about my own family, and how all families are different, diverse and special. I showed photos of my mum and dad and talked about how they are of different ethnicities and different religions. I asked, 'That's OK… right?'. Children enthusiastically replied 'Yes!'. I then showed a photo of my sister and her daughter and talked about single-parent families and asked, 'That's OK… right?', to a resounding 'Yes' from the children. Finally I showed a photo of my brother and his husband and talked about same-sex families and asked, 'That's OK… right?'. My heart was beating fast and I honestly didn't know what I would have done if the children had shouted 'no', but they didn't. Again, they enthusiastically shouted 'Yes!' and my heart smiled because I was again reminded of the beauty of children and how powerful sharing personal experiences can be. We then went on to sing 'Born This Way' by Lady Gaga and it was wonderful. Note: I am not suggesting that you have to bare your soul and everything about your life to children; of course there need to be boundaries. This is something that I *chose* to do: I chose to share my family in an appropriate manner, as a way to discuss diversity and equality. Sometimes, when we

share things about our lives, we create a safe space for others to do so. And if one child in that room felt represented, accepted or safe to talk about their own lives, I can rest happy.

After the assembly, with my Year 6 class we listened to 'Same Love' by Macklemore, and read through the lyrics. It was a beautiful session, where children were very reflective about how to treat people and 'gayness'. We used it as a platform to discuss why we don't call people 'gay' as an insult. I asked, 'Would you call someone Black as an insult?'. They then wrote their own rap verses to the song and performed. This use of music was extremely powerful as a provocation to discuss human rights.

Here is a list below of some songs I have used*, separated by human rights issue:

Environment

'The 3 Rs' by Jack Johnson

'Big Yellow Taxi' by Counting Crows and Vanessa Carlton

'Truth to Power' by One Republic

'Mercy Mercy Me (The Ecology)' by Marvin Gaye

Race

'Blowin' in the Wind' by Bob Dylan

'A Change Gonna Come' by Sam Cooke

'What's Going On' by Marvin Gaye

'Changes' by Tupac

Female empowerment and self love

'Brown Skin Girl' by Blue Ivy, SAINt JHN, Beyonce and Wizkid

'Fight Song' by Rachel Platten

'Respect' by Aretha Franklin

'Beautiful' by Christina Aguilera

*Please note that this section is heavily weighted towards English songs and singers – these are some tried and tested songs that I have used. There are, of course, songs in all languages and from all cultures that deal with rights-based political issues. Ask your community for suggestions: staff, children and parents. There have been thousands of performers, artists, bands and songs inspired by human rights and injustice!

Drama

Drama is such a fabulous opportunity for expression, especially for children who struggle to express themselves in the day to day. Drama and spoken language objectives are found within the subject of English. Here, the National Curriculum describes 'the importance of spoken language in pupils' development across the whole curriculum – cognitively, socially and linguistically. Spoken language underpins the development of reading and writing. The quality and variety of language that pupils hear and speak are vital for developing their vocabulary and grammar and their understanding for reading and writing.' (DfE, 2014a) As educators, we therefore need to ensure the continual development of children's confidence and competence in oracy, spoken language and listening skills. They should develop the capacity to explain their understanding of issues, books and other reading and provocations, and be able to prepare their ideas before they write. Of course, it is our job to support children in articulating their thoughts through words, and to make sure that they are in a learning environment that allows a safe space for this.

Pupils should also be taught to:

- understand and use conventions for discussion and debate
- participate in and gain knowledge, skills and understanding associated with the artistic practice of drama
- adopt, create and sustain a range of different roles and how to appropriately respond to others in role
- have opportunities to improvise, devise, write and script drama for a range of audiences and each other
- rehearse, refine, share and respond thoughtfully to drama and theatre performances.

The objectives that underpin the different aspects of spoken language are reflected and contextualised within the reading and writing domains that are indicated in the literacy chapter (Chapter 3).

A curriculum entrenched in social justice and human rights allows children the space and opportunity to discuss issues and develop their voice and opinions.

The teaching of drama

There are some essential elements to the teaching of drama that are necessary to structure the learning in a way that is effective. Here are some examples of the structures, alongside ideas that celebrate diversity and promote equality.

Role play

Students take on the role of another person. This is particularly effective if they take on the role of someone who is being treated badly or being discriminated against, as it allows for empathy and reflection from a different perspective.

Examples:

- A child has just been called 'gay' on the playground.
- A lady wearing a hijab was walking down the street and someone shouted something about what she was wearing.
- Another student in your class has their phone in the class and they took a photo of you without consent.

Freeze-frames

These are when you give the children a title and have them work in groups to create a tableau or frozen 'frame' of the moment or image. Students can be humans, animals or inanimate items.

Examples:

- a child starting a new school and who speaks a different language from most other children there
- one child who has a different lunch from other children
- different types of families
- hope
- hate
- love.

Clay freeze-frames

Children can work in pairs, each with clay or play dough. Give one child an image or an idea to create. Then the other child sees whether they can guess, and it creates a stimulus for a rich conversation.

Flashback/flash-forward

This structure starts with a freeze-frame. Children are then given a moment to think about what has happened just before this freeze-frame and act it out. Similarly, children can think about what happens afterwards too.

Phone calls

Children move around the room. When you signal to them, students stop and pretend to hear their phone ring. They 'pick up' the phone and tell the person next to them their thoughts and ideas about a given concept. If they hear something they like, they can either stick with their own ideas or share another person's ideas next time.

Soundscapes

This is an activity where children are challenged to think about the many different sounds that may be heard in a specific place. This makes use of voice and body expression and even body percussion. Sounds can be repeated, like motifs, and children can explore pitch, rhythm and volume. Children record their ideas on a grid, and then one child can become the conductor of the group, using the ideas written down/drawn.

Examples for soundscapes:

- acceptance
- inclusion
- kindness.

Diversity through drama

Drama is a brilliant way in which to teach empathy and understanding of other people. Key books (some of which are mentioned in the Chapter 3) can be used as a basis to celebrate difference and promote equality.

Here is an example of an LGBT equality drama unit from Allens Croft Primary School.

Character in Character: LGBT Equality Units

	Session 1	Session 2	Session 3
Rec	• To understand that different people like different things • To act out experiences with other people • To review how well an approach worked		
	Red Rockets and Rainbow Jelly by Sue Heap and Nick Sharratt To create simple representations of events, people and objects	**The Artist Who Painted a Blue Horse** by Eric Carle To represent ideas, thoughts and feelings through role play and stories	**Elmer** by David McKee Begin to "perform" through play-based activities
Year 1	**Something Else** by Kathryn Cave • To understand what it feels like to be left out • To take part in "pretend" activities to explore situations and stories through imaginative improvisation and role play. • To reflect on the situation or character both in and out of role		
	To pretend to be a **character**	To demonstrate **emotion** through action and language	To work with others to present their own situations
Year 2	**And Tango Makes Three** by Justin Richardson • To understand there are different kinds of family • To present a devised performance based on the themes of the book with a group using simple theatrical techniques (narration, still image) • To talk about why they made certain decisions and discuss how their work and that of others could be improved		
	To work together to create **Freeze Frames** based on given scenarios	To understand what makes for good **Narration** of a story	Use Freeze Frames and Narration to **present a devised performance** in an original way
Year 3	**Troll Swap** by Leigh Hodgkinson • To celebrate that everyone is different • To collaborate to produce a piece of theatre that "flows" without interruption in order to explore a story • Both in and out of role, comment thoughtfully on the drama and suggest ways of improving it		
	To act out **improvised dramas**, creating characters that are clearly different from themselves	To reflect on the action taken by characters in the drama and **consider alternative responses**	To collaborate to produce a piece of theatre that "flows" without interruption in order to explore a story

Philosophy 4 Children

Philosophy for children – or P4C – is a pedagogy that develops children's oracy through exploring issues such as equality, diversity, inclusion, truth and beauty. This provides a learning structure for children to experience reasonable and rational dialogue about the world around them. 'All participants work together in a "community of enquiry". The aim for each child is not to win an argument but to become clearer, more accurate, less self-contradictory and more aware of other arguments and values before reaching a conclusion.' (P4C, n.d.).

> **Top tip!**
>
> Teach children the language of debate, how to agree or respectfully disagree or challenge, and how to build upon others' ideas. You could use ABC (agree, build, challenge) and put posters in your classroom as visual aids. You could build ABC into your morning routine, whilst you're doing the register; have a statement on the board and then ask children to respond afterwards.
>
> An example of an ABC conversation from my class is:
>
> Given statement: 'Our society is equal.'

> **A:** *I agree with this statement. (Child 1)*
> **B:** *I would like to build upon this. Our society is more equal than it used to be, but there is still some work to do – for example, equal pay for men and women. (Child 2)*
> **C:** *I challenge this statement – our society is not equal, men and women are not paid equally, people with disabilities are not empowered to travel as much due to accessibility in transport and don't get me started on racism. (Child 3)*

The arts are powerful. They represent happiness, pain, struggle and everything in between. Songs, performances and art reflect society, and therefore the study of the arts is actually the study of people and how they live. A high-quality arts education allows a platform for children to understand both the society in which they live in and global societies in a deeper way.

Key takeaways

- The arts are a brilliant way for children to express themselves, explore empathy and connect with other perspectives.
- Ensure that you explore a range of artists and their historical contexts – match this to your history and geography topics.
- Music is a great way to explore human rights, culture and historical context.
- Ensure that there's a link between your music curriculum and your singing assemblies.
- Use drama as a platform to explore different perspectives and teach empathy.

7 STEM: Science, maths and technology

This chapter looks at STEM (science, maths and technology), and how to develop more inclusive and diverse practice. Great STEM teaching provides the intellectual foundation for our future engineers, scientists and inventors, and it is extremely important because it allows understanding of how everything in our daily world works. Children who are good at STEM are able to think critically and problem solve – STEM subjects power the world! This is why it is imperative to demonstrate the broad range of role models who have made and are currently making waves in the STEM world!

In this chapter, I will explore some topics for science, maths and design technology that allow a platform to explore diversity, role models and different perspectives.

What does the research say?

The professional field of STEM is dominated by White males, meaning that many other groups (women and ethnic minorities) are significantly underrepresented. In terms of STEM professions, a more diverse team is more likely to perform better than a homogeneous team, as people from different backgrounds bring a wealth of perspectives, experiences and approaches. More diversity ultimately means more innovative solutions (Rollins, 2020)!

The APPG on Diversity and Inclusion in STEM (British Science Association, 2020) found that 65 per cent of the STEM workforce are White men and also that, proportionally, White women are less likely to be STEM workers than women from an ethnic minority. In addition, the number of academic staff with a known disability is far lower for STEM staff than for non-STEM careers, with disabled people, irrespective of ethnicity, being greatly underrepresented within the STEM workforce. Furthermore, there is a significant underrepresentation of women across all seniority levels. Interestingly, the report found that 'ethnic minority workers make up a larger share of higher managerial roles (17%) than they do non-managerial roles – this reflects the fact that within STEM, ethnic minority workers are more likely to be found in disciplines with a high rate of managerial employment, disciplines outside engineering' (British Science Association, 2020, p. 7).

When looking at the different workforces, the science and maths workforce:

'has a broadly representative proportion of people from ethnic minorities, overall, and it is significantly more gender balanced than both engineering and technology... This overall figure for ethnic minorities masks imbalances for particular ethnicities, though the share of people of Indian and "other" ethnicities is significantly higher than that in the non-STEM workforce, whereas the share of people of Bangladeshi and Pakistani and Black ethnicities is significantly lower.' (British Science Association, 2020, p. 12).

However, in the technology workforce:

'the technology workforce is predominantly male and middle-aged, but has more ethnic diversity than other parts of the STEM workforce. Just one-in-five workers in the technology workforce are female, and disabled workers are also underrepresented in this part of the STEM workforce. But… people from ethnic minorities make up a larger share of the technology workforce than in the rest of the labour market (16% compared to 12%). This is driven by an over-representation (relative to the rest of the workforce) of Indian workers in this part of STEM: 7% of workers in technology are of Indian ethnicity, compared to 2% in the rest of the workforce.' (British Science Association, 2020, p. 13).

They also found that:

- The STEM workforce is less diverse than the wider workforce.
- Only 27 per cent of the STEM workforce is female, compared to 52 per cent of the wider workforce.
- Disabled people working in STEM are likely to be male.
- Twelve per cent of the STEM workforce are from ethnic minorities.
- There is very little difference in the gender balance of the STEM workforce at younger ages.
- Women and ethnic minority employees are overrepresented in the health workforce.
- Eleven per cent of STEM workers have a disability, compared to 14 per cent of the wider workforce. (British Science Association, 2020)

In STEM, diversity is critical to innovation and excellence. STEM ultimately comes down to group problem-solving – making the world better. A more diverse group of people being part of that problem-solving means more innovation to improve and touch the lives of more people. This underlines the importance of our role as educators to open up the world of STEM to children, in order to tackle this lack of diversity through excellent teaching practice and curriculum planning.

Science

'A high-quality science education provides the foundations for understanding the world through the specific disciplines of biology, chemistry and physics. Science has changed our lives and is vital to the world's future prosperity, and all pupils should be taught essential aspects of the knowledge, methods, processes and uses of science. Through building up a body of key foundational knowledge and concepts, pupils should be encouraged to recognise the power of rational explanation and develop a sense of excitement and curiosity about natural phenomena. They should be encouraged to understand how science can be used to explain what is occurring, predict how things will behave, and analyse causes.' (DfE, 2013e, p. 3).

Working scientifically

In order to work scientifically, children need to know the different types of scientists. This in itself is a wonderful lesson at the start of the year (and a good display for your classroom/corridors). Teach children about the different areas of science (not just chemistry, biology and physics). When you then study the skeletons of birds, you can say to the children, 'Today we are going to be ornithologists – let's see whether we can remember what they do.' This develops children's language around the different science areas and allows room for researching and finding out about role models in the areas.
Examples

- botanist: studies plants
- ecologist: studies the relationship between living things and the environment
- ichthyologist: studies fish
- astronomer: studies outer space, the solar system and its objects
- herpetologist: studies amphibians and reptiles

- zoologist: studies animals
- neuroscientist: studies the nervous system.

Teach children about the field of science first. Get them to generate questions about it. I like to do a little quiz at the end of each day/half-term to reinforce remembering a wealth of different science areas and role models.

> **Top tip!**
>
> If your school is near a GP, dentist or hospital, get in touch with them and see whether you can organise a visit from a doctor/specialist to come and talk to the class or take an assembly! This is a lovely way to make science real. Ask your parent/carer community and staff – the chances are that someone will know someone whom they can call in to talk.

Project ideas

There are so many different branches of science about which we can make children aware through exploring role models in science. Here are some project ideas:

Great scientists

When studying role models, be sure to give key information about scientists who have had an impact on the world. Here are some scientists that you could include:

Percy Lavon Julian, 1899–1975 (chemistry): One of the first African Americans to achieve a doctorate in chemistry, he developed drugs to help people, including synthesising progesterone.

Charles Kao, 1933–2018 (physics): Kao was a Chinese electrical engineer and physicist who won the Nobel Prize for groundbreaking work in using fibre optics for telecommunication.

Kusala Rajendran, 1954– (seismology): Kusala is a seismologist and researcher into tsunamis and earthquakes. She is from India. Her research has been pioneering!

Mae C Jemison, 1956– (astronaut): Mae Jemison was the first Black woman astronaut to travel into space. She was actually initially trained as a doctor, before becoming an astronaut. She orbited the Earth 126 times!

Farida Bedwei, 1979– (software engineer): A highly successful software engineer, Farida is a Black, female scientist with cerebral palsy from Nigeria. She says, 'Disability is still largely misunderstood and a bit of a taboo in various parts of Ghana and other African countries.' She has also said, 'Accept and love yourself for who you are' and 'Don't waste your time wishing you didn't have this condition. Rather, find ways to attain greater heights with your disabilities.' She has even written children's books, such as *Definition of a Miracle*, which is about an African girl called Zaara with cerebral palsy, and a comic book called *Karmzah* (about a superhero with cerebral palsy).

Did you know that it is thought that Einstein had dyslexia, as his teachers at primary school reported that he couldn't grasp concepts as quickly as others?

Did you also know that Thomas Edison was hearing-impaired? He lost much of his hearing by his early twenties!

Women in STEM

Ada Lovelace, 1815–1852: Ada was an English writer and mathematician, who is known for being the first computer programmer. She is also mentioned in more detail in the maths section!

Dame Anne McLaren, 1927–2007: Anne was a geneticist whose work pioneered development in the genetics of mammals and embryology.

Florence Nightingale, 1820–1910: Florence was a British nurse, statistician and social reformer who helped British and Allied soldiers during the Crimean War.

Katherine Johnson, 1918–2020: Katherine was a mathematician who worked for more than 30 years at the US Space Program, and her work helped to send astronauts to the moon through calculating the flight paths of spacecraft (www.britannica.com/technology/spacecraft).

> **Top tip!**
>
> The film *Hidden Figures* is about Katherine Johnson, Dorothy Vaughan and Mary Jackson, and there is a beautiful book with the same name too. This could be displayed on your maths board. You could even create a QR code link to clips from the movie, for children to use tablets to scan them and watch for inspiration.

Tu Youyou, 1930–: Tu Youyou was a Chinese scientist who helped to discover the cure for malaria, using both Chinese and Western medicine. During the Vietnam War, Tu tested plants, creating a herbal treatment against malaria. This became the world's first effective medicine and defence against malaria.

Marguerite Perey, 1909–1975: A physicist from France, Marguerite was Marie Curie's student, who in 1939 discovered francium. She was also the first woman to be elected to the French Académie des Sciences, which amazingly was an honour that was denied to her mentor Curie.

British Science Week

British Science Week happens every year, and there is always a wealth of free published resources for teachers found on their website. There are brilliant resources for 'Smashing stereotypes' too, including posters of role models, their areas of science and their contribution to science.

'Smashing stereotypes' underlines the importance of diversity in STEM subjects and careers, and invites STEM employees to share stories about their day-to-day work. The British Science Association aims to showcase the broad range of careers in STEM and the fact that scientists and mathematicians can be… well, anyone!

Case study: STEM fair

At my school, we held a STEM Career Fair, which was at the end of Science Week. During Science Week, each class was given a STEM career, and they had an investigation to explore, complete and present. Careers included computer programming, volcanologist, astronaut, biomedical engineer, paediatrician and many more. We then invited role models from those careers in to speak with children and to inspire them. My class looked at medicine, and I had asked one of my secondary school friends – who studied medicine – to come in and speak to the children. She did and they loved it! She brought her stethoscope in and the children listened to heartbeats. One of our parents was a computer programmer, so he came and spoke to another class about his job.

At the end of the week, each class had a large table in the hall, demonstrating their learning for the week, and the children got to see what others had been learning. We also invited parents in to share the learning.

> The whole community loved it, including my friend, who said that she got a lot of joy sharing her career and passion with the next generation.

Maths

The National Curriculum states that:

> 'Mathematics is a creative and highly inter-connected discipline that has been developed over centuries, providing the solution to some of history's most intriguing problems. It is essential to everyday life, critical to science, technology and engineering, and necessary for financial literacy and most forms of employment. A high-quality mathematics education therefore provides a foundation for understanding the world, the ability to reason mathematically, an appreciation of the beauty and power of mathematics, and a sense of enjoyment and curiosity about the subject.' (DfE, 2021)

As maths is predominantly about skill, rather than knowledge, how to diversify maths teaching feels less obvious, as numbers… are numbers. However, there are a few ways in which you can build diversity and inclusion into maths. And, similarly to the other core subjects, ensure that your teaching and learning policy explains the importance of diversity and inclusion in maths.

What does the research say?

As educators, we know that there is a gender gap in STEM careers; only six per cent of maths professors in the UK are female (London Mathematical Society, 2013). Pearson researched teachers in 2021 in relation to their perceptions and experiences of maths. They found that 'Students who are disadvantaged, have special educational needs and disabilities (SEND), or are girls are more likely to think that maths, and associated careers, are not accessible or appealing.' They also found that '67% of primary maths teachers think more positivity about maths in popular culture would help them to inspire students with the power of maths' and that many believe 'more diverse role models in maths would inspire their students'. (Pearson, 2021).

Inclusive maths practice

Ensure that you use visual symbols (consistent across the school) for the meanings of the operations such as add, subtract, multiply and divide, etc. I would suggest

Communicate: In Print or Widget, which are online platforms where you can create such content.

> **Top tip!**
>
> Ask your maths leader to create a class set so that all year groups are using the same symbols. This will really support children with SEND/EAL (but also all pupils) to develop a really fluent understanding of the meaning of maths vocabulary.

Ensure that you have the appropriate concrete resources available in your classroom to support the needs of all children.

The learning environment

Maths displays in primary school tend to be the least creative displays in classrooms, as they demonstrate process rather than creativity. Think about displaying posters of role models; perhaps you could display a model of the role model!

- There are some great diverse role model posters on the Pearson Maths website, showing a range of different famous mathematicians, both past and present.
- Check out the website Mathematically Gifted and Black for more posters and information recognising a wide range of mathematicians.
- Add photos of real-life people (or, better yet, of children in the class) and events that demonstrate that maths is part of everything that we do! These could be photos of:
    - children cooking and baking (measurement)
    - cutting pizza (parts of a circle, fractions)
    - paying money in the local shop (money, calculation)
    - aiming for a penalty kick (angles)
    - street dance (time)
    - gymnastics (angles)
    - waiting for the bus (timetables).

> **Top tip!**
>
> Get children to collect cash receipts from home (with parental permission, of course) and keep a box of receipts. These are always good to get out during lessons to provide real-life context to lessons.

Investigation ideas

Maths4Girls

Maths4Girls is an initiative that aims to help teachers to increase the number of girls pursuing maths beyond GCSE level. It is provided for free by Founders4Schools, an ed-tech charity. They provide a platform of current role models in the field and connect girls with professional women in maths careers. It has resources to support role model events and lots of tips – it's a great resource to tap into.

Use student interest in reasoning and investigative tasks

Think back to what you found out when auditing the community of your school – which communities and interests are represented in your context? Are these represented in the problem-solving and reasoning tasks that you set for children? Research has demonstrated that pupils are far more motivated in learning when it is applicable to their own interests and communities (Carlone and Johnson, 2007; Jones et al., 2000 as cited by Hobson, 2017). Use what you learn about your students when framing the mathematical tasks and problems. Be sure to consider whether the tasks that you assign represent *all* of those interests in your classroom and make sure that there are not groups of pupils who are left out. Consider diversifying problem-solving and investigative tasks.

I did this as a staff meeting, and as a team we came up with a number of maths investigations per year group, which were representative of our community. Here are some examples:

- **Shop, shop, shop!** I live with my foster mum and two siblings. Where is the cheapest local shop to buy my food shopping list? [Insert list of shopping items.]
- **It's travelling time:** We are travelling to see family in Europe. Where is the best place locally to exchange my pounds to euros?

- **Hair-raising:** My two sisters and I are going to my auntie's wedding on Saturday and we need our hair braided. Our budget is [insert budget]. What hairstyle combinations can we get? [Provide price list.]
- **Ramadan maths investigation:** How many days does Ramadan last? How many hours does Ramadan last? If daylight hours are from 4.40 am to 9.05 pm, how many hours are spent fasting?
- **Symmetry and Islamic art:** Take a look at the patterns and beautiful images that decorate mosques and palaces. Can you find art symmetry or repeated patterns and geometric shapes?
- **Zero:** Did you know that the concept of zero was created in India? Let's find out more!
- **World of tan:** Chinese tangrams – through studying tangrams, children can develop the embedding, visualisation and manipulation skills required for a smooth transition to secondary mathematics. Check out World of Tan and Shapely Tiling from the Nrich website.

Mathematical games from around the world

Use different mathematical games from different countries to help to develop number fluency and strategic problem-solving skills. Games could include chess (thought to have originated in India); Alquerque or Qirkat from the Arabic القرقات, a strategy game thought to have been taken by the Moors to Spain (but watch out for being 'huffed'); Pumpkin Patch (from Somalia); Two Stones or 'Ou-moul-ko-no' from Korea; and Achi (Ghana). And of course there is Sudoku (Japan), which children (and their parents/carers) may already be familiar with.

Technology: Computing and design and technology

Computing

The aim of computing is to deliver:

'a high-quality computing education [that] equips pupils to use computational thinking and creativity to understand and change the world. Computing has deep links with mathematics, science, and design and technology, and provides insights into both natural and artificial systems. The core of computing is computer science, in

which pupils are taught the principles of information and computation, how digital systems work, and how to put this knowledge to use through programming. Building on this knowledge and understanding, pupils are equipped to use information technology to create programs, systems and a range of content. Computing also ensures that pupils become digitally literate – able to use, and express themselves and develop their ideas through information and communication technology – at a level suitable for the future workplace and as active participants in a digital world.
(DfE, 2013f)

Teaching and learning in computing

Here are some ways in which to engage all students in computing, regardless of their gender, ethnicity, disability, socio-economic status or any other individual identities that can be traditionally underrepresented in computing. It is important to say that these strategies benefit *all learners*, such as reviewing exactly how you ask questions, develop confidence and establish routines to reduce anxiety. The strategies provide many ways for pupils to engage with and express their learning, allowing lessons to be more inclusive for all.

Think about how you present content/lessons to children. Make sure that you:

- Present smaller chunks of information, using image support.
- Change the layout of content to include plenty of white space and features such as lists, titles or infographics to help students to make sense of the content and what they can see.

Pedagogical tools

When introducing new concepts, use familiar contexts to help to illustrate and reduce the amount of new information being presented to the pupils. For instance, introduce the idea of algorithms as a sequence of instructions to get dressed in the morning or brush your teeth – something that all children have an experience of.

- The 'Use-Modify-Create' framework is great because it provides all pupils with different ways to engage with content, scaffolding for different levels of both confidence and understanding. Some children may want to investigate working code, whilst others can make simple changes to a program, and another group may be designing and creating their own version of an activity. This allows all learners to be included in a lesson, but at a level suitable to their current understanding.

- Use physical computing devices to engage learners, for eliciting quick wins and providing a concrete, sensory output for an abstract program – such as playing a sound, making a robot move or being able to light up LEDs.

Enhancing diversity

We know that every pupil brings their individuality, experiences and interests to our classrooms. These wonderful differences must be acknowledged and celebrated, and used to provide a safe space for learners to engage, especially in computing.

The following are ways to do this:

- pair programming – this has been proven to engage girls
- celebrating diverse and relevant role models, helping students to 'see' themselves represented in computing-related careers
- words matter: consider your language – is it gender-neutral and culturally sensitive?
- making sure that homework is accessible and not relying on students having access to specific technology at home; this is particularly important as many children will not have access to devices at home – many children from my school were sharing a parent's phone with their siblings to access online learning during the pandemic.

Computing role models

It is also good to weave computing role models into your learning and displays in classrooms. Here is a list of some great role models that you might like to include:

Ada Lovelace, 1815–1852 (computer programmer): Born in 1815 in London, Ada is thought to be the world's first ever computer programmer, after writing an algorithm intended to be carried out by a machine. Lovelace recognised the significance of the development and what it could lead to in the future.

Marie Van Brittan Brown, 1922–1999 (inventor): Marie was a Black nurse who developed the first prototype of CCTV. This contributed to a safer society, as it was the first home security system.

Juliana Rotich, 1977– (software developer): Juliana Rotich is originally from Kenya and studied IT at university. Whilst there, she became a well-known and popular blogger. She now works for a not-for-profit company called

Ushahidi, which develops free open-source software, and she has pioneered new tools from crowdsourcing crisis information.

Marc Regis Hannah, 1956– (electrical engineer): Marc was an electrical engineer who had expertise in computer graphics and developed the 3D special effects systems used widely in movies – for example, *Terminator 2* and *Beauty and the Beast* – and also in scientific research settings, such as aerospace and biotech engineering labs.

Design and technology

Design and technology or DT is:

'an inspiring, rigorous and practical subject. Using creativity and imagination, pupils design and make products that solve real and relevant problems within a variety of contexts, considering their own and others' needs, wants and values. They acquire a broad range of subject knowledge and draw on disciplines such as mathematics, science, engineering, computing and art. Pupils learn how to take risks, becoming resourceful, innovative, enterprising and capable citizens. Through the evaluation of past and present design and technology, they develop a critical understanding of its impact on daily life and the wider world. High-quality design and technology education makes an essential contribution to the creativity, culture, wealth and well-being of the nation.' (DfE, 2013g, p. 1)

Teaching and learning

DT is important because it provides opportunities for children to develop their knowledge, skills and ability; by combining their design and making skills with knowledge and understanding, they learn to create quality products. Children enjoy making decisions for themselves and carrying out practical work. They love creating new products that they can see and touch – and even taste – for themselves. It is a motivating context for discovering literacy, maths, science, art, PSHE and computing. Primary design and technology also provides a firm basis for later learning in the subject and a platform for further developing skills in literacy and numeracy.

Here are some tips for ensuring diverse practice in DT:

- When introducing a new product, always make reference to the contribution of many cultures to the development of technology and its importance in all societies.

- Ensure that activities, tasks, projects, materials and examples reflect the multicultural nature of society and relate to the everyday experiences of pupils.
- Representations of people engaged in technology should reflect a broad range of people from diverse ethnic backgrounds. Throughout each topic, teachers should expose children to the works from designers from a diverse range of ethnic backgrounds, age, gender and people with disabilities.
- The response of people from diverse cultures in their design solutions should be reflected on and valued. When appropriate to the product focus, teachers should encourage children to consider the impact that their design may have on people from diverse cultures and backgrounds, including people with disabilities.
- Teach pupils to appreciate the range of technologies, both simple and complex, in all societies, past and present.
- Teach pupils to appreciate the historical and political factors involved in product development.
- Teach a global perspective regarding the need for all to use materials in a creative, non-harmful and non-wasteful way.

Wonderful project ideas

It is important to say that many of the projects mentioned in the geography and history chapters have cross-curricular links to DT. Design and technology provides excellent opportunities for children to think critically and creatively about solving problems and, furthermore, helping others. Here are some projects to add into your long-term plans and explore with your pupils.

Global food project

This is a wonderful project designed so that pupils can discover the exciting and diverse choice of food available around the world. Perhaps there is a range of different cultures represented in your class – have a family food afternoon! Ask parents to bring in some food from their culture and all children can share, chat and learn. From there, children can learn where different ingredients grow, and build an understanding of the Eatwell plate and food groups. This will enable learners to understand that, although food can be varied, it still all comes under the same basic food groups. Children can then go on to learn some cooking techniques (basic and advanced) and apply these to making some traditional dishes from different countries. Then hold a food festival in your class!

Homes

This is an opportunity to look at designing, making and evaluating homes. Look at homes from around the world, and how they are fit for purpose: climate, terrain and materials.

African instruments: Kalimba

This is a wonderful project that can be found on PlanBee, where children study different instruments and how they are able to make different-pitched sounds. Children can then go on to make their own kalimba, ensuring that different pitches are achieved.

Bread

There are many cross-curricular links with a breadmaking DT unit – for example, looking at the cultural significance of bread and sharing it. From French baguettes to Jewish challah to Jamaican bammy and Ethiopian injera, children can explore different types of bread and their significance to culture. Then look at food hygiene in baking and finally they can bake their own bread. Children get a wonderful sense of achievement at the end of this project.

Chinese inventions

During this project, children can look at various different Chinese inventions, such as Su Song's astronomical clock, the kite and the compass. This is an insight into how and why designs were invented and, furthermore, their impact upon the world. Children can design and create their own kites as part of this project.

Inventors

Here is a list of inventors from a range of backgrounds that you might like to share with your class:

Chieko Asakawa, 1958–: Japanese-born woman who lost her sight at a young age, who became frustrated at the inaccessibility of learning. She went on to study computer programming, was hired by IBM and developed a word processor for braille documents and, furthermore, a braille library network.

Ralph Braun, 1940–2013: Braun was a mechanical engineer with muscular dystrophy who invented the first wheelchair-accessible van with hand controls in the 1960s. He then went on to found the company BraunAbility. In 1991, the company created the first accessible minivan by devising a way to integrate a wheelchair lift onto commercial vans. This was transformative for a more accessible world for wheelchair users.

Dr Maggie Aderin-Pocock MBE, 1968–: Maggie is an inventor, space scientist and science communicator who has worked on many influential projects throughout her career, including developing instruments to detect landmines and other instruments to help us to investigate and understand climate change.

Garrett Morgan, 1877–1963: Morgan was an African-American who invented both the traffic lights and the gas mask! He felt that the lights moving from red to green gave no interval to change, and so developed the red, yellow and green system that many places use to this day. The gas mask started off as a smoke hood, which then became the prototype and precursor for the gas masks used during the First World War.

Case study: *Dragons' Den* Week

After looking at a range of inventions and their inventors with my Year 4 class, we decided to hold a *Dragons' Den*-style week, where children had to think about a problem in their life and create an invention to address it. The results were wonderful: one child designed a robot to do the dishes, as there was a build-up of dishes in their house due to having lots of siblings. One child designed a 'Jollof Rice Cooker', as they felt that a 'normal' rice cooker was not inclusive enough and often her mum was too busy to cook jollof rice, the family's favourite. My absolute favourite design, however, was a girl who designed a walking stick with GPS and earphones, so that 'blind people could have more independence and not always feel helpless', an experience she shared that her parent had felt. She designed the prototype and presented it to the class, and received 'investment' from the Dragons (me and my TA!) for such a creative, thoughtful and innovative design.

Design and technology is a great subject when taught well, as it allows the link between creativity and wellbeing to be fostered. Ultimately, DT is about making lives better, and there are many people around the world who have done amazing and innovative work to support all the things that we do today, and it is important that we know about them and their contributions!

Key takeaways

- Diversity of thought is essential to innovation.
- Learning about inventors, scientists, engineers and mathematicians from different backgrounds allows for a more rounded understanding of the world and its needs.
- Celebrate culture through learning about and from role models: ensure that your medium-term plans have opportunities to reflect on people in STEM who have made a difference from all walks of life.
- Build creativity and diversity in maths through problem-solving.
- Build technology opportunities into your cross-curricular humanities projects.

8 Physical education

This chapter looks at PE (physical education), and how to develop more inclusive and diverse practice. I am genuinely shocked at the number of adults I meet who hated PE when they were at school – this is a huge failure of our system. Children should love PE because its purpose is to help to develop fitness and good health. Exercise makes us feel good! The National Curriculum states that:

> 'A high-quality physical education curriculum inspires all pupils to succeed and excel in competitive sport and other physically-demanding activities. It should provide opportunities for pupils to become physically confident in a way which supports their health and fitness. Opportunities to compete in sport and other activities build character and help to embed values such as fairness and respect.' (DfE, 2013h)

In this chapter, I will explore some ways in which to develop the teaching practice of physical education, where everyone feels safe and valued.

What does the research say?

It is no surprise that the World Health Organization states that 'in children and adolescents, physical activity confers benefits for the following health outcomes: improved physical fitness (cardiorespiratory and muscular fitness), cardiometabolic health (blood pressure, dyslipidaemia, glucose, and insulin resistance), bone health, cognitive outcomes (academic performance, executive function), mental health (reduced symptoms of depression); and reduced adiposity' (World Health Organization, 2020, p. 3).

Physical education is a traditionally gendered subject, and an area of formal education where there are many debates around participation and inclusion, particularly surrounding gender. Stonewall found that 20 per cent of sport fans think that anti-LGBTQ+ language is harmless if it's just meant as banter, 43 per cent of LGBTQ+ people think that public sporting events aren't a welcoming space for them and 33 per cent of LGBTQ+ people who participate in or follow sport are not out to anyone in their sporting life (Menzel et al, 2019). Similarly, 'most female rugby players in the UK and Canada say people automatically assume they are lesbians for playing the sport' and 'a recent BBC documentary highlights how this stigma is particularly challenging for women and girls from non-Anglo backgrounds in developing countries. However, researchers have also found this to be the case in western countries for girls with cultural backgrounds that have outdated norms related to gender.' (Out on the Fields, 2020).

Sport England's (2016) research into disability found that nearly one in five people have a long-standing limiting disability or illness in England, and that, by comparison to other groups, disabled people are far less likely to take part in physical activity or sports. Their research also found that 43 per cent of disabled people are twice as likely to be physically inactive (Sport England, 2016) – all the more reason to ensure that the teaching of PE includes all learners irrespective of abilities.

There is also much fatphobia within sport and PE; athletes with larger bodies are often stigmatised, ridiculed and made to feel left out. If professional athletes are made to feel this way, imagine how children with larger bodies feel. There is an idea – certainly in the Western world – that thinness equals fitness. There are many sports, however, where bigger bodies are better, such as strength sports (weightlifting), shot put, rugby, etc. Often, fatphobia intersects with anti-Blackness and transphobia. Global Sport Matters (de la Cretaz, 2022) published an article noting that 'cultural ideas about whom sports are for (thin people) and which kinds of bodies can be good at sports (thin ones) continue to exclude fat people – despite the fact that fat people are participating (and often excelling) at all levels of sport', and that, furthermore, 'these attitudes can be incredibly harmful. Not only do the beliefs discourage fat people from getting involved in sports from the outset, but also the belief that thin bodies will be better at sports does a ton of harm, even to non-fat athletes. The pressure to maintain certain body fat percentages or to drop weight to "improve" at their sport takes an incredible toll on athletes, and eating disorders are rampant in sports of all levels.' (De La Cretaz, 2022)

There is also still widespread racism in sport, particularly evident in football. One just has to think back to the 2021 European Championship, England vs Italy, and the racist abuse that the three players who missed their penalties received.

PE, in my opinion, should be recognised as a core subject, and it is our responsibility to ensure that it is truly inclusive. We have a wealth of gender-diverse, neuro and physically diverse children in our schools. We have to work as hard at differentiating for all pupils as we would in a reading lesson – and do our research.

Teaching and learning

Differentiating for learners with different needs

Youth Sport Trust have produced some brilliant guides on how to include learners with different needs, from physical disabilities to neurodiverse students.

Here are some tips from their guide '10 top tips to adapt activities for young people':

- Think carefully about the balls you use – could you use larger balls which are easier to catch? Could you use softer balls which are less intimidating for those who struggle with catching?
- Slower moving balls are good for young people who are developing their reaction time.
- Use balls containing things that make a sound such as bells or seeds, so that young people can track where they are through sound.
- Use flashcards to demonstrate skills to young people. These could be colour coded depending on the skills – this really helps children who have EAL, cognitive impairment or struggle with lengthy verbal instructions.
- Make channels for rolling items – you could use two benches as a channel for rolling a ball down.

Here are some other tips for including children with SEND in sport and PE lessons:

Children with Down's syndrome

Good to know…

- Sometimes children with Down's syndrome can experience hypertonia (relaxed muscle tone) and hypermobility.
- Sometimes children with Down's syndrome have poorer visual acuity and may struggle with depth perception.

Ways to include in PE…

- Use appropriate equipment, e.g. beach balls for throwing and catching if they struggle with basketball, for example.
- Develop a routine for PE; it builds confidence and reduces anxiety.

- Use slight and gradual progressions in learning new skills.
- Single commands and points help with communication.

Children with amputations or limb difference

Good to know…

- In some cases, mobility and balance may be affected.
- Children with amputations or limb difference can have low confidence and self-esteem.

Ways to include in PE…

- Think about your language and offer adaptations. For example, if you are teaching hockey to your whole class and you have a child with one arm, show everyone techniques for holding the stick with either one or two hands.
- Communicate with the child. Say, 'Show me what feels comfortable.'
- Praise and celebrate! Develop the child's confidence through praise and recognition.

For more information, check out www.limbformation.com and www.limbpower.com.

Children with cerebral palsy (CP)

Good to know…

- All children with CP are different, so don't categorise them into the same box. Learn about the child's needs and abilities.
- CP affects children's motor ability in different ways.
- In some children, it causes weaker arms or legs.
- In some children, it causes hypertonia (seeming too stiff or too floppy).

Ways to include in PE…

- Adapt equipment, e.g. using balloons instead of balls if it fits the child's needs better.
- Think about the space that your lesson is in – is it inclusive? Does it allow room for children to move safely? Is there an appropriate rest space if needed? Are the toilets nearby?

> **Top tip!**
>
> Find out what your students *can* do. Speak with their parents and carers. Praise them for progress. Create a culture in your PE lessons where everyone is praised on their effort and progress, so it is not simply the 'best kids at PE' who get praised and awarded.

Inclusive PE training

Sainbury's run an Active Kids for All inclusive PE training programme, which provides a high-quality curriculum for PE for all learners, and active inclusion of young people with physical difference or neurodiversity. There is an online portal with many resources, some interactive and some downloadable, which complement the face-to face training. It is a great resource for CPD training.

There is also a resource on Youth Sport Trust called Elements, which is for young people with multiple and profound learning difficulties. There are links with the National Curriculum on adapted activities to fit the needs of learners.

> **Case study: Find the *can*, not the *can't***
>
> A friend of mine has a son with Perthes disease. This is a condition where the supply of blood to the thigh bone is disrupted, which causes the bone to deteriorate and limits movement of the hip joint. It is a condition that affects children generally between the ages of three and 11 years old. One evening I received a phone call from my friend, who was upset because her son had been left out of his PE lessons and asked to sit and watch the other children do PE. She wondered whether this was normal practice in a primary school. I informed her that it isn't! The teacher obviously didn't know how to include him in the PE lesson; it broke my heart to hear of a young, disabled person being left out of a lesson. There were many things that the teacher *could* have done, firstly doing some research on the condition and speaking with the parents. They could have had him join in the lesson from a chair, and partnered with the teacher or support staff. I am pleased to say that he is now included and joining in differentiated PE lessons.

> Furthermore, he has gone above and beyond. This young man is particularly passionate about car racing and go-karts. He now takes part in regular go-kart racing… and is exceptionally good at it! This is a wonderful example of finding out exactly what a child *can* do rather than excluding them because they *can't*. He even has a successful Facebook page, documenting his racing success, at 'Racing with Perthes Disease'… check it out!

LGBTQ+ inclusive teaching

As educators, our language is so important. Ensure that in PE you are using inclusive language, and no phrases such as 'man up' or 'run like a girl'. You may chuckle to yourself and think that you would never use language like that, but I have observed people making comments that they didn't even really realise they were saying. Instead, you can use language like 'sportsperson' instead of 'sportsman' and 'dig deeper' or 'keep on going'.

Top tip!

> Be sure that everyone who teaches PE gets training on inclusive practice – in some schools there is a PE coach who plans and teaches all PE, and often they are not contracted to be part of all staff meetings, etc. Be sure that your teaching and learning policy for PE explicitly lays out the expectations surrounding language and that it is shared with all.

Having mixed teams (all genders) in sport and PE makes it more inclusive for LGBTQ+ students and pupils who are gender-diverse. It fights against reinforcing the traditional gender binary and allows for progress and development of self-esteem.

Call out abuse: homophobic, transphobic or sexist language is not acceptable. It's not acceptable in your lessons and it is not acceptable in sport itself. Show your stance as an ally!

> **Top tip!**
>
> Put your pronouns on your email signature; this again shows people awareness and acceptance and opens a conversation for others to share theirs with you. It creates a culture where gender is not assumed.

Stonewall Rainbow Laces Campaign

The Stonewall Rainbow Laces Campaign is one that shows support of LGBTQ+ inclusion in sport. This campaign has brought visibility and awareness to LGBTQ+ people in sport. Everyone should be able to feel comfortable, confident and included in sport. However, that is not always the case, as many LGBTQ+ people have experienced bullying and being made to feel uncomfortable. Sport and physical exercise improves both our physical and mental wellbeing and health. All people should be engaged with this.

The campaign is simple: Lace Up and Speak Up. You can buy the rainbow laces from the Stonewall website at a price of £2.00. They come in all different colours: rainbow, trans flag colours (pink, blue and white), bi flag colours, lesbian colours, non binary, ace and pan colours. Wearing the laces provokes conversations surrounding equality and inclusion.

Racism in sport

Unacceptable racist abuse and behaviour still overshadow sports. A YouGov survey in 2021 found that 92 per cent of ethnic minority football fans in Great Britain say that racism exists in professional football, with a further 78 per cent saying that racism is a serious issue affecting the sport (YouGov, 2021).

Brendon Batson, a West Bromwich player during the 1970s, told the *Guardian* in 2014:

> 'We'd get off the coach at away matches and the National Front would be right there in your face. In those days, we didn't have security and we'd have to run the gauntlet. We'd get to the players' entrance and there'd be spit on my jacket or Cyrille's shirt. It was a sign of the times. I don't recall making a big hue and cry about it. We coped. It wasn't a new phenomenon to us.' (Rees, 2014)

Unfortunately, racism still continues in football. It is important that, as teachers, we call it out. Read through *Newsround* articles on the issue and prompt children to discuss their thoughts about it. If we do not call out racism, we are complicit in racism.

There is also racism in other sports, such as cricket. Azeem Rafiq, a British Asian cricketer, spoke out in 2020 about teammates and, furthermore, captains who were openly racist, hearing comments like 'There's too many of you lot. We need to have a word about that' and other unacceptable abuse (Hashim, 2020).

Ask children to respond with metacognitive stems like:

- I'm thinking…
- I'm wondering…
- I'm seeing…
- I'm noticing…
- I'm feeling…

Get children to come up with a charter of acceptable behaviour in sport – they could make posters of these and display them in the playground and in the corridors.

Top tip!

Like all other subjects, the images that you use of sportspeople are important. For example, show images of women wearing the hijab playing sports. The Nike video advert 'Equality has no boundaries' is a great video to show young people.

Project ideas linked with PE

History of legislation against racism in football

After many incidents of racism in football throughout the 1970s, '80s and '90s, legislation was written and used to respond to repeat incidents. Learning about this makes an interesting project for upper Key Stage 2, as well as serving as good knowledge for educators.

The Public Order Act of 1986 meant that anyone who was intentionally behaving and speaking in an abusive way, with the intention of causing distress to another, was fined or imprisoned. This was followed by the Football Spectators Act in 1989, which included football banning orders. Indecent or racial football chants were banned at football matches.

'Between 2010/11 and 2018/19, the UKFPU reported an average of just 24 arrests, although this is an improvement on the early impact of the provision, when annual arrests across England and Wales only just reached double figures. […] It is difficult to see how the [Law] Commission will not recommend reform here, particularly under pressure from groups like Kick It Out. Section 3 is flawed on many levels, and […] is outdated in the context of the contemporary norms of football fandom.' (Lewis, 2021)

Racial justice protests in sports

Raised gloved fists

During the 1968 Olympics, which took place a few months after Martin Luther King Jr was assassinated, American athletes John Carlos and Tommie Smith raised their gloved fists as the US national anthem played, to protest against racism and show solidarity with Martin Luther King's plight.

Taking the knee

Taking the knee was made mainstream by NFL players Colin Kaepernick, Eli Harold and Eric Reid, who knelt down on one knee during the American national anthem just before a game. Kaepernick said that he wouldn't stand proud to the national anthem in a country where Black people were being killed in the streets every day, at the behest of the police. It was originally used as a symbol by Martin Luther King Jr, to show solidarity with anti-racist protestors during the civil rights movement in the 1960s.

Following the death of George Floyd in 2020 members of the England football team took the knee at the Euros 2020 to show solidarity with the Black Lives Matter movement.

This too is an interesting conversation and project to look at with children.

By Angelo Cozzi (Mondadori Publishers) - This file has been extracted from another file, Public Domain, https://commons.wikimedia.org/w/index.php?curid=40937149

Case study: Class names

After the three Black England players missed the penalty kicks in the decisive European Championship shootout against Italy in 2021, my class (and I) were shocked at the disgusting racist abuse that the players received as a result of it. The children directed me to teach an assembly about racism, which they presented, and they wanted to create 'say no to racism' and 'give racism the red card' placards.

They organised a school-wide 'wear red' day to give racism the red card, and they created videos about being anti-racist and what to do if you experience racism.

Finally, they decided that they wanted to honour the players, and so we named one of our classes Bukayo Saka class, and designed a mural of Marcus Rashford and Jadon Sancho for our Key Stage 2 playground.

This warmed my heart, because it showed that we had done something right as a school. We *should* be outraged by racism – or any type of discrimination. We *should* actively make steps to fight it.

Inclusive PE initiatives

Kick it Out @kickitout

Kick it Out is a fantastic organisation that fights, educates and challenges all forms of discrimination in football, from a grassroots level to professional teams. On their website, there are many education and training resources, such as an Equality Charter and an Equality Calendar for the Year, including a range of events across the year to celebrate diversity and promote equality.

There is also a 'Report It' function, where anyone can report discrimination seen in football, either online, grassroots, non-league or professional games.

Black Girl Hike @UkBgh

For anyone who has been on a residential school journey, you may also have noticed that there are very few instructors of colour at the centres. I've been to many different residential providers across the UK, from north to south, and have actually never experienced a Black instructor. As we know, representation matters; we want all children to feel included and like they have a place and space for outdoor adventure. Black Girl Hike is a fantastic organisation that aims to 'develop services and projects to increase the participation and development of Black women in the outdoors, and opportunities to engage', and they work with 'the wider outdoor industry to meet the needs of our community, tackling the lack of inclusion and representation'.

This Girl Can @ThisGirlCanUK

This Girl Can is a campaign funded by the National Lottery, which encourages girls and women into sport. It celebrates women of all shapes and sizes, ages and backgrounds getting involved in sport and exercise and shaking off confidence and self-esteem issues. It aims to rid them of the fear of judgement in taking part in physical activity, and feelings of not feeling good enough. There are wonderful real stories from women from all walks of life – fabulous to share with your girls… and your parents/carer community!

Using social media

Your school social media platforms are great to engage families and the local community in sport and PE at the school – with parental permission, of course. I usually send out a Google Form to parents/carers at the start of each year and ask permission for social media platforms. This information is then stored on the MIS. You can deliver the message of fun and inclusive physical activity to promote school sports and reach the local community.

> **Top tip!**
>
> Get your PE coach to organise a parent/carer fitness class every week. My amazing PE coach started this after lockdown and it was hugely successful; you could see the parents who attended (who were all women) build in confidence and pride in themselves. We gave out certificates in our celebration assembly to celebrate the fact that they had completed a term's worth of fitness classes, and they were beaming from ear to ear (as were their proud children, who watched their parent/carer receive an award). I also used to teach Zumba to the staff and parent community once per week, and it was a lovely way to get people together and shake off some stress.

Kit

Ensure that your kit is inclusive for all children – for example, allowing children to swim in leggings if they wish or to do PE in long trousers as well as shorts.

> **Top tip!**
>
> Think about who is teaching PE and ensure that children over their time at your school get taught PE by people of different genders, so that they can see that PE is not inherently for 'boys', for example. This could be by getting different staff members or sports coaches to deliver after-school clubs, for example.

Living a healthy life, both physically and mentally, supports growth and development as people. However, so many adults hate PE because of unhappy memories or shame from their own PE education. We need to do better. Nurturing a love for looking after our bodies and emotions is so important, as it gives children the toolkit to succeed in adult life. Let's create a space where everyone can succeed and grow together and, furthermore… love PE!

Key takeaways

- Physical education is key to children's physical and mental health development.
- Find out what children *can* do and work from there.
- Do your research – find inclusive teaching CPD for staff to do.
- Work with the parent and carer community – get them involved in physical activity.
- Call out discrimination with children.
- Be an ally! Show your support of anti-racist, anti-homophobic, anti–transphobic, anti-sexist, anti-ableist and anti-fatphobic physical education.

9 SMSC: Collective worship, assemblies and charity work

SMSC (spiritual, moral, social and cultural development) is part of the Ofsted inspection framework and is essentially about preparing children to be active citizens and lead full lives as part of the community. This chapter is about weaving global and diverse celebrations into the curriculum and your collective worship or assembly timetable – not as tokenistic celebrations but to complement the taught curriculum. When events and celebrations are discussed and shared, as part of a wider ethos of inclusion, it allows for whole-school discussions about relevant issues. It also allows you as a leader (if you are one) to model how to talk about issues that some staff members may feel less confident to talk about.

What is SMSC?

SMSC is the beating heart of everything that we do as educators. We teach hearts as well as minds. A curriculum designed to actively teach human rights, social justice, and identity and diversity is already rich in SMSC. Your curriculum maps should be laced with opportunities to critically think about inclusion and raise awareness of issues that affect the world and its people, and to develop young people's hearts and minds.

During Ofsted inspections, how a school develops children's SMSC identities is really important. Ofsted currently inspect four areas: quality of education, behaviour and attitudes, personal development, and leadership and management. As part of this inspection, SMSC plays a huge role in these areas, particularly behaviour and attitudes, and personal development.

Let's break SMSC up to understand fully what it means.

Spiritual

Spiritual development means providing opportunities for children to develop spiritually, to formulate and reflect on their own beliefs and the beliefs of those around them, to show empathy and to develop understanding of religion.

Reflection, self-awareness and the development of creativity and imagination come as a result of spiritual development. Ways to develop this are:

- RE lessons
- collective worship/assemblies
- trips to places of religious significance
- reflecting upon the beauty of language, art and music.

Moral

Moral development is supporting children to know the difference between right and wrong – both in the eyes of the law and also from a humanitarian standpoint. Essentially, moral development is about choices. Ways to develop this are:

- school values
- class charter
- PSHE
- Philosophy4Children: an enquiry-based programme of critical thinking for children, where they are given provocations to discuss, question and reflect, and given a framework
- visits from local community: police, fire service, etc.
- raising money for charity.

Social

Social development is actively teaching children social skills, how to engage with others and accept people's differences. The aim is to develop young people who can communicate and socialise effectively, to develop emotional intelligence and to build self-esteem and maintain good mental health. Ways to develop this are:

- PSHE
- cooperative learning
- oracy
- social skills intervention groups
- family board games events
- school council and pupil leadership team

- social justice events: Earth Day, Save the bees!, climate change protests, etc.
- relationships and sex education (RSE).

Cultural

Cultural development is teaching the appreciation and understanding of different cultures, beyond the five Fs of food, fashion, famous people, festivals and flags. It's understanding who is in our society and how our society has been formed and the appreciation and development of music, art, sports and other cultural pursuits. This includes understanding democracy and the British parliamentary process. Ways to develop this are:

- quality RE lessons
- themed weeks: Black History Month, Roma Gypsy Month, LGBTQ+ History Month
- art exhibitions, museum trips, musical concerts and performances
- Culture Day, where everyone dresses up in colours or clothing to reflect their personal culture
- all the wonderful history projects that you design!

Top tip!

Sign up to Newsthink from the British Red Cross, which emails through topical teaching resources about how to explore news from a humanitarian perspective. They include brilliant photos and questions to prompt critical thinking and in-depth discussions.

British Values (or my preferred term, 'human values')

The government's 'Prevent Strategy' in 2011 articulated that, through SMSC provision, schools are to promote 'British Values' of:

1. democracy
2. the rule of law
3. individual liberty
4. mutual respect
5. tolerance of different faiths and beliefs.

Of course, referring to the above as 'British Values' is problematic in itself – my preferred term is 'human values', but that's a whole other book! I'm fairly sure that the British didn't invent democracy….

Anyway, through SMSC provision, the aim is to:

- enable students to develop self-esteem, self-awareness and confidence
- support children to distinguish between right and wrong
- understand the elements of criminal law in the UK
- support children to accept responsibility for their own behaviour, choices and actions
- develop a respect and broad general knowledge of public institutions and services in the UK
- further develop tolerance, harmony and appreciation between different groups of people and cultural traditions
- develop respect and empathy for one another
- understand and further democracy.

Rights Respecting Schools

Unicef runs Rights Respecting Schools Awards (RRSA), which are awarded to schools in which children's rights are taught, promoted and realised by and for children. It is based on the United Nations Convention on the Rights of the Child (1990), and Unicef is the world's leading organisation working for children and their rights. Schools can apply for bronze, silver and then the gold award. When you sign up to apply for the RRSA, you get access to the Rights Respecting Schools website, which has a plethora of amazing resources teaching children about the big issues of the world today, from war to migration to climate change.

There are four key areas of impact for children at a Rights Respecting School: wellbeing, participation, relationships and self-esteem.

The difference that a Rights Respecting School makes goes beyond the school gates, having a positive impact on the whole community:

- Children are healthier and happier.
- Children feel safe.
- Children have better relationships.
- Children become active and involved in school life and the wider world.

Case study: Culture Day

Over the lockdown of 2020, one of the children who was in my class suggested that we have a Culture Day. She wanted to celebrate all the different cultures that make up the diverse tapestry of our school community. She also said that it was 'important that people take some time to think about where they come from, wherever that is'. Unfortunately, we were in the middle of lockdown, so it didn't get organised until this child was in Year 6. Right at the end of the summer term, she and I organised it together; she was leaving Year 6 and I was leaving to move into my first headship in a different school.

We talked about how we could include everyone in the day. We discussed how some cultures have traditional dress and how others may not know their traditional dress. We talked about how people of mixed heritage may want to show more than one culture. We agreed that children, staff, parents and carers could wear:

- traditional clothing
- colours from the flag of their country/ies
- football/sports kit from their country/ies
- dress like a role model from their culture/country.

I then did an assembly to tell the school about it. Everyone was excited and I must say that I was bursting with pride watching this fantastic young woman talk confidently in assembly to her peers about something that she was passionate about. She told everyone that if they weren't sure what to wear, they could come and talk to her or me about it. She talked about her Nigerian heritage and what she *could* wear. I talked about my mixed heritage and how I planned to show a range of cultures and countries through the colours I planned to wear. Us modelling the thought process of what to wear opened up opportunities for others to think and discuss openly with their peers and teachers. It didn't need to be new clothes – this was about showing who you are, accessible to all.

We then set the date and made flyers to go home and be displayed in each classroom and corridor. She also got a group of Year 6s together to create a 'promotion video' for it.

The night before the Culture Day, I received a message from a worried parent whose heritage was Russian; she was concerned that her daughter might have some unkind comments thrown her way if she dressed as such. I encouraged her that we were an inclusive community, and that we had done a lot of work surrounding the war in Russia and how we treat each other. We had taught the children that we can disagree with the war but this did not mean that we treat Russians with any less respect than anyone else. We had even sent out a parent/carer leaflet on how to speak with your children about the war in Russia. This eased her worry. I messaged the staff team to keep an eye out for this particular girl to make sure that she was OK and feeling safe all day.

Well, the day came along. I went out slightly earlier on gate duty because I was excited, and I wasn't let down. Children (and parents/carers) were already waiting outside the gate, in their own clothes. In fact, the first parent who greeted me was wearing a sombrero (and, considering that this parent was generally quite hard to reach, it warmed my heart that she had made an effort to show her Mexican heritage). The girl mentioned above, whose mum was worried, proudly walked through the gates in the morning with her Russian flag around her shoulders, and was embraced by her friends, who were also dressed up.

Children came into school beaming. There were children wearing a range of outfits, from Algerian football kit, to a knitted poncho in Colombian colours, to blue-striped dresses to represent Scotland, to Nigerian agbadas, to Ghanaian kente cloth, to traditional Polish folk attire. It provided a platform for children, parents/carers and staff to have open conversations about their heritage, simply by saying, 'Tell me about your outfit…'.

We had an assembly in the morning where children were able to see the clothing of all classes, excitedly spot others wearing similar colours/

patterns to them and learn about outfits that were unfamiliar to them. At the end of the day we had our summer fair, and it was wonderful to see parents/carers arrive to collect their children, also dressed up. We organised food stalls – some run by parents/carers or staff and some by local businesses – selling a range of different food types (for example, jerk chicken, falafel and jollof rice).

It was a wonderful day – a great celebration of diversity and development of SMSC, and a wonderful way to bring the term to an end. The girl who organised the day with me felt such a sense of pride, and her dad thanked me at the end of the day too. I will be sure to start Culture Day at my new school!

COMBER GROVE PRIMARY SCHOOL

SUMMER FAIR
and
CULTURAL DAY

Wednesday 13th July 3:30pm to 5pm

At Comber Grove we celebrate all the wonderful cultures that make up our community. We invite children, staff and parents to come to school in clothing or colours from their culture. Then our Summer Fair starts at 3:30pm on the KS2 playground.

Foods and stalls from different cultures!

Bouncy Castle!
Book Fair!
Raffle!

Whole-school practices

Here are some ways to think holistically about whole-school practices and events that you can plan to bring together the wonderful learning that children have done. This links with the 'British Value' (though I find that term problematic, as mentioned earlier) of the rule of law. Children can show moral development by understanding that every action has a reaction, the consequences of their actions and behaviour, and each other's viewpoints (both moral and ethical).

Celebration days and weeks across the school year

Every year, The Key publishes a whole-school calendar, including celebration weeks and days. You can also download it straight onto your Google Calendar (which I have found extremely useful). Of course, there is simply not enough time to celebrate every single individual day, but sit at the start of the year and work out which days/weeks fit into learning and/or the school's needs and map it out.

Here are some examples of celebration weeks, by month:

September

- International Day of Peace
- National Inclusion Week
- Holy Cross Day (Christian)
- Rosh Hashana (Jewish New Year)
- Macmillan Coffee Morning
- Jeans for Genes Week
- European Day of Languages

October

- Black History Month
- Yom Kippur (Jewish)
- Sukkot (Jewish)
- Dussehra (Hindu)
- Diwali (Hindu)
- Down's Syndrome Awareness Month

- Dyslexia Awareness Week
- World Mental Health Awareness Day
- Anti-Slavery Day
- International Pronouns Day
- Halloween
- Birthday of Guru Ram Das (Sikh)
- International Day for the Eradication of Poverty

November

- Armistice Day
- Birthday of Guru Nanak (Sikh)
- UK Disability History Month
- Islamophobia Awareness Month
- Elimination of Violence Against Women Day
- Transgender Day of Remembrance
- World Kindness Day
- St Andrew's Day (Christian)
- Interfaith Week

December

- Hanukkah (Jewish)
- Christmas Day (Christian)
- World AIDS Day
- Human Rights Day
- International Day of People with Disabilities
- International Day for the Abolition of Slavery
- Bodhi Day (Buddhist)

January

- Martin Luther King Jr Day
- Burns Night
- Holocaust Memorial Day

February

- LGBT History Month
- Safer Internet Day
- Children's Mental Health Week
- World Cancer Day
- Isra and Mi'raj (Islam)
- Shrove Tuesday, Ash Wednesday and Lent (Christian)

March

- World Book Day
- Women's History Month
- Purim (Jewish)
- Holi (Hindu)
- World Water Day
- Ramadan (Islam)
- World Poetry Day
- World Down Syndrome Day

April

- Eid al-Fitr (Islam)
- Passover (Jewish)
- Easter (Christian)
- World Health Day
- Earth Day
- Stephen Lawrence Day

May

- World Asthma Day
- VE Day
- International Day Against Homophobia, Transphobia and Biphobia

- Global Campaign for Education Action Day
- World Trade Day
- Christian Aid Week

June

- Gypsy, Roma and Traveller History Month
- World Environment Day
- World Oceans Day
- World Refugees Day
- Windrush Day
- Make Music Day

July

- Mandela Day
- Eid al Adha (Islam)
- International Day of Friendship
- Plastic Free July
- National Transplants Week

August

- International Youth Day
- World Water Week
- National Zoo Awareness Week

Of course, this list is not exhaustive, and you may want to change (some of) the celebrations that you focus on from year to year, so that by the time a child leaves your school, they have had exposure to a wide range of celebrations and causes.

At the start of the year, delegate the organisation of each day/week to staff members, so that there is ownership over championing it.

Here are some suggestions to make the celebration days as successful as possible:

- I have introduced the celebration day/week in assembly. We discussed *why* we are celebrating it and why it matters.
- I have set up a competition for children to do some home learning surrounding the issue. I started off by doing poster competitions, but I seemed to have the same group of children (mainly girls) entering. I then opened it out to be a 'creativity competition' and had many more children engaged. Children would write a rap about ending racism or create a 'how to' video, as well as beautiful posters. The prize would be a book about the issue. The children loved it!
- I then sent out information (websites, PowerPoints, sources for further learning) to the teachers and, during their PSHE session that week, children would learn about more about it.
- It is up to the smaller teams in your school (key stages) to run their own follow-up assemblies, etc.
- I wrote a parent/carer newsletter about the issue or celebration, to make sure that everyone was aware of the learning. Sometimes parents/carers do have a good understanding of celebrations/world issues, and it's important that we include them in the learning too!
- Use the work created by children to build a working display about the issue – over the course of the year, you will have a wealth of relevant corridor displays about current world issues.
- Tweet, Tweet, Tweet! Tweet children's reflections and learning about the issues. Find out the trending hashtag for the celebration or the organisation's Twitter handle and show your support online for the issue. This gives the school a wonderful online presence, showcasing exactly what you care about, and it also makes links with others.

> **Top tip!**
>
> At the start of the year, plan a whole-school calendar or event and give it to staff. This avoids overwhelming or surprising people, ensures that you don't overplan events and means that you can run events as well as possible. There are so many different celebrations each year that *could* be celebrated – choose the ones that work best to complement your taught curriculum for the year.

Case study: The power of Twitter

In early 2022, when Russia invaded Ukraine and tensions began to rise again between the two countries, we had a couple of incidents at school. In my school, there was one Russian family, and one day the girl had been subject to some nasty comments from other children on the playground. Upon investigating it with the children, those children saying horrible things to her had been watching videos on TikTok about how 'all Russians were evil' and even tutorial videos on 'how to spit at a Russian'. I knew that we needed to act quickly before it got out of hand, and it became glaringly obvious that children were getting their sources of learning about this issue from the wrong places. So, firstly I called the parent of the girl and informed her of what was happening and what we were doing about it. I made sure that the girl was OK and I let her know that we would keep her safe and told her the plan. After lunchtime, I pulled the whole school together for an assembly. First, I asked the children what they knew and then, perhaps more importantly, I asked where they got their sources of information from. It was mainly from social media or, for younger pupils, from their older siblings, who also got it from social media. I also asked them how they were feeling, and most said 'scared' or 'worried about World War III'.

We discussed reliable and child-friendly sources of information – for example, *Newsround*. I opened the website on the board in assembly, so that children could see what it looked like. We talked about speaking openly with people at home about feeling scared. We talked about showing empathy to all: both Ukrainians and Russians. We discussed how the war was caused by people in power, and not all Russians felt the same. We talked about how it might feel to be Ukrainian at the moment and how it may feel to be Russian. Children were very reflective and spoke about the feeling of fear or shame. One child said, 'Well, I guess Russians actually need more of our love at the moment', which was lovely! Many children shared the fact that when they asked their parents/carers, they did not know any information, and this made them feel more scared.

After the assembly, I put together a 'Talking to your child about war' parent/carer guide and sent it home that afternoon.

It included:

What's happening in Ukraine?

An attack on Ukraine has been launched by Russia, and the leader of Russia, Vladimir Putin, has sent forces across the borders to fight. Many Ukrainians have lost their lives and have been displaced (had to move to somewhere else). Some children at school have been talking about this, so we wanted to support you to discuss it with your children if they bring it up.

Should I talk to my child about this?

Children are exposed to lots of information online, whether they are browsing the internet, watching the news or on apps such as TikTok or YouTube (particularly for older children). Hearing words such as 'bombing' or 'war' online may make children feel worried or anxious. If your child asks you about what is happening, there are several things that you can do to support them: this is a guide to help. Start with finding out what they know. If your child brings it up, first ask what they already know. You could ask:

- What do you think is happening?
- Do you know why it's happening?
- What do you think about it?

Let them know that if they have any questions they can ask you, and if you don't know, you can find out together.

Where can I find unbiased information?

Look at age-appropriate children's websites to find out more information together. *Newsround* is great place to find child-friendly information. Reassure children that Ukraine and Russia are far away from England.

Protection from bullying

There will be people within our school and local community who are Ukrainian, Russian or have family and friends in either country. We must make sure that we prevent all forms of bullying. If a child were to say 'I don't like Russia', for example, correct them and talk about how they may not like what's going on in Russia, but it's not OK to say that they don't like 'Russia' or 'Russians'.

Key words and what they mean

Here are some child-friendly explanations of words that children may be hearing around this issue:

- Displaced: If someone is displaced, it means that they have been forced to leave their home because it isn't safe anymore.
- Refugee: A refugee is someone who leaves their country because it has become unsafe for them to stay there.
- Invasion: An invasion is when an army enters another country by force. It's usually done to take control of the area or country that they're entering.
- Kremlin: The Kremlin is a big fortress in Moscow containing government buildings and is the official residence of Vladimir Putin.
- NATO: NATO stands for the North Atlantic Treaty Organisation. It is an international organisation that brings together the armies of various countries, including the UK, the United States and France.

Worried or want to discuss in more detail?

If you want to speak in more detail about this or have any concerns, please do not hesitate to get in contact with Ms Wordlaw.

The feedback from the family of the child who received nasty comments that day for being Russian was that they felt extremely supported by the school. There were no further comments made towards the pupil, and that pupil received regular mental health check-ins to make sure that she felt safe. I also checked in regularly with the family, to make sure that they were OK too.

After I sent home printed copies of the parent newsletter, I also Tweeted it. The response that the school received was amazing. Within minutes, Sky News got in contact and wanted to interview children. The following day, the

Pupil Leadership Team (which consisted of four Year 6s) were interviewed by Sky News. They were asked what they knew about the war and how their school had prepared them and made sure that pupils were safe. The children were able to speak confidently and with empathy and pride about what was happening between Ukraine and Russia and, furthermore, how to alleviate fears and educate themselves in an age-appropriate and unbiased manner. The interviewer from Sky News was extremely impressed with their knowledge and ability to articulate their thoughts. This shows the power of acting swiftly but in an informed manner, always starting with finding out first *what* children know and secondly *how* they know it, so that you can appropriately support children and families.

Top tip!

If you can link your celebration days into your whole-school learning themes, it weaves a rich tapestry of global citizenship learning and development of SMSC.

Global citizenship

'We must foster global citizenship. Education is about more than literacy and numeracy. It is also about citizenry. Education must fully assume its essential role in helping people to forge more just, peaceful and tolerant societies.' (Ban Ki-moon, United Nations Secretary-General, 2012, quoted in Oxfam, 2015a, p. 2)

Global citizenship means being part of and aware of the wider world and your place in it. It is about taking an active role in the local, national and international community and working together to make the world a better place. Oxfam has produced two brilliant documents: Education for global citizenship: A guide for schools (2015a) and Global citizenship in the classroom: A guide for teachers (2015b). I have got a lot of inspiration for curriculum design from these documents and they are a great place to start. Oxfam's definition of education for global citizenship is as follows:

'A transformative vision of education… for global citizenship is a framework to equip learners for critical and active engagement with the challenges and opportunities of life in a fast-changing and interdependent world. It is transformative, developing the knowledge and understanding, skills, values and attitudes that learners need both to participate fully in a globalised society and economy, and to secure a more just, secure and sustainable world than the one they have inherited… Oxfam believes that young people's learning, thinking and actions – both now and in their adult lives – are integral to the achievement of that more just, secure and sustainable global future. Therefore, alongside a rigorous development of global understanding and multiple perspectives, an education for global citizenship should also include opportunities for young people to develop their skills as agents of change and to reflect critically on this role.' (Oxfam, 2015a, p5)

Oxfam (2015, p5) express that a global citizen should:

- *Be actively aware of the world around them and what it means to be a good citizen.*
- *Know, understand and seek to find out how the world works and its systems.*
- *Highly value diversity and inclusion, understanding its worth and why it is needed.*
- *Commit fully to ideas of social justice.*
- *Be actively engaged in both the local and global community.*
- *Take full responsibility for their actions.*
- *Be able to work with others around them.*
- *Be committed to being sustainable with their actions and the way they live their life.*

Oxfam explains that this idea of Global citizenship is imperative because:

- Children must be taught to understand and process the world around them, including ideas of poverty, equality, sustainability.
- Children must be taught to critically think and develop empathy for others.
- This empathy is needed for children to grow into adults who understand and can act upon the vision to make the world a better place.
- Our world is deeply interconnected, and understanding the complex nature of this is essential for navigating societal challenges and pursuing social justice (Oxfam, 2015a).

The 'guide for schools' document (Oxfam, 2015a) lists the knowledge and understanding, skills, values and attitudes that are developed through ideas and projects – and is absolutely brilliant.

Some of these include:

- Social justice and equity: Looking at the idea of fairness and inequality at different levels (local, national and global).
- Identity and diversity: Looking at individual uniqueness, self-identities and belonging.
- Globalisation and interdependence: Looking at similarities and differences between different parts of the world.
- Power and governance: Looking at rules, laws, structures and systems at different levels (local, national and global).

This guide can be used by teachers to inform classroom practice or by leaders to inform long-term planning and project ideas. It provides ideas and structure with which to plan amazing classroom projects or a whole-school approach to diverse and inclusive education and, furthermore, development of children's SMSC identities.

Key takeaways

- Celebrating and learning about world issues through your assembly or collective worship schedule is powerful and a great way to develop children's SMSC identities.
- Plan and give out a yearly plan of celebrations at the start of the year, so staff have time and space to plan great learning,
- Be sure to support your staff to learn about it too – they may not be confident or have a great deal of subject knowledge on the matter.
- Add parent/carers into the mix – create a platform where everyone is learning together and give them tools to discuss issues with their children when they come home from school.
- Utilise PSHE sessions to deliver further age-appropriate learning surrounding the issue.
- This also supports children learning 'British Values'.

PART 3

Remapping the curriculum

10 Mapmaker, mapmaker, make me a map… A practical guide to mapping out curriculum

This chapter is a guide to taking the research from previous chapters and mapping it out to create a whole-school curriculum map and individual subject curriculum maps. These maps ensure progression from Early Years up to Year 6. A curriculum map is the road map – the journey – that children's learning takes throughout the school. They are essential for you, the planner, the teachers delivering it and also the children and their parents/carers to see what they are going to learn in their time with you.

This process takes time. It's a good idea to split your team into groups. Subject leads and subject champions can make up little breakaway groups. At the start of the year, I ask *all staff* (support staff, office staff, teachers and leaders) where their personal passions lie outside of their leadership area. You may have an admin officer who is passionate about sewing, for example, or a governor who plays semi-pro football! I call these 'subject champions' and they are part of designing, reviewing and monitoring that subject alongside the subject lead. These diverse groups of educators can get together, over the course of an inset day, and complete the following process. It cannot be rushed; good curriculum design takes time and headspace.

How to remap your curriculum

Step 1

You have your school vision for your curriculum: your curriculum intent. This is the basis for all further planning. This could include the whole-school themes for each term.

Here is an example from my school:

	Autumn 1	Autumn 2	Spring 1	Spring 2	Summer 1	Summer 2
School global curriculum theme	Power and governance	Social justice and equality	Identity and diversity	Human rights	Sustainable development	Peace and conflict

Step 2

Ensure that you have a progression of skills document for each subject. You do not need to design this from scratch; there are lots of great examples online. Your local council may have their own progression of skills documents or, failing that, you can find them on TES or Twinkl.

Step 3

Now, with your whole-school themes and your progression of skills, the next step is to create your subject long-term plan. This maps out the learning/projects in which the skills mentioned above will be taught, across the whole school year, and ensures that the National Curriculum objectives are covered. Think about mapping out a diverse range of projects, across each year group but also across the key stages. For example, under 'sustainable development', you could include a wealth of projects across the year groups, like climate change, growing and planting, carbon footprint, plants, etc.

On page 173 there is an example of a **long-term history map**.

Top tip!

Get together as a leadership team and decide how to best map out the curriculum. Will you have cross-curricular projects that encompass skills from various subjects? Or will you have half-terms that focus on particular subjects for a depth of learning? Either is effective when done well and alongside your classroom timetables.

School global curriculum theme	Autumn 1 Power and governance	Autumn 2 Social justice and equality	Spring 1 Identity and diversity	Spring 2 Human rights	Summer 1 Sustainable development	Summer 2 Peace and conflict
Year 1	Gunpowder plot	Sarah Forbes Bonetta Nelson Mandela (significant individuals)	Emily Davison and women's suffrage	Food technology – changes in living history	Nurturing Nurses – Florence Nightingale and Marie Curie	Walter Tull and World War 1
Year 2	Queen Victoria What was London like then?	Elizabeth Fry and social activism	Ibn Battuta the explorer	The school day – changes in living memory	Mary Seacole and healthcare	Great Fire of London
Year 3	Iron Age	Martin Luther King and Jesse Owens	Ancient Egypt		Anglo Saxons and Settlements	Julius Cesar
Year 4/5	Shang Dynasty	History of British Civil Rights: LGBT, Race, Disability	A local history study: Camberwell's Black History		The Roman Empire	World War 1
Year 6	Ancient Greece	The *Windrush*	Leisure and Entertainment	Medicine and Disease	The Roman Empire and its impact on Britain	Ancient Benin

Step 4

Once you have the long-term plans for each subject, you can then create year group long-term plans, so that the teachers have an overview for each subject, for their class, for the year.

On pages 175–178 is an example of a **Year 6 curriculum map**.

Step 5

Medium-term plans – these are the specifics of what is being taught from week to week within a topic. These must include learning objectives, skills covered, resources, key questions, challenge and key concepts. In my experience, these are what take the time to design. Not all need to be created from scratch. There is a wide range of great resources out there to find and use, and edit where necessary. See previous chapters for great places to find medium-term plans.

Step 6

Create your knowledge organisers! Knowledge organisers are the summary of the essential knowledge, key facts and specific vocabulary that you would like children to know over the course of a project/topic. It should fit on an A4 page, and children should use them as a basis of reference to know what they've learned so far and what they are still to learn. Again, you can find many of these online, on Twinkl or TES, and edit them to include more diversity and inclusive language rather than starting from scratch.

Step 7

Lesson plans – these are for the teachers to plan, based upon the long- and medium-term plans that you have given them. Give teachers a template and structure to use for this. You may already find resources for short-term plans in the places mentioned in previous chapters. Where your school currently is on its curriculum journey is important here, and the quality of education in your establishment. You may have teachers who are keen and able (and fabulous) at lesson planning – great! Or you may have practitioners who need more support, are early career or are unconfident at planning. You know your staff. Put in the correct support for each practitioner.

Year 6 curriculum map 2021/22

	Autumn 1 (8 weeks)	Autumn 2 (7 weeks)	Spring 1 (6 weeks)	Spring 2 (6 weeks)	Summer 1 (6 weeks)	Summer 2 (6 weeks)
Schools global curriculum theme	Power and governance	Social justice and equality	Identity and diversity	Human rights	Sustainable development	Peace and conflict
Positive role models	David Lamy MP Harriet Harman MP Alexandria Ocasio-Cortez	Harvey Milk Rosa Parks Marcus Rashford	Sam King Una Marson	Malala Leslie Thomas	Greta Thunberg Licypriya kangujam	Walter Tull Olaudah Equiano
National and whole-school events	Black History Month (Oct) Ethiopian New Year's Day 11th Sept Harvest Festival 27th September Sukkot 3rd Oct	Diwali 4th Nov Anti-Bullying Week 15th – 19th Nov	Martin Luther King Day 18th Jan LGBTQI+History Month (Feb) Safer Internet Day 9th Feb World Poetry Day 21st March	World Book Day 3rd March Holi 19th March Easter 17th April Ramadan begins 2nd April	Earth Day 22nd April Stephen Lawrence Day 22nd April VE Day 8th May	World Ocean Day 8th June Windrush Day 22nd June Mandala Day 18th July
Project-Based Learning Theme	What is democracy?	Has the UK achieved equality?	What is our identity as Earthlings?	How has the *Windrush* generation been treated?	How can we reduce our carbon footprint?	Did British spies win the war?

Mapmaker, mapmaker, make me a map… A practical guide to mapping out curriculum

Time to Shake Up the Primary Curriculum

Year 6 curriculum map 2021/22

	Autumn 1 (8 weeks)	Autumn 2 (7 weeks)	Spring 1 (6 weeks)	Spring 2 (6 weeks)	Summer 1 (6 weeks)	Summer 2 (6 weeks)
Subject areas						
Whole-class reading	*Percy Jackson and the Lightning Thief*	*Black and British* Black London Trips book	*Origami Yoda*	*Windrush Boy* *The Other Side of the Truth*	*The Hidden Forest* by Jeannie Baker	*My Story: Noor-un-Nissa Inayat Khan*
Writing	Recount text (2 weeks) Diary (2 weeks) Instruction (2 weeks)	Formal letter (2 weeks) Newspaper (2 weeks) Narrative (3 weeks)	Biography (2 weeks) Narrative (2 week) Non-chronological report (2 weeks)	Explanation (2 weeks) Persuasive speech (2 weeks) Narrative (2 weeks)	Narrative (2 weeks) Persuasive speech (2 weeks)	Character description (2 weeks) Debate (2 weeks) Poetry (1 week) Letter (1 Week)
Quality Texts	*Percy Jackson and the Lightning Thief*	*Black and British* Black London Trips book	*Origami Yoda*	*Windrush Boy* *The Other Side of the Truth*	*The Hidden Forest* by Jeannie Baker	*My Story: Noor-un-Nissa Inayat Khan*
Mathematics	Place value Number: four operations	Number: fractions	Number: Fractions (Year 5), Ratio (Year 6) Decimals and Percentages Algebra (Year 6)	Measurement: converting units, Perimeter area and volume statistics	Geometry: properties of shape position and direction	Investigations and consolidation

Year 6 curriculum map 2021/22

	Autumn 1 (8 weeks)	Autumn 2 (7 weeks)	Spring 1 (6 weeks)	Spring 2 (6 weeks)	Summer 1 (6 weeks)	Summer 2 (6 weeks)
Science	Animals, including humans	Properties and changes of materials	Earth and Space	Forces	Living things and their habitats	Electricity
Geography	Modern day Athens vs London	The Americas		Migration across the UK Climate refugees		
History	Ancient Greece	The *Windrush*	Leisure and Entertainment	Medicine and Disease		The Roman Empire and its impact on Britain
Art	Printing	Collage	Drawing	Sculpture	Painting	Textiles
D&T	Ancient Greece Fairground ride	Fashion and textiles – create a Caribbean style bag				Create an Italian dish!
PE	Invasion games	Gym/dance	Invasion games	Net games	Striking games OAA	Athletics
Computing	Text and graphics Google Docs	Digital creativity Google Draw	Multimedia authoring producing multimedia videos	Data and programming algorithms and coding	Research and communication	Design your own app project

Time to Shake Up the Primary Curriculum

Year 6 curriculum map 2021/22

	Autumn 1 (8 weeks)	Autumn 2 (7 weeks)	Spring 1 (6 weeks)	Spring 2 (6 weeks)	Summer 1 (6 weeks)	Summer 2 (6 weeks)
Spanish	Ask and give personal information, reading and pronunciation, Spanish grammar, describing yourself and others, bilingual dictionary skills					
Music	Charanga music programme Being happy!	Charanga music programme Jazz and improvisation and composition	Charanga music programme Benjamin Britten's music and cover versions	Charanga music programme The music of Carole King	Charanga music programme Create Your own music inspired by your identity and	Charanga music programme Classical

Step 8

Keep all your planning documents in a central place, in clearly labelled folders, consistent across each year group, so that they can be used, edited and built on year upon year. Personally, I love Google Drive!

Step 9

Publish your curriculum intent, progression of skills, subject long-term plans and year group long-term plans on your website. Let the world (and Ofsted!) know what you're doing.

Case study: Being led by driving questions

In one school I worked in, our projects were led by driving questions, encouraging children to think about the world. The questions were related to the whole-school theme, and were the overarching basis for cross-curricular projects. In the projects, children would then demonstrate a wide range of skills from different subjects and showcase their learning at the end of the half-term to the parent/carer community, other children and the wider community, whom we would invite in.

At the end of the term, children would reflect on the learning across those few weeks, and think about how they wanted to show their understanding and response to the question and make choices on how to present. They could do this in a range of ways: a piece of extended writing, creating a video/film, a presentation, a diorama, writing and performing a play, designing a restaurant and cooking food, a fashion show and much more!

Examples of driving questions:

- What is fairness?
- How can we reduce our carbon footprint?
- What if everybody had a home?
- What is diversity?
- Who am I?

- Is there enough for everyone? (Renewable energy)
- Is war ever just?
- What is the importance of home?
- Is monarchy important?
- How do we fight for education for everyone, everywhere?
- What should healthcare look like?
- How can good come from disasters?
- How do we save our planet from climate change?
- How do we create peace?
- Why is law important?
- Why is housing a right?

An inclusive curriculum that celebrates diversity and embraces difference is invaluable in supporting the next generation to be more enlightened than us. It helps to change life chances, to develop critical thinkers and young citizens who care about the world around them. Great curriculum design and mapping helps to support consistent teaching and learning, where children can build on their skills and develop their knowledge further. Moving from curriculum design to consistently great implementation takes time, honest and reflective practice and creativity. But the impact is powerful. Teaching is a privilege – let's make everything that we say and do count. Let's create a better world!

Key takeaways

- Curriculum mapping takes time – do not rush. Plan out time and headspace!
- Mapping can be done with a diverse range of staff, which allows for diversity of thought.
- Complete long-term subject maps first, and then year group long-term plans.
- Include your curriculum intent at the top of all maps, to ensure that you're constantly reminded of the 'why'.
- Use resources that already exist, and then edit and build on them.
- Be sure to publish your hard work on your website.

11 Learning environments: Inside, outside and dress code

The classroom and school building is an extension of the taught curriculum, and displays, resources and environments must be rich, enabling and inclusive. Learning environments should be arranged to support learning and play. They should build upon and extend the learning and thinking without being overbearing and distracting. The classroom design can impact the way in which children socialise, feel and behave and can either positively or negative impact behaviour for learning. The classroom set-up should support social interaction, in addition to allowing children to make independent choices about the resources that they need. They must be decluttered; cluttered classrooms (and offices) cause stress and heavily cluttered classrooms disrupt the mind's attention from learning and distract pupils – tidy space, tidy mind.

When I first started teaching, I found it really hard to keep my classroom clean and tidy. In fact, I was constantly getting feedback from my deputy head to sort it out! It's something that I've worked really hard on over the years, and my classrooms now – and the classrooms in my school – are beautiful, purposeful and set up to support wellbeing and learning. Be patient with teachers – some people find this harder than others. Roll your sleeves up and help out any staff who are struggling to keep it tidy. Support them to build routines.

Learning environment

In each chapter of this book, there are tips for how to ensure that your learning environment is reflective of the learning, which is diverse and inclusive. Building upon that, here are some final tips to ensure that you are doing everything you can to create stimulating environments, accessible to all:

- Review your class library – in Chapter 3, there is a guide to revamping the school library. Ensure furthermore that classroom libraries include texts that reflect both the children within that class and also a wide range of different cultures, peoples and beliefs. Have a 'Book of the Week' or 'Author of the Month' working display in your room.

- Diverse role models display – include photos and biographies of role models on your subject displays. This makes up a nice working display within your core subject display and allows children to see a range of diverse role models within subjects.
- Name your classes after role models… and then create a working display for that person. This can be added to across the year, the more that children find out about them.
- Celebrate and display students' heritages. A great way to do this is to take a photo of each child at the start of the year, and then give them a blank globe template to write on – something along the lines of 'My name is… and my heritage is…. I believe…' etc.
- Make sure that your classroom/corridor/school is physically accessible. Ensure that desks are arranged in a way that allows plenty of space to move around the room. The same goes with corridors, and make sure that resources are stored at arm's length for children to use (for example if you have a child in a wheelchair).
- Display photos of children learning around the room – this sets up the space as a celebration of learning that children can feel proud of.
- Make sure that you have a diverse range of dolls and toys in play areas. Check out Diverse Dolls 4 All (@diverse_dolls), who make multicultural dolls, and Bright Ears, who make inclusive dolls for the deaf community.
- Consider gender-neutral bathrooms – this makes sure that all children can safely and comfortably use the bathroom without being forced to use a toilet that doesn't match their gender identity.

Top tip!

Set out your learning environment expectations list at the end of the year, and give it to teachers before the summer. This allows time for teachers to think about their space before the holidays start. Organising an inset day at the end of the summer term is great for teachers to be able to set up their rooms so that when they start in September they can focus on learning. Include photos of good practice from your school on your expectations list, so that teachers can see what it looks like.

Year 6 display after a local walk combined with reading the text
The Boy in the Tower

Classroom display about how we show that we are inclusive and stand united

Case study: Classroom non-negotiables

In a previous school, classrooms were definitely a key focus as, when I started there, to say that they were cluttered would be an understatement. Every classroom had a range of bright, in-your-face coloured backgrounds, which did not match or complement each other. I'm talking oranges, reds, yellows… and don't get me started on decorated borders. Behaviour for learning was also poor. When I spoke with groups of children for each class, the overwhelming feedback was that classrooms were 'stressful'. So we started again. Here are some of the non-negotiables:

- Everything is useful or beautiful – if it's neither, it's gone!
- Boards should have neutral backing, e.g. hessian or painted white (I actually went around the school with a roller and tin of paint, much to the dismay of my premises manager).

- Borders are plain black or artificial leaves.
- Classrooms must contain a variety of plants (this was from feedback from children).
- Displays **must** contain photos of children learning, pieces of work and the flipchart notes from lessons to make it a working display.
- Libraries must be beautiful – I provided new books and natural-feel storage for them, such as wicker baskets.

I set my classroom up as a model room and worked with the Key Stage 1 lead to set up a model classroom lower down the school. This meant that staff could see what it should look like, rather than it simply being an abstract list. The impact of this was much calmer learning spaces, reducing classroom behaviour incidents by nearly 95 per cent, and much happier children upon speaking to them. I also reorganised my office to reflect the same vibe, and the staff room, with plants and new furniture from Freecycle. Learning spaces are powerful!

School accessibility plans

All schools must have an accessibility plan in order to increase the extent to which pupils with disabilities can access and participate in the delivered curriculum. Your school's plan must be reviewed every three years and you can find out more about how to design and review this plan in the DfE's advice for schools in the Equality Act (DfE, 2014b, p. 29).

Outdoor environment

Outdoor learning opportunities broaden children's learning horizons and enhance the school's curriculum, further developing children's SMSC identities. A creative outdoor setting allows children to engage with the natural environment, nurturing self-esteem, team-building, confidence and an ability to form positive relationships with others. Any school – urban or rural – can develop an outdoor space suitable for children to learn in, even on a limited budget. Provide children with access to natural areas and opportunities to plant, grow, tend to a garden, care for the environment, engage with the weather and the seasons, as well as with wildlife, and be given access to the great outdoors.

> **Top tip!**
>
> Get your PTA (parents and teachers association) involved in developing the outdoor space if yours needs improvement. They can fundraise and feel a sense of pride in seeing the space grow and develop. They will love being part of creating the opportunity for children to develop both academic and social skills, whilst embracing the natural world.

Ways in which to develop the outdoor space (even if you don't have much space!):

- wild flower garden
- wooded wilderness area
- roof garden if you don't have much outdoor space
- pizza oven
- mud kitchen
- vegetable patch
- greenhouse – made from recycled plastic bottles
- animals – chicken coop and ducks (I worked in a school where we had old bathtubs on the rooftop where our ducks used to bathe… the duck eggs were also delicious!).

All of the above provide an environment for children to broaden their learning horizons and enhance the school's curriculum. Opportunities for outdoor learning support all pupils, particularly those with additional needs.

> **Top tip!**
>
> Ask your staff team who is passionate about gardening or animals. The likelihood is that you will have at least one person who would be thrilled

> to lead on developing the outdoor space alongside a group of parents/carers or the PTA.

There are some great resources for CPD or schemes of work to help you to develop your outdoor learning practice. Here are a couple:

Forest School @ForestSchools
Forest Schools offer level 1, 2 or 3 training courses, leading to a facilitator becoming a Forest School Practitioner. This is available to anyone working with children or young people. It allows a practitioner to deliver nature-based learning and exploration through the outdoors. The Forest School website has a wealth of information and tips on how to do this.

Natural Thinkers @NatThink
The Natural Thinkers programme supports schools in connecting children to nature, and is a framework incorporating lots of different subjects, from science to maths to art. It is a whole-school approach to nature-based learning, and helps to educate children on how to look after their world and sustainable development. It was created with the aim that children from Reception through to Year 6 are given stimulating, thought-provoking, curriculum-linked activities, also linked with the changing seasons. In order to become a 'natural thinkers' setting, schools must embed their '10 commitments to becoming a "natural thinkers" setting', so that children can learn how to sow, grow, harvest, celebrate and engage with all weathers (and understand how to dress for them!).

Top tip!

> In EYFS classrooms, we often find raincoats and wellies for children to explore outside; however, this seems to be lost as we move higher up the school. In my opinion, children should have a permanent raincoat and welly boots from Reception to Year 6. If you are in a community that is underserved, scour charity shops, ask parents/carers to donate their children's coats and wellies when they no longer fit and keep a bank of wet-weather clothing so that all children can engage with all weather. If it were up to me, 'wet playtimes', with children being stuck inside, would not exist!

Outdoor learning enables children to overcome many different barriers towards school and learning. They gain newfound confidence: I have seen this myself in previous schools, where children who have normally been shy and seemingly disengaged in the classroom have flourished in the outdoors. They then bring this developed self-esteem back into the classroom and it becomes visible in all other learning.

It gives them the opportunity to gain a fresh and positive outlook on their lives, as well as with the social interactions that they have with others, and offsets the amount of time that children spend indoors on devices!

School trips

When planning school trips, ensure that they are also accessible to all, including the journey to get there. This sounds obvious, but sometimes it is hard to find full accessibility information for school trips. Look for ways in which all children can be included fully on trips.

Dress code

The dress code should be one that is inclusive to everyone, and needs to be reviewed regularly. Dress code can be upsetting, restricting and uncomfortable for trans and/or gender-diverse pupils.

Ask yourself:

- Is the dress code inclusive to all genders, i.e. can anyone choose to wear a skirt or trousers and it not be sex- or gender-specific? Ensure that your uniform allows for children to wear whatever affirms their gender identity.
- Is all religious dress allowed: dreadlocks, turbans, patka, cross, hijab, etc.? Ensure that children are not restricted from showing their faith identity through the school dress code.
- Are hairstyles mentioned on your dress code? Is this inclusive to all cultures and hair types?

The Halo Code @TheHaloCode

Racial-based hair discrimination exists and happens more often than you think. Dress codes are responsible for some of this discrimination (even though this is illegal through the 2010 Equalities Act). Many Black people have been told that their hair/hairstyles do not look 'tidy' or 'professional'. The Halo Code is a code to follow to end hair discrimination in schools and places of work; it has been created by The Halo Collective, an organisation that aims to end hair inequality. One of the co-organisers of The Halo Code is the sister of a student whom I taught. Their website is incredibly informative, including the historical background of hair discrimination for Black people and personal stories.

Schools can adopt The Halo Code, where they promise that:

'Our school champions the right of staff and students to embrace all Afro-hairstyles. We acknowledge that Afro-textured hair is an important part of our Black staff and students' racial, ethnic, cultural, and religious identities, and requires specific styling for hair health and maintenance.

We welcome Afro-textured hair worn in all styles including, but not limited to, afros, locs, twists, braids, cornrows, fades, hair straightened through the application of heat or chemicals, weaves, wigs, headscarves, and wraps.

At this school, we recognise and celebrate our staff and students' identities. We are a community built on an ethos of equality and respect where hair texture and style have no bearing on anyone's ability to succeed.' (Halo Collective, 2020)

The learning environment is an extension of the classroom, and is bigger than simply the displays on the walls. The learning environment is the atmosphere that is created by the people and things in and around it. It is the provocation of thinking, creativity and questioning. It is a space in which children feel supported in their quest for knowledge and feel safe emotionally and physically. It is a space where everyone is seen and heard. Make sure that all of your environment aspects deliver the message that you are trying to put across: inclusion matters. Diversity matters.

Key takeaways

- The learning environment is an extension of learning.
- Cluttered and disorganised spaces cause disruption and stress.
- Try a more neutral theme, where the focus is the current learning.
- Develop the outdoors – remember that, for some children, this may be the only outdoor space that they have access to. They deserve it to be beautiful and to challenge them physically.
- The outdoors is a classroom too – find and use resources that teach children about the natural world, as this supports wellbeing.
- Dress code matters – make sure that what you are asking of children and staff is fair and inclusive for all.

12 Implementation and monitoring impact of your wonderful new curriculum

Implementation

How things are done is almost as important as what is being done. In the school inspection handbook (2019), Ofsted describes curriculum implementation as how 'the curriculum is taught at subject and classroom level'.

It is important to get this right, or else your hard work on curriculum design is all for nothing. When I implemented the new curriculum that I designed, I looked to the Education Endowment Foundation (EEF) for advice. The EEF is an independent charity that aims to break down the link between family income and educational achievement, through evidence-based school support to better teaching. They have written an excellent guide called 'Putting evidence to work: A school's guide to implementation' (Sharples et al., 2019), which explores how introducing new ideas and concepts can be managed in a way that actually makes a real change, rather than jumping in with haste and not really achieving the intended goal. What you don't want is for diversity and inclusion to just be buzz-words thrown around and not implemented in a way that facilitates true innovation. Great implementation is key, and here are some recommendations from the EEF (Sharples et al., 2019) to support this.

The six key recommendations

> **'1: Treat implementation as a process, not an event; plan and execute it in stages'** *(Sharples et al., 2019, p. 3)*

Give yourself time. If you have a teaching commitment, by all means try out elements of your new curriculum design with your class so that you have working examples for other staff, but the best time to implement new things is at the start of the year, and it will take time to embed properly. Be patient!

'2: Create a leadership environment and school climate that is conducive to good implementation' *(Sharples et al., 2019, p. 3)*

This cannot be done by one person – delegate, delegate, delegate! Distributed leadership is needed in order for effective implementation. Meet as a leadership team regularly, with clear purpose and meaningful actions. This is not a one-person job!

'3: Define the problem you want to solve and identify appropriate programmes or practices to implement' *(Sharples et al., 2019, p. 3)*

Use research (for example from EEF) to make evidence-based decisions on implementation. Build upon and develop – you do not always need to start from scratch. For example, you may find existing planning schemes of work for some of the wonderful new texts that you've added to your writing long-term plan. Use and build upon what exists, so that you and the teaching staff are not overwhelmed with new planning.

'4: Create a clear implementation plan, judge the readiness of the school to deliver that plan, then prepare staff and resources' *(Sharples et al., 2019, p. 3)*

'Develop a well-specified implementation plan by setting appropriate implementation targets linked to outcomes and monitor it closely using pragmatic and robust measures. Ensure that the implementation process is shared with all and carefully plan the introduction of new knowledge and skills with high quality CPD.

'5: Support staff, monitor progress, solve problems, and adapt strategies as the approach is used for the first time' *(Sharples et al., 2019, p. 3)*

Motivate staff with a flexible and supportive approach to monitoring, ensure you deliver (or get experts to deliver) highly skilled coaches, provide coaching and peer collaboration and make thoughtful adaptations throughout the process.

Staff voice is really important. Keep checking in and finding out how it's going. I don't mean through a Google Forms questionnaire – go and speak with people and listen. Find out who your champions of implementation are, and support them to support others. Empower your staff to grow and develop.

'6: Plan for sustaining and scaling an intervention from the outset and continually acknowledge and nurture its use' *(Sharples et al., 2019, p. 3)*

Think out how to scale up the project, and the scaling up itself becomes part of the new implementation process. Keep an eye out for great practice, ensuring you acknowledge support and praise it.

Sometimes the things that we do naturally with children we forget with adults. Change is tricky. It can be stressful and exhausting. Notice when staff do something good or make good progress with implementing the new curriculum. This makes a difference. I have a staff WhatsApp group, where we do shout-outs; we also have a staff Star of the Week, who is celebrated alongside the children, as voted by the school council.

So what? Monitoring the impact

So… you have designed your new curriculum and you now need to know the impact. How well is it being taught and what impact is it having on children's learning – and lives?

What does the research say?

In a 2018 Ofsted research report called 'An investigation into how to assess the quality of education through curriculum intent, implementation and impact', the indicators of having a **strong curriculum intent alongside strong implementation** were:

- Ensuring that accountability is high.
- Ensuring that assessment is rigorous and that teachers know how to regularly check what pupils know and can do.
- Ensuring that subject knowledge of teachers is consistently excellent across the school at all phases.
- Ensuring leaders regularly check the content of the curriculum and that all children are able to access it.
- Ensuring that all strands of the National Curriculum are understood by leaders through planning and evaluating. (Ofsted, 2018, p. 28)

Compared to a strong curriculum intent but weak implementation:

- 'Leaders focus on planning and paperwork but do not check its implementation or its impact.
- Subject leaders have complete autonomy. This goes unquestioned by the headteacher.
- Subject leadership does not check the implementation of the curriculum and so the building blocks within units of work or schemes are not secure. This has an adverse impact on curricular implementation.
- Accountability (knowing what is implemented and learned) is narrowly focused on Year 2 and 6 in primary schools, and key stage 4 in secondary schools.
- There are weaknesses in other non benchmark years. These are not tackled in a timely way'. (Ofsted, 2018, p. 28)

Monitoring impact

In terms of monitoring, you want to ensure that you have a monitoring schedule planned out and shared with all staff at the beginning of the year. The monitoring should include input from senior leaders and phase and subject leaders. Make sure that you focus on the targets set out in the school development plan – you cannot simply monitor everything! It could be, for example, that you look at the quality of questioning across all subjects, or that you have chosen to focus on historical enquiry. Your subject leaders' action plans should include targets aligned with the school development plan and whole-school priorities. Clear priorities will mean avoiding unnecessary monitoring.

> **Top tip!**
>
> Be sure to give subject/phase leaders time to carry out monitoring – be clever with your organisation of timetables to allow for effective monitoring that is not rushed and provides timely feedback to those involved.

At the start of the year, make sure that you:

- Outline the monitoring activities for the year, being explicit and clear on why you are doing it.

- Give staff dates, being mindful of busy time periods, e.g. close to parents' evening, report writing, etc.
- Think carefully about when in the year to monitor which subjects/priorities, e.g. end of terms vs start of terms.
- Encourage staff to reflect on the previous year's monitoring, specifically discussing workload and stress vs impact.
- Listen to the staff!
- Delegate – monitoring impact is not a one-person job!
- Meet as a wider leadership team and discuss the plan.

> **Top tip!**
>
> Develop your monitoring forms to be consistent and reflective of what you are trying to achieve. Write the curriculum intent at the top and include both yes/no tick boxes and also space to write reflections and next steps. This will help to frame your feedback to staff and ensure consistent practice. This is a good activity to do in a leadership meeting at the start of the year.

Questions to ask when monitoring

Monitoring refers to all the activities undertaken with the purpose of gathering information or evidence about teaching and learning standards, and the many factors affecting them. Effective monitoring is imperative, as it leads to an informed evaluation of the school's strengths, next steps and areas for further development. The main purpose of monitoring is to inform the school's strategic decision-making for school improvement.

Here are some questions that you might like to ask when monitoring:

For school leaders:

- How well are pupils learning the content outlined in the curriculum? What evidence do you have?
- How well are learners prepared for the next stage of education (i.e. key stage, secondary school, etc.) or even working life?

- How do you know that the curriculum is having a positive effect across all pupils, including those who are disadvantaged, SEND or have low starting points or attainment?

For teachers:

- How well is key subject knowledge – and skills – consolidated before moving onto the next objective/topic? What evidence do you have?
- How well-developed are the learning habits and learning skills of students? What evidence do you have?
- How is pupils' learning evidenced and what does it tell you?
- How is this evidence used to feed into the planning, adaptation and moulding of the curriculum?

Ways to monitor

Monitoring – or growth and development (my preferred term) – should be done at all levels:

- **Planning:**
    - curriculum maps
    - schemes of work
    - individual/weekly lesson plans.
- **Pupil book study:** This is an alternative to 'book looks' and is a systematic, research-informed way to evaluate the quality of learning and the curriculum through dialogic and metacognitive talk. It acts as a window into seeing learning through the experience of the child, rather than the observed experience of the adult. Essentially, this involves sitting with groups of children and their learning books and talking with them about what and how they have learned. Book recommendation: *Pupil Book Study: An evidence-informed guide to help quality assure the curriculum* by Alex Bedford (2021).
- **Learning walks:** Ensure that these are purposeful and have a focus, e.g. diverse learning environment, classroom library, etc. Include your governing body in this – get governors in for school visits and to see what is going on in the school.

> **Top tip!**
>
> Create your learning environment expectations/tick list. Ask your Year 6 pupil leaders to do the learning walk with you and see what elements they can find. Ultimately, they are the reason why we are all here. It's all well and good us as adults being able to spot great practice around the classroom, but can the children?

- **Pupil voice:**
  - Speak with pupils about what they have learned: Do they actually know the information that you set out on your knowledge organisers? Do they know why they are learning their topics? Do they know what they have made progress with and what they need to work on further? You could meet with the school council for this, or small groups from each class could meet with the subject leads and champions.
  - Pupil surveys to look at attitudes towards learning.
  - Monitor *with* children. In one of my schools, I did learning walks with the two head pupils, and it was really interesting to hear what they noticed and celebrated. It gives an additional layer of voice to your practice.
- **Team up with other schools:**
  - Challenge Partners – this is an organisation that collaborates with schools to challenge, support and improve practice. They aim to improve the life chances of young people through education. @ChallengePartnr
  - Compare standards and practices with other similar and/or local schools.
- **Look at the data:** Analyse tracking data and assessment to measure attainment and progress against pupil targets.
  - Look at trends for different groups, e.g. how well are your most vulnerable children doing and how does this compare to this time last year?
  - How much progress have children made from starting points (i.e. prior attainment)?
  - Link attainment and progress data to attendance and/or behaviour. For example, if children are more engaged in learning, are there fewer

behaviour incidents as a result? Has attendance improved due to better wellbeing practice?
- Quantitative data would be the percentage of children at each standard, or making good or better progress.
- Qualitative data would be how engaged children are in lessons or classroom observation notes.

> **Case study: Improvement in Key Stage 2 SATs results**
>
> In July 2022, the Year 6 cohort at my school got the best reading Key Stage 2 SATs results that they had achieved at the school since I started there as deputy head. I was so proud that nearly a quarter of the children reached greater depth, most of whom had incredibly low starting points (and a pandemic in between). Tracking back, these children started the new curriculum when they were in Year 3. This meant that their entire Key Stage 2 learning was that of human rights and global citizenship. The girl who organised Culture Day was part of this cohort. The child who spoke out against culturally and racially inappropriate practice on a school journey (mentioned in the introduction) was also part of this cohort. The children who were interviewed by Sky News about their understanding of the war between Russia and the Ukraine were part of this cohort.
>
> Not only did the children's understanding of the world, social justice and equality stand out amongst others, but their academic standards had been positively impacted by the successful implementation of the curriculum, and the high standards of teaching and learning had been maintained.

Using your findings

It must be said that monitoring alone does not lead to school improvement. It is the *evaluation* of the information gathered and your next steps that support school improvement. Use your evidence to identify the needs and which strategies to address said needs.

What to do with findings:

- Targets and findings can be fed into teachers' performance management.
- General trends found can be built into subject action plans.

- Staff meetings can be focused around what needs to be improved – you may find that you have a practitioner who is excellent at delivering a certain part of the curriculum, so get them to support another teacher who may be less confident.
- Use trends to inform your subject policies.

Key takeaways

- Implementation is a process – be patient and time it right.
- Support staff through modelling, praising and checking in regularly outside of monitoring.
- Be transparent with your monitoring timetable from the get go – share at the start of the year and be clever with your timing of monitoring.
- Use findings to put in support and CPD, amend policies and review the targets set on subject action plans/the school development plan.

A final word

Developing a new curriculum is not a quick fix. It is a journey, one of which we are all on together. We all need to continually improve our practice, review our words and language, and have frank and honest conversations about when things are not right. Do we always get it right? No. Do we keep striving to? Yes.

All we can hope for is that the next generation are more enlightened than us: Young people who are comfortable and articulate about their own identities and accepting of others. Critical thinkers who have the language and tools to fight for social justice, equality and sustained positive change to our world.

Thank you for taking the time to read this book. You are a hero – keep shining bright!

I will leave you with a quote from a child from my Year 6 class, upon leaving the school. When asked 'What's next for you?' for the yearbook, she responded, 'Well isn't it obvious? I'm going to change the world!'

Appendices

Curriculum maps

Appendices

Nursery curriculum map

	Autumn 1	Autumn 2	Spring 1	Spring 2	Summer 1	Summer 2
School global curriculum theme	Power and governance	Social justice and equality	Identity and diversity	Human rights	Sustainable development	Peace and conflict
Positive role models	David Lamy MP Harriet Harman MP Alexandria Ocasio-Cortez	Harvey Milk Rosa Parks Marcus Rashford	Sam King Una Marson	Malala Leslie Thomas	Greta Thunberg Licypriya Kangujam	Walter Tull Olaudah Equiano
National and whole-school events	Family Feast Black History Month (Oct) Ethiopian New Year's Day Harvest Festival Sukkot	Diwali Anti-Bullying Week	Martin Luther King Jr Day LGBTQI+ History Month (Feb) Safer Internet Day World Poetry Day	World Book Day Holi Easter Ramadan begins	Earth Day Stephen Lawrence Day VE Day	World Ocean Day Windrush Day Mandela Day
Topic theme	Ourselves – who am I?	Who helps us?	What's at the end of the rainbow?	Where do people live? Homes and habitats	How do things grow?	Peace and quiet by the seaside!

	Autumn 1	Autumn 2	Spring 1	Spring 2	Summer 1	Summer 2
Linked books/ stimulus	- *Hair Love* - *Amazing* - *From Head To Toe*	- *Hats of Faith* - *The Best Diwali Ever* - *Busy People* series - *People who help us* series	- *Brown Bear, Brown Bear*	- *All Are Welcome* - *Five Minutes Peace* - *Six Dinner Sid*	- *New Baby* - *Fruits: A Caribbean Counting Poem* - *Jim and the Beanstalk* - *I Really Wonder What Plant I'm Growing*	- *Lubna and Pebble* - *Treasure Map*
Literacy (phonics throughout)	Mark making activities Little Wandle – Phase 1: Fill in missing word or phrase in a known rhyme, story or game, e.g. 'heads, shoulders, knees and…?' Listen and join in with stories, join in with repeated refrains, suggest how a story might end		Mark making activities Little Wandle – Phase 1–2: Enjoy rhyming and rhythmic activities, show awareness of rhyme and alliteration Letter formation, name writing Talk about setting, events and characters in stories, look at books independently and hold them the correct way around, handle books carefully, show an interest in print and illustrations in books		Mark making activities Little Wandle – Phase 2–3: Enjoy rhyming and rhythmic activities Understand that stories have a beginning, middle and end, listen to stories with increasing attention, understand that books are read from left to right, retell a story Letter formation, name writing, recognise own name and familiar logos Link sounds to letters, name and sound the letters of the alphabet	

Appendices

Appendices

	Autumn 1	Autumn 2	Spring 1	Spring 2	Summer 1	Summer 2
Maths **Continuous:** Number recognition, ordering, 1:1 counting, numeral writing and number-related songs and rhymes, time	Recite some number names in sequence, use number names and number language spontaneously Use some language of quantities, categorise objects by shape and size, begin to use the language of size Use some number names accurately in play, recite numbers in order to 10, realise that anything can be counted, e.g. clap Show an interest in representing numbers, ask questions/make comments about numbers Show an interest in shape and space by making arrangements with objects		Represent numbers using fingers, marks on paper or pictures, identify how many objects are in a set Show interest in shapes in the environment Identify numerals in the environment and begin to represent numbers Make arrangements with objects through construction Describe shape of everyday objects Use positional language		Sometimes match numeral and quantity correctly, show an interest in number problems, compare two groups, saying when they have the same number, recognise numbers 1–5, count objects that cannot be moved, select the correct numeral to represent up to 10 objects Recognise and name 2D shapes, recognise similarities of shapes in the environment, use shapes appropriately for tasks Order by length from shortest to longest	

	Autumn 1	Autumn 2	Spring 1	Spring 2	Summer 1	Summer 2
Communication and language *Continuous:* Through general daily communication with peers, literacy and role-play work	Talking about themselves and their family Developing listening skills Following simple directions Using talk in their play Retelling a simple past event in the correct order	Talking about people who help us, e.g. doctors, nurses, police, fire fighters, vets, teachers, etc. Listening to others one-to one and in small groups Understanding use of objects Joining in with repeated refrains in stories and rhymes	Listening to others one-to one and in small groups Understanding use of objects Joining in with repeated refrains in stories and rhymes	Talking about their own experiences of animals/minibeasts that they have found Questioning why things happen and giving explanations Responding to simple instructions Listening to stories with increasing attention and recall Using talk to connect ideas Displaying focused attention Making meaning clear to others	Talking about the signs of spring and summer Using more complex sentences to link thoughts and ideas Following a story without pictures Questioning why things happen and giving explanations. Showing understanding of prepositions	Talking about their own experiences of the seaside, focusing on objects and people that are important to them Using a range of tenses Linking statements and sticking to a main theme or intention Listening and responding to ideas expressed by others in discussion

Appendices

	Autumn 1	Autumn 2	Spring 1	Spring 2	Summer 1	Summer 2
Physical development **Continuous:** Games/ gymnastics, adventure playground, trikes, bikes and scooters	Kosmic Yoga Squiggle while you wiggle – drawing lines and circles using gross motor movements Moving to music in different ways Dressing ourselves Ability to tell an adult when hungry or tired Washing and drying own hands	Developing fine motor skills Emergency transport vehicles – negotiating space, adjusting speed and direction to avoid obstacles Movement to music	Developing fine motor skills Movement to music	Ball games, throwing and catching Squiggle while you wiggle Movement to music Using one-handed tools and equipment Understanding the importance of safety when using equipment	Understanding the effects of activity on our bodies Movement to music Squiggle while you wiggle Pencil control – copy some letters from their name	Sports Day Park play equipment – able to climb using alternate feet Movement to music Squiggle while you wiggle Movement to music Pencil control – copy some letters from their name

	Autumn 1	Autumn 2	Spring 1	Spring 2	Summer 1	Summer 2
Understanding the world: **People** **The world** **Technology**	Marvellous Me activities Show interest in the lives of familiar people Recognise and describe special times for family or friends Know some of the things that make them unique Purple Mash – know that information can be retrieved from computers	People who help us activities How to stay healthy activities Show interests in different occupations and ways of life How can we make our local areas safe? Purple Mash	Children to build their own rainbow/fairy garden and to look after their creation	Can talk about some of the things they have observed such as plants, animals natural and found objects Show care and concern for living things and the environment Purple Mash	Gardening activities – vegetable/flower growing Talk about why things happen and how things work Investigating our local area Talk about how plants grow and change over time Purple Mash	Remember and talk about significant events in their own experiences Comment and ask questions about aspect of their familiar world Purple Mash

Appendices

Appendices

	Autumn 1	Autumn 2	Spring 1	Spring 2	Summer 1	Summer 2
Expressive art and design, including: Exploring and using media and materials, being imaginative, role play	Marvellous Me art activities Enjoy joining in with dancing and ring games Notice what adults do and imitate when adult is not there	Explore colour and how colours can be changed Imitate movement in response to music – Bangra dance Sing a few familiar songs – Spanish songs Engage in imaginative role play – use available props to support role play Capture experiences and responses with a range of different methods i.e. photo, video, work	Colour mixing to make butterflies Artist: Frank Bowling Use various construction materials Begin to construct stacking blocks vertically, horizontally and using them to create enclosures and spaces, join construction pieces together to build and balance	Movement as minibeasts Understand that they can use lines to enclose a space Use shapes to represent objects Begin to show interest in and describe the texture of things Use tools for a purpose	Growing-themed craft activities Responding to sound stimuli (loud/soft) Recreating rhythm/beats/tempo (fast/slow)	Use movement to express feelings, begin to move rhythmically, create movement in response to music Make up simple rhymes and songs Build stories around toys

210

	Autumn 1	Autumn 2	Spring 1	Spring 2	Summer 1	Summer 2
Personal, social and emotional development, including: Self-confidence and self-awareness, managing feelings and behaviour, making relationships	Establishing some class rules and learning to follow them. Learn about our School Values. Speak about own home and community. Form good relationships with friends and adults. Play together cooperatively, taking turns and sharing. Manage and adapt own behaviour during changes in routine. Select and use activities and resources with help.		School Values *Golden Rules* Book Series by Donna Luck Build up a role-play activity with other children. Invite others to join them in play. Confidently ask adults for help. Enjoy taking on responsibility of carrying out small tasks. Tolerate delay when needs are not immediately met, and understand that wishes may not always be met.		School Values *Golden Rules* Book Series by Donna Luck *Our Class is a Family* *The Colour Monster* Confident to speak to others about own needs, wants, interests and opinions. Able to adapt behaviour to different events, social situations and changes in routine. Become more outgoing.	
Assessment	Baseline assessments					

Appendices

211

Appendices

Reception curriculum map

	Autumn 1	Autumn 2	Spring 1	Spring 2	Summer 1	Summer 2
School global curriculum theme	Power and governance	Social justice and equality	Identity and diversity	Human rights	Sustainable development	Peace and conflict
Positive role models	David Lamy MP Harriet Harman MP Alexandria Ocasio-Cortez	Harvey Milk Rosa Parks Marcus Rashford	Sam King Una Marson	Malala Leslie Thomas	Greta Thunberg Licypriya Kangujam	Walter Tull Olaudah Equiano
National and whole-school events	Family Feast Black History Month (Oct) Ethiopian New Year's Day Harvest Festival Sukkot	Diwali Anti-Bullying Week	Martin Luther King Jr Day LGBTQI+ History Month (Feb) Safer Internet Day World Poetry Day	World Book Day Holi Easter Ramadan begins	Earth Day Stephen Lawrence Day VE Day	World Ocean Day Windrush Day Mandela Day
Topic theme	Marvellous me – who am I?	Festivals and cultural celebrations – why do we celebrate?	On the move! Countries around the world/transport – where am I?	Blue planet: Sea, pollution, animals How do I take care of the sea?	Ready, steady, cook! Food, nutrition and sports – what should we eat?	Fantasy and adventure: Superheroes! How can I be amazing?

212

	Autumn 1	Autumn 2	Spring 1	Spring 2	Summer 1	Summer 2
Linked books/ stimulus	- I Like Myself - Timmy on the Toilet - Daisy the Hedgehog - Masai and I - Ally and the Sea Stars	- So Much - Sweet Dates to Eat: A Ramadan and Eid Story - Lighting a Lamp: Diwali - Mog's Christmas	- Iggy Peck, Architect - Funny Bones - Lima's Hot Chilli - Playtime (Around the World)	- Blue Planet clips and photos - Where's the Starfish - Commotion in the Ocean	- Last Stop on Market Street - Goldilocks - The Very Hungry Caterpillar	- Eliot, Midnight Superhero - Mummy Sayang - Superhero ABC - Charlie's Superhero Underpants - Super Duck - How to be a Superhero
Literacy (phonics throughout) *Literacy Tree*	Myself stories Oral retelling Own versions narrative (*Where the Wild Things Are*)	Labels and captions Descriptive posters Simple explanations (*Anansi The Spider*)	Thought bubbles/ lists Letters of advice (*I Am Henry*) Labels, writing in role, own version narrative (*The Magic Paintbrush*)	Statements, writing in role (*I Will Not Ever Never Eat A Tomato*) Recount (*So Much*)	Poetry, own version narrative Cooking instructions Menu writing	Traditional tales and fairytales: role play, hot seating, story writing, sequencing and retelling Captions and labels, own version narrative (*Oi Frog*) Transition to Year 1 letter

Appendices

Appendices

	Autumn 1	Autumn 2	Spring 1	Spring 2	Summer 1	Summer 2
Maths (part 1) **Continuous:** Number recognition, ordering, 1:1 counting, numeral writing and number-related songs and rhymes, time *White Rose*	Getting to know you: key times of the days, class routines Recite number names in order, 1–10 Count reliably up to 5 objects Begin to recognise none and zero in stories and rhymes Find 1 more than (up to 5 objects) Sort and match objects, justifying decisions made Use language such as round, circle, square to describe shapes	Recite number names to 20 and beyond Count reliably up to 10 objects or actions Use language such as more/less or greater/smaller to compare 2 numbers up to 5 Begin to use language of doubling and halving Name 3D shapes: cube, sphere, cone Put objects in order of size Use everyday language to describe position	Recite number names to 20 and beyond Recite number names in order, counting from 2, 3, 4 Recite number names in order counting back from 6, 5, 4 Count reliably up to 12 objects Begin to use the language involved in addition and subtraction Relate addition to combining sets and subtraction to taking away Use the language of doubling and halving, review addition and subtraction with the same digits, i.e. 2+2 is the same as doubling Name 3D shapes	Recite number names to 20 and beyond Recognise numerals 1–10 and select correct numeral to represent quantities Compare 2 numbers Say a number that lies between 2 given numbers up to 10 Recognise small numbers without counting Count an irregular arrangement of objects Talk about, recognise and recreate simple patterns	Recite number names to 20 and beyond Recognise numerals 0–10 and select correct numeral to represent quantities Ordering numbers Counting on Estimation Remove a smaller number from a larger and use counting back to find out how many are left Use vocab of subtraction Solve problems including doubling and halving	Recite number names to 20 and beyond Recognise numerals to 20 and beyond and begin to write them Count in 2s and 10s Select 2 groups to make a given total Estimation beyond 10 Use ordinal numbers Find 1 more/less Use developing mathematical ideas and methods to solve practical problems Use language such as more/less/ longer/shorter/ heavier/lighter to compare more than 2 quantities

	Autumn 1	Autumn 2	Spring 1	Spring 2	Summer 1	Summer 2
Maths (part 2) *Continuous:* Number recognition, ordering, 1:1 counting, numeral writing and number-related songs and rhymes, time *White Rose*	Use words such as bigger and smaller to describe size Use 2D shapes to make pictures and patterns	Talk about and describe symmetrical patterns Fill and empty containers, using language such as full, empty, holds more, holds less Begin to use language of time and sequence familiar events	Use shapes to make pictures and patterns Solve simple puzzles in practical context Use language such as more or less, longer or shorter, heavier or lighter to make direct comparisons of 2 quantities	Understand and use vocab relating to money Make direct comparisons of 2 then 3 lengths or masses Know days of the week in order Use everyday words to describe position and direction	Name 2D and 3D shapes and use them to make patterns, including symmetrical ones Use vocab of position, time and money Know days of the week, months of the year, seasons	Use shapes to make pictures, models and patterns

Appendices

Appendices

	Autumn 1	Autumn 2	Spring 1	Spring 2	Summer 1	Summer 2
Communication and language *Continuous:* Through general daily communication with peers, literacy and role-play work	Children will be exposed to new vocabulary linked to ourselves. The children will have an opportunity to use appropriate language in the hospital role-play area. Children will develop their concentration skills in different contexts and listen for longer periods. Children will have the opportunity to discuss their personal experiences, e.g. when they were a baby.	Children will learn how to ask appropriate questions and listen to different visitors. Children will use what they have heard to take part in discussions and apply it to their independent play. Eye contact when speaking.	Children will learn to use story language in their play and use repeated refrains. They will talk about their favourite stories and say what they like and don't like. Children will begin to attend whole-school assemblies and develop their concentration skills. Eye contact when speaking.	Children will learn how to recall events using the correct tense and use more complex sentences to link their ideas. Children will develop their skills in answering how and why questions related to their experiences. Eye contact when speaking.	Children will focus on asking and answering questions in relation to tadpoles and changes they observe. Children will make predictions about what they think might happen using correct tenses and vocabulary. Eye contact when speaking.	Children will be exposed to new vocabulary linked to Space. Children will be involved in the EYFS/Key Stage 1 sports day, where they will be supported to follow instructions involving several ideas or actions. Eye contact when speaking.

	Autumn 1	Autumn 2	Spring 1	Spring 2	Summer 1	Summer 2
Physical development **Continuous:** Games/ gymnastics, adventure playground, trikes, bikes and scooters	Children will be encouraged to become independent in managing own needs, e.g. undressing/dressing themselves for PE. Children will play stopping and starting games and explore different ways of travelling using different parts of their body. Children will start a regular PE lesson. Children will learn about classifying healthy and unhealthy foods and the effects they have.	Children will be encouraged to become independent in managing own needs, e.g. undressing/dressing themselves for PE. Children will be developing their pencil grip and control. Children will learn how to use tools to shape different materials. Children will develop their skills in using small apparatus.	Children will experiment with different ways of moving and adjusting speed and direction. Children will play sending and receiving games with bats, balls, bean bags. Children will learn how to transport equipment safely and will be discussing the effects of exercise on their bodies. Children will be developing their independence in managing their own hygiene and personal needs.	Children will continue to develop their pencil control and independently forming recognisable letters. Children will be developing their balance and coordination skills. Children will be developing their independence in managing their own hygiene and personal needs. Visit from doctor.	Children will continue to develop their pencil control and independently forming recognisable letters. Teamwork! Children will be given the opportunity to work as part of a team in their PE lessons. Children will discuss and learn about sun safety, e.g. wearing suntan lotion and sun hats.	Sports Day! Children work in mixed teams. Children will continue to develop their pencil control and independently form recognisable letters. Children will have opportunities to manage their own needs as they come up.

Appendices

217

Appendices

		Autumn 1	Autumn 2	Spring 1	Spring 2	Summer 1	Summer 2
Understanding the world	People	Children will look at their own bodies and look at similarities and differences between them, which will be recorded using simple computer programs.	Compare how people celebrate their birthday/Christmas, celebration of Diwali, Christmas.	Children will explore key workers: bus drivers, train drivers, etc. Visit from bus driver.	Foods people eat in different countries and cultures, favourite foods. Feast festival in EYFS playground (parents to bring food in).	Describing and sorting materials, plants and animals, minibeast hunt. Animals and their habitats. Looking after the environment – informative videos using Puppet Pals, posters.	Children will talk about different superheroes and their powers. What's my power?
	The world	Children will learn about their new school environment. Journey around the school! Children will explore and compare the local environments.	Exploration – day and night. Animals we see in the day and at night time. Guy Fawkes story.	Science investigation – how things move. Different types of transport. Making their own boat and testing it. Learn about the differences and similarities with other countries that children have links with.	Growing vegetables – where food is grown around the world.	Recycling and deforestation.	Making up own fantasy characters (hero) and land. Homes and buildings.

		Autumn 1	Autumn 2	Spring 1	Spring 2	Summer 1	Summer 2
Understanding the world	Technology	Using simple computer programs.	Use of age-appropriate software on computer. Programmable toys, CD player, Smartboard.	Bee-Bots and other vehicles. Explore a vehicle.	Chromebooks, e-safety, Puppet Pals on tablet.	Children can take photos of the natural environment outside – gardens, local park.	Hansel and Gretel – designing their own sweet house (use Chromebooks on 2Paint) (link to literacy).
Expressive art and design, including: Exploring and using media and materials, being imaginative, role play		Children will be looking at self-portraits by Van Gogh, Frida Kahlo and Picasso. Children will be using different textures to create different body parts. Children will be learning and singing new songs linked bodies.	Celebrations–Diwali/birthday party. Food preparation. Decorations for party. Christmas – food preparation, Christmas cards focus, pattern making. Create own birthday party songs. Dance – celebration link: birthday party, toy shop, food festival, songs from different countries, Spanish songs.	Design a vehicle/something that moves. Build vehicles using different materials. Junk modelling. Music journey – sound walk. Down at the station song.	Children will explore the life cycles of tadpoles, chicks, plants and beans. Children will have the opportunity to learn about what living things need to grow. Painting with rubbish. Collage of under the sea. Making their own sea creature. Under the sea music (*The Little Mermaid*).	Printing and patterns with food. Still life painting with flowers and fruit. Designing and making something with dry pasta (e.g.).	Junk modelling. Link to chalk – chalk pictures. Making potions. Superhero songs.

Appendices

Appendices

	Autumn 1	Autumn 2	Spring 1	Spring 2	Summer 1	Summer 2
Personal, social and emotional development, including: Self-confidence and self-awareness, managing feelings and behaviour, making relationships.	The children will be supported in their transition into Reception and will make new friends. Children will be supported to explore stories they read to explore feelings and emotions. By talking about their baby photos children will develop their confidence to speak in larger groups.	Showing respect, celebrating things differently, respect for the environment.	Group/teamwork games. Turn-taking. Talking about feelings and emotions. Following instructions.	Taking care of others and animals. Speaking and listening activities. Helping – them helping others and others helping them, when to ask for help.	Healthy foods and healthy living – how to look after ourselves. Being safe out and about. Challenges – persevering through challenges (CoEL). Instruction drawing (drawing back to back) with Duplo.	Transition and feelings about next year. Reflection on year. Little Miss Proud – what are they proud of?
Assessment	Baseline assessments					

Year 1 curriculum map

	Autumn 1	Autumn 2	Spring 1	Spring 2	Summer 1	Summer 2
School global curriculum theme	Power and governance	Social justice and equality	Identity and diversity	Human rights	Sustainable development	Peace and conflict
Positive role models	David Lamy MP Harriet Harman MP Alexandria Ocasio-Cortez	Harvey Milk Rosa Parks Marcus Rashford	Sam King Una Marson	Malala Leslie Thomas	Greta Thunberg Licypriya Kangujam	Walter Tull Olaudah Equiano
Project-based learning theme	What is right and what is wrong?	What is fairness?	Who am I?	One for you, one for me – why is fooc important?	How do we look after each other?	How do I find peace?
Whole-class reading	*Look Up* by Nathan Byron	*Splash* by Claire Cashmore	*The Proudest Blue* by Ibtihaj Muhammad, S. K. Ali and Hatem Aly	*The Blanket Bears* by Samuel Langley-Swain	*A Boy and a Jaguar* by Alan Rabinowitz	*Leo and the Octopus* by Isabelle Marinov

Appendices

Appendices

	Autumn 1	Autumn 2	Spring 1	Spring 2	Summer 1	Summer 2
Writing	Letters Wanted poster Labels and lists Fact file	Character description Instructions Non-fiction writing	Retelling a story (2 weeks) Explanation (2 weeks) Instructions (2weeks)	Diary (2 weeks) Letter (2 weeks) Non-fiction (2 weeks)	Poetry (2 weeks) Narrative (2 weeks) Explanation (2 weeks)	Narrative (3 weeks) Poem (2 weeks) Instructions (2 weeks) Letter to my new teacher
Quality texts *Literacy Tree	- *The Naughty Bus* - *Where the Wild Things are*	- *Beegu* - *Man on the Moon* Non-fiction moon book	- *Weirdo**	- *The Odd Egg*	- *We are the Water Protectors**	- *Izzy Gismo**
Mathematics	Number: place value (within 10), addition and subtraction	Geometry: shape Number: place value (within 20)	Number: addition and subtraction, place value (within 50)	Measurement: length and height, weight and volume	Number: multiplication and division, fractions Geometry: position and direction	Number: place value (within 100) Measurement: money, time
Science	Seasonal changes Everyday materials	Seasonal changes Everyday materials	Animals, including humans	Seasonal changes Plants	Plants	Seasonal changes Animals, including humans

	Autumn 1	Autumn 2	Spring 1	Spring 2	Summer 1	Summer 2
Geography	Map out the Houses of Parliament	Where is South Africa? London vs Johannesburg		Locational knowledge – Black History Archives, Camberwell, Black History Walk		WWII – maps, atlases and globes
History	Gunpowder plot	Nelson Mandela and social justice	Princess Sophia Duleep Singh, Emily Davison and women's suffrage	Food and technology – changes in living history	Marie Curie, Mary Seacole and healthcare	Anne Frank and conflict
Art	Textiles	Toyin Ojih Odutola Drawing	Sculpture	Painting	Printing	Claudette Johnson Collage
DT	Moving bus pictures Moving wheels	Nigerian food – make a dish!		Make a piece of playground equipment		Make an Anderson shelter
PE	Invasion games: sending and receiving	Gym Dance	Invasion games: throwing towards a target	Net games: using a racquet	OAA: problem-solving	Athletics
Computing	Text and graphics	Digital creativity	Multimedia authoring	Data and programming	Research and communication	Project

Appendices

Appendices

	Autumn 1	Autumn 2	Spring 1	Spring 2	Summer 1	Summer 2
Spanish	Spanish songs: numbers, colours, classroom instructions					
Music	Charanga music programme How pulse, rhythm and pitch work together	Charanga music programme Pulse, rhythm and pitch, rapping, dancing and singing	Charanga music programme How to be in the groove with different styles of music	Charanga music programme Pulse, rhythm and pitch in different styles of music	Charanga music programme Using your imagination	Charanga music programme The history of music
RE	What does it mean to belong: What does it mean to belong to Islam?	What does it mean to belong: Why do Christians celebrate Christmas?	What does it mean to belong: What can be special about living with family and friends?	What does it mean to belong: What does it mean to belong to Hinduism?	What does it mean to belong: What does it mean to belong to Christianity?	What does it mean to belong: What does it mean to belong to Sikhism?
PSHE and wellbeing	Jigsaw Being me in my world	Jigsaw Celebrating difference	Jigsaw Dreams and goals	Jigsaw Healthy me	Jigsaw Relationships	Jigsaw Changing me
Assessment	Starting point assessment: Phonics screening Maths assessment	Assessment week Summative tests	Formative assessment – objectives on Insight	Assessment week Summative tests	Formative assessment – objectives on Insight	Phonics screening Assessment week Summative tests

Year 2 curriculum map

	Autumn 1	Autumn 2	Spring 1	Spring 2	Summer 1	Summer 2
School global curriculum theme	Power and governance	Social justice and equality	Identity and diversity	Human rights	Sustainable development	Peace and conflict
Positive role models	David Lamy MP Harriet Harman MP Alexandria Ocasio-Cortez	Harvey Milk Rosa Parks Marcus Rashford	Sam King Una Marson	Malala Leslie Thomas	Greta Thunberg Licypriya Kangujam	Walter Tull Olaudah Equiano
National and whole-school events	Family feast Black History Month (Oct) Ethiopian New Year's Day Harvest Festival Sukkot	Diwali Anti-Bullying Week	Martin Luther King Jr Day LGBTQI+ History Month (Feb) Safer Internet Day World Poetry Day	World Book Day Holi Easter Ramadan begins	Earth Day Stephen Lawrence Day VE Day	World Ocean Day Windrush Day Mandela Day
Project-based learning theme	Is monarchy important?	What is fairness?	Do I belong?	How do we fight for education for every child, everywhere?	What should healthcare look like?	How can good come from disasters?

Appendices

Appendices

	Autumn 1	Autumn 2	Spring 1	Spring 2	Summer 1	Summer 2
Whole-class reading	*Astro Girl** by Ken Wilson Max	*Emmanuel's Dream* by Laurie Ann Thompson	*Tadpole's Promise* by Jeanne Willis	*I have the Right to be a Child* by Alain Serres	*The Visible Sounds* by Yin Jianling	*The Day the War Came* by Nicola Davis
Writing	Recount (2 weeks) Information text (2 weeks) Poetry (2 weeks)	Instructions (2 weeks) Character description/ narrative (3 weeks) Non-chronological leaflet (2 weeks)	Narrative (2 weeks) Explanation (2 weeks) Letter (2 weeks)	Diary/writing in role (2 weeks) Information leaflet (2 weeks) Setting description (2 weeks)	Narrative (3 weeks) Informal (2 weeks) Setting description (1 week)	Explanation (2 weeks) Recount (2 weeks) Narrative (3 weeks) Letter to new teacher
Quality texts *Literacy Tree	- *Julian is a Mermaid**	- *Wolves**	- *The Snail and The Whale*	- *Rosie Revere*	- *Anancy and Mr Dry Bone*	- *Vlad and the Great Fire of London*
Mathematics	Number: place value, addition and subtraction	Number: multiplication and division Measurement: money	Number: multiplication and division, statistics	Geometry: shape Number: fractions	Measurement: length and height Geometry: position and direction	Measurement: time, mass, capacity and temperature
Science	Uses of everyday materials	Animals, including humans	Living things and their habitats	Animals, including humans	Plants – be a botanist	Plants
Geography	What is London like now?		Where is America?	The geography of the school and its grounds	Locational knowledge – UK vs Jamaica	

	Autumn 1	Autumn 2	Spring 1	Spring 2	Summer 1	Summer 2
History	Queen Victoria – what was London like then?	Elizabeth Fry and social activism	Rosa Parks	The school day – changes in living memory	Mary Seacole and healthcare	Great Fire of London
Art	Yinka Shonibare Sculpture	Textiles	Jenny Sampson Drawing	Nahem Shoa Painting	Printing	Collage
DT		Design and make a flag for a cause!		Make a healthy smoothie		Make a stable structure (house)
PE	Invasion games: attack and defence	Gym Dance and expression through movement	Invasion games: dribbling	Net games: using hand/s and tennis racquets	OAA: problem-solving	Athletics
Computing	Text and graphics	Digital creativity	Multimedia authoring	Ada Lovelace Data and programming	Research and communication	Project
Spanish	Spanish songs: Classroom instructions, numbers, colours						
Music	Charanga music programme South African music	Charanga music programme Festivals and Christmas	Charanga music programme Playing together in a band	Charanga music programme Reggae and animals	Charanga music programme A song about being friends	Charanga music programme The history of music

Appendices

Appendices

	Autumn 1	Autumn 2	Spring 1	Spring 2	Summer 1	Summer 2
RE	Can stories change people: Why did Jesus tell stories?	Can stories change people: How does special food and fasting help people in their faith?	Can stories change people: How is forgiveness important to people's lives?	Can stories change people: How do we know that Easter is coming? What special story is told at Easter?	Can stories change people: Where did the world come from and how should we look after it?	Can stories change people: Why are different books special for different people?
PSHE and wellbeing	Jigsaw Being me in my world	Jigsaw Celebrating difference	Jigsaw Dreams and goals	Jigsaw Healthy me	Jigsaw Relationships	Jigsaw Changing me
Assessment	Starting point assessment: Reading speed test Prodigy Maths Placement Test	Assessment week Summative tests	Formative assessment – objectives on Insight	Assessment week Summative tests	SATs	Formative assessment – objectives on Insight

Year 3 curriculum map

	Autumn 1	Autumn 2	Spring 1	Spring 2	Summer 1	Summer 2
School global curriculum theme	Power and governance	Social justice and equality	Identity and diversity	Human rights	Sustainable development	Peace and conflict
Positive role models	David Lamy MP Harriet Harman MP Alexandria Ocasio-Cortez	Harvey Milk Rosa Parks Marcus Rashford	Sam King Una Marson	Malala Leslie Thomas	Greta Thunberg Licypriya Kangujam	Walter Tull Olaudah Equiano
National and whole-school events	Family Feast Black History Month (Oct) Ethiopian New Year's Day Harvest Festival Sukkot	Diwali Anti-Bullying Week	Martin Luther King Jr Day LGBTQI+ History Month (Feb) Safer Internet Day World Poetry Day	World Book Day Holi Easter Ramadan begins	Earth Day Stephen Lawrence Day VE Day	World Ocean Day Windrush Day Mandela Day
Project-based learning theme	Why is the law important?	What is equality?	What is identity?	How do we save our planet from climate change?	Why is housing a right?	How do we create peace?

Appendices

Appendices

	Autumn 1	Autumn 2	Spring 1	Spring 2	Summer 1	Summer 2
Quality texts – whole-class reading *Literacy Tree	*Cloud Tea Monkeys* by Mal Peet*	*I am Martin Luther King Jr* by Brad Meltzer	*Leon and The Place Between* by Angela McAllister and Grahame Baker-Smith*	*The Tin Forest* by Helen Ward*	*Flotsam* by David Wiesner	*Roman Diary: The journey of Iliona* by Richard Platt
Writing	Recount (2 weeks) Setting description (2 weeks) Information leaflet (3 weeks)	Speech (I have a dream) (2 weeks) Narrative (3 weeks) Non-chronological report (2 weeks)	Narrative (2 weeks) Explanation (2 weeks) Instructions (recipe)	Diary (2 weeks) Letter (2 weeks) Discussion (2 weeks)	Poetry (1 week) Informal letter (2 weeks) Mystery narrative (3 weeks)	Discussion (2 weeks) Letter (2 weeks) Non-chronological report (2 weeks) Letter
Mathematics	Number: place value, addition and subtraction	Number: multiplication and division	Number: multiplication and division, fractions	Statistics Measurement: money, length and perimeter	Number: fractions Measurement: time	Geometry: shape Measurement: mass and capacity
Science	Rocks	Forces and magnets	Animals, including humans	Marie M. Daly Plants	Plants Sound (introduction to Year 4 unit)	Light
Geography	Map and globe work		Physical geography of Egypt	Single-use plastics	Housing and shelters (human geography)	
History	Iron Age	Martin Luther King and Jesse Owens	Ancient Egypt		Anglo-Saxons and settlements	Julius Cesar

	Autumn 1	Autumn 2	Spring 1	Spring 2	Summer 1	Summer 2
Art	Amrita Sher-Gil Painting	Collage	Printing	Stephen Wiltshire Drawing	Textiles	Anish Kapoor Sculpture
DT	Iron Age cooking! Iron Age tools		Baking Egyptian bread		Design and build a shelter	
PE	Invasion games: passing and moving with hands	Gym Dance	Invasion games: dribbling, passing with feet	Net games: throwing and hitting a ball	OAA: problem-solving	Athletics
Computing	Text and graphics	Digital creativity	Multimedia authoring	Data and programming	Research and communication	Project
Spanish	Greetings, Spanish songs, ask/give personal information, family members, classroom objects, parts of the body, days of the week					
Music	Charanga music programme R&B and other styles	Charanga music programme Exploring and developing playing skills	Charanga music programme Reggae and animals	Charanga music programme Music from around the world, celebrating our differences and being kind to one another	Charanga music programme Disco, friendship and hope	Charanga music programme The history of music
RE	How are symbols and sayings important in religion: What can we learn about special symbols and signs used in religions?	How are symbols and sayings important in religion: How do Jews celebrate their beliefs at home and in the synagogue?	How are symbols and sayings important in religion: What do Sikh sayings tell us about Sikh beliefs?	How are symbols and sayings important in religion: How and why do Hindus celebrate Holi? What celebration can we design to mak a special time in our class?	How are symbols and sayings important in religion: How did Jesus and Buddha make people stop and think?	How are symbols and sayings important in religion: What is the significance of light in religion?

Appendices

Appendices

	Autumn 1	Autumn 2	Spring 1	Spring 2	Summer 1	Summer 2
PSCHE and wellbeing	Jigsaw Being me in my world	Jigsaw Celebrating difference	Jigsaw Dreams and goals	Jigsaw Healthy me	Jigsaw Relationships	Jigsaw Changing me
Assessment	Starting point assessment: Reading speed test Prodigy Maths Placement Test	Assessment week Summative tests	Formative assessment – objectives on Insight	Assessment week Summative tests	Formative assessment – objectives on Insight	Assessment week Summative tests

Year 4 curriculum map

	Autumn 1	Autumn 2	Spring 1	Spring 2	Summer 1	Summer 2
School global curriculum theme	Power and governance	Social justice and equality	Identity and diversity	Human rights	Sustainable development	Peace and conflict
Positive role models	David Lamy MP Harriet Harman MP Alexandria Ocasio-Cortez	Harvey Milk Rosa Parks Marcus Rashford	Sam King Una Marson	Malala Leslie Thomas	Greta Thunberg Licypriya Kangujam	Walter Tull Olaudah Equiano
National and whole-school events	Family Feast Black History Month (Oct) Ethiopian New Year's Day Harvest Festival Sukkot	Diwali Anti-Bullying Week	Martin Luther King Jr Day LGBTQI+ History Month (Feb) Safer Internet Day World Poetry Day	World Book Day Holi Easter Ramadan begins	Earth Day Stephen Lawrence Day VE Day	World Ocean Day Windrush Day Mandela Day
Project-based learning theme	Why is democracy important?	What is justice?	What is diversity?	The water fight – why is water vital?	How do we take less from our planet?	Is peace the only way to stop war?
Subject areas						
Quality texts – whole-class reading	*Shackleton's Journey* by William Grill	*Tar Beach* by Faith Ringgold	*Hidden Figures* by Margot Lee Shetterly	*Malala: My story of standing up for girls' rights* by Malala Yousafzai	*The Incredible Eco Systems of Planet Earth* by Rachel Ignotofsky	*Charlotte's Web* by E. B. White

Appendices

Appendices

	Autumn 1	Autumn 2	Spring 1	Spring 2	Summer 1	Summer 2
Writing	Recount (2 weeks) Newspaper (2 weeks) Myth (3 weeks)	Explanation (2 weeks) Character description (2 weeks) Narrative (3 weeks)	Non-chronological report (2 weeks) Biography (2 weeks) Diary (2 weeks)	Narrative (3 weeks) Persuasive (2 weeks) Poetry (1 week)	Instructions (2 weeks) Explanation (2 weeks) Letter (2 weeks)	Narrative (2 weeks) Diary (2 weeks) Play (2 weeks) Letter (1 week)
Mathematics	Number: place value, addition and subtraction	Number: multiplication division Measurement: length and perimeter	Number: multiplication and division Measurement: area	Number: fractions, decimals	Number: decimals Measurement: money, time	Statistics Geometry: properties of shape
Science	Charles Kao Sound	States of matter	States of matter	Animals, including humans	Kusala Rajendran Living things and their habitats	Electricity
Geography	World map work	*Titanic* journey from Belfast to New York		The water cycle, rivers	Taking less from our planet	
History	Ancient Greece	*Titanic*	Civil rights in UK and USA			World War II
Art	Agatharchus Painting	Collage	Yinka Shonibare Textiles	Drawing	Nancy Holt Printing	Sculpture
DT	Greek restaurant – making a healthy dish!		Pop-up story book		Create a bag for life	
PE	Invasion games: attack vs defence, football	Gym Dance	Invasion games: benchball	Net games: tennis	Striking games: batting, bowling	Athletics

234

Appendices

	Autumn 1	Autumn 2	Spring 1	Spring 2	Summer 1	Summer 2
Computing	Text and graphics	Digital creativity	Multimedia authoring	Data and programming	Research and communication	Project
Spanish	Numbers 1–50, days/months/dates, reading and pronunciation, likes and dislikes, rainforest animals, ask/give personal information, describe yourself					
Music	Charanga music programme ABBA's music	Charanga music programme The Beatles, equality and civil rights	Charanga music programme Soul/gospel music	Charanga music programme Writing lyrics linked to a theme	Charanga music programme Exploring and developing playing skills	Charanga music programme Classical
RE	What is special to me and the people in my community: What religions are represented in our community?	What is special to me and the people in my community: Why is the Bible special for Christians?	What is special to me and the people in my community: What makes me the person I am?	What is special to me and the people in my community: Why is Easter important to Christians?	What is special to me and the people in my community: How and why do Hindus worship at home and in the mandir?	What is special to me and the people in my community: What happens when someone gets married? All religions/world views.
PSHE and wellbeing	Jigsaw Being me in my world	Jigsaw Celebrating difference	Jigsaw Dreams and goals	Jigsaw Healthy me	Jigsaw Relationships	Jigsaw Changing me
Assessment	Starting point assessment: Reading speed test Prodigy Maths Placement Test	Assessment week Summative tests	Formative assessment – objectives on Insight	Assessment week Summative tests	Formative assessment – objectives on Insight	Assessment week Summative tests

Appendices

Year 5 curriculum map

	Autumn 1	Autumn 2	Spring 1	Spring 2	Summer 1	Summer 2
School global curriculum theme	Power and governance	Social justice and equality	Identity and diversity	Human rights	Sustainable development	Peace and conflict
Positive role models	David Lamy MP Harriet Harman MP Alexandria Ocasio-Cortez	Harvey Milk Rosa Parks Marcus Rashford	Sam King Una Marson	Malala Leslie Thomas	Greta Thunberg Licypriya Kangujam	Walter Tull Olaudah Equiano
National and whole-school events	Family Feast Black History Month (Oct) Ethiopian New Year's Day Harvest Festival Sukkot	Diwali Anti-Bullying Week	Martin Luther King Jr Day LGBTQI+ History Month (Feb) Safer Internet Day World Poetry Day	World Book Day Holi Easter Ramadan begins	Earth Day Stephen Lawrence Day VE Day	World Ocean Day Windrush Day Mandela Day
Project-based learning theme	What is power?	How do we fight for social justice?	What does it mean to belong to a country?	Why should trade be fair?	What does it mean to be free?	Punishment or rehabilitation – which helps more?

Appendices

	Autumn 1	Autumn 2	Spring 1	Spring 2	Summer 1	Summer 2
Whole-class reading quality texts	*The Boy in the Tower* by Polly Ho Yen	*Suffragette: The battle for equality* by David Roberts *The Promise* by Nicola Davis	*The Other Side of Truth* by Beverley Naidoo *The Arrival* by Shaun Tan	*The Three Little Pigs Project*	*Can We Save The Tiger?* by Martin Jenkins	*Otto – the Autobiography of a Teddy Bear* by Tomi Ungerer
Writing	Recount text (2 weeks) Diary (2 weeks) Instructions (2 weeks)	Formal letter (2 weeks) Newspaper (2 weeks) Narrative (3 weeks)	Biography (2 weeks) Narrative (2 week) Non-chronological report (2 weeks)	Explanation (2 weeks) Persuasive speech (2 weeks) Narrative (2 weeks)	Narrative (2 weeks) Persuasive speech (2 weeks)	Character description (2 weeks) Debate (2 weeks) Poetry (1 week) Letter (1 week)
Mathematics	Place value Number: four operations	Number: fractions	Number: fractions, decimals and percentages	Measurement: converting units, perimeter, area and volume Statistics	Geometry: properties of shape, position and direction	Investigations and consolidation
Science	Animals, including humans Dame Anne McLaren	Evolution and inheritance	Evolution and inheritance	Electricity	Living things and their habitats	Light
Geography	London vs Mexico		Migration across the UK Climate refugees	Fair trade	The slave trade – trade links	

Appendices

	Autumn 1	Autumn 2	Spring 1	Spring 2	Summer 1	Summer 2
History	Ancient Maya QT: History in infographics: The Maya	Sushama Sen, Emmaline Pankhurst and suffragettes	Migration in Southwark (trip) Baghdad: early Islamic civilisation		The slave trade	Anglo-Saxon crime and punishment
Art	Printing Frida Kahlo	Collage	Drawing Shepard Fairey street art	Sculpture	Lubaina Hidid Painting	Textiles
DT	Mexican food – make a Mexican dish!		Food from your heritage! Making healthy dishes	Circuits, electronics and mechanics	Make your own djembe drum	Anglo-Saxon fashion (textiles/stitching)
PE	Invasion games	Gym/dance	Invasion games	Net games	Striking games OAA	Athletics
Computing	Text and graphics Google Docs	Digital creativity Google Draw	Multimedia authoring Producing multimedia videos	Data and programming Algorithms and coding	Research and communication	Project

	Autumn 1	Autumn 2	Spring 1	Spring 2	Summer 1	Summer 2
Spanish	Ask and give personal information, reading and pronunciation, Spanish grammar, describing yourself and others, bilingual dictionary skills					
Music	Charanga music programme Rock anthems	Charanga music programme Jazz and improvisation	Charanga music programme Pop ballads	Charanga music programme Old-school hip hop	Charanga music programme Motown	Charanga music programme Classical
RE	How do beliefs influence actions: What inner forces affect how we think and behave?	How do beliefs influence actions: How is Christmas celebrated around the world?	How do beliefs influence actions: Why is Muhammad and the Quran important to Muslims?	How do beliefs influence actions: What do religions believe about God? All faiths	How do beliefs influence actions: Animal lawsuit	How do beliefs influence actions: How do Christians try to follow Jesus's example? Karma
PSCHE and wellbeing	Jigsaw Being me in my world	Jigsaw Celebrating difference	Jigsaw Dreams and goals	Jigsaw Healthy me	Jigsaw Relationships	Jigsaw Changing me
Assessment	Starting point assessment: Reading speed test Prodigy Maths Placement Test	Assessment week Summative tests	Formative assessment – objectives on Insight	Assessment week Summative tests	Year 6 SATs week Year 5 mock SATs week	Formative assessment – objectives on Insight

Appendices

Appendices

Year 6 curriculum map

	Autumn 1	Autumn 2	Spring 1	Spring 2	Summer 1	Summer 2
School global curriculum theme	Power and governance	Social justice and equality	Identity and diversity	Human rights	Sustainable development	Peace and conflict
Positive role models	David Lamy MP Harriet Harman MP Alexandria Ocasio-Cortez	Harvey Milk Rosa Parks Marcus Rashford	Sam King Una Marson	Malala Leslie Thomas	Greta Thunberg Licypriya Kangujam	Walter Tull Olaudah Equiano
National and whole-school events	Family Feast Black History Month (Oct) Ethiopian New Year's Day Harvest Festival Sukkot	Diwali Anti-Bullying Week	Martin Luther King Jr Day LGBTQI+ History Month (Feb) Safer Internet Day World Poetry Day	World Book Day Holi Easter Ramadan begins	Earth Day Stephen Lawrence Day VE Day	World Ocean Day Windrush Day Mandela Day
Project-based learning theme	What is democracy?	Has the UK achieved equality?	What is our identity as Earthlings?	How has the *Windrush* generation been treated?	How can we reduce our carbon footprint?	What did the Romans ever do for me?

240

	Autumn 1	Autumn 2	Spring 1	Spring 2	Summer 1	Summer 2
Whole-class reading *Literacy Tree	*Children of the Benin Kingdom* by Dinah Orji	*Black and British* by David Olusoga Black London trips book	*Origami Yoda* by Tom Angleberger *Hidden Figures* by Margot Lee Shetterly	*Windrush Child* by Benjamin Zephaniah	*The Hidden Forest* by Jeannie Baker	*My Story: Noor-un-Nissa Inayat Khan* by Sufia Ahmed
Writing	Recount text (2 weeks) Diary (2 weeks) Instructions (2 weeks)	Formal letter (2 weeks) Newspaper (2 weeks) Narrative (3 weeks)	Biography (2 weeks) Narrative (2 week) Non-chronological report (2 weeks) Based on *Hidden Figures*	Explanation (2 weeks) Persuasive speech (2 weeks) Narrative (2 weeks)	Narrative (2 weeks) Persuasive speech (2 weeks)	Character description (2 weeks) Debate (2 weeks) Poetry (1 week) Letter (1 week)
Mathematics	Place value Number: four operations	Number: fractions	Number: fractions (Year 5), ratio (Year 6), decimals and percentages, algebra (Year 6)	Measurement: converting units, perimeter, area and volume Statistics	Geometry: properties of shape, position and direction	Investigations and consolidation
Science	Animals, including humans	Classifying organisms	Earth and Space Mae Jemison Maggie Aderin-Pocock	Healthy bodies	Evolution and inheritance	Seeing light
Geography	Abuja vs London	The Americas	Longitude and latitude	Migration across the UK	Natural resources and sustainability	Geographical skills and fieldwork

Appendices

Appendices

	Autumn 1	Autumn 2	Spring 1	Spring 2	Summer 1	Summer 2
History	Ancient Benin	Medicine and disease	Leisure and entertainment	The *Windrush*		The Roman Empire and its impact on Britain Aballava and the Black Romans Ivory Bangle Lady
Art	Àsìkò Photography Drawing	Street art Mr Cenz and Love Pusher	Collage	Denzel Forrester Painting	Tan Zi Xi Textiles	Express yourself Sculpture Huma Bhabha
DT	Ancient Benin Fairground ride	Fashion and textiles – create a Caribbean-style bag	Creating models of the planets and phrases of the moon			Create an Italian dish!
PE	Invasion games	Gym/dance	Invasion games	Net games	Striking games OAA	Athletics
Computing	Communication	Webpage creation	Variables in games	Introduction to spreadsheets	3D modelling	Sensing
Spanish	Numbers 0–10, greetings, classroom instructions, ask for and give name, ask for age, Christmas		Revision of numbers 0–10, colours	Fruit, food items, Easter (spring time)	Days of the week, months of the year	Weather conditions

	Autumn 1	Autumn 2	Spring 1	Spring 2	Summer 1	Summer 2
Music	Charanga music programme Being happy!	Charanga music programme Jazz and improvisation, composition	Charanga music programme Benjamin Britten's music and cover versions	Charanga music programme The music of Carole King	Charanga music programme Create your own music inspired by your identity and women in the music industry	Charanga music programme Classical
RE	What is the best way for a Muslim to show commitment to God?	How significant is it that Mary was Jesus's mother?	Is anything ever eternal?	Is Christianity still a strong religion 2,000 years after Jesus was on Earth?	Does belief in Akhirah (life after death) help Muslims lead good lives?	
PSCHE and wellbeing	Jigsaw Being me in my world	Jigsaw Celebrating difference	Jigsaw Dreams and goals	Jigsaw Healthy me	Jigsaw Relationships	Jigsaw Changing me
Assessment	Starting point assessment: Reading speed test Prodigy Maths Placement Test	Assessment week Summative tests	Formative assessment – objectives on Insight	Assessment week Summative tests	Year 6 SATs week	Formative assessment – objectives on Insight

Appendices

Further reading

Key reports

- Equality Act 2021
- 'Framework for developing an anti-racist approach' (NEU, 2021)
- 'Reflecting realities: Survey of ethnic representation within UK children's literature' (CLPE, 2021, www.clpe.org.uk/research/clpe-reflecting-realities-survey-ethnic-representation-within-uk-childrens-literature-0)

> **Top tip!**
>
> Print off some key reports and leave them in the staff room. You could have a 'staff book club' or a 'recommended reads' section in your staff room. Alternatively, you could give your staff a section of a report to read before a staff meeting and have professional discussions around evidence/key research to make your professional development more purposeful.

History

Key books

Here are some suggestions for further reading to enhance subject knowledge of areas such as Black history, British Asian history, women's history, queer history, history of people with disabilities and much more!

- *Why I Am No Longer Talking To White People About Race* by Reni Eddo-Lodge
- *How to Be an Antiracist* by Ibram X. Kendi
- *The Good Immigrant* edited by Nikesh Shukla

- *White Fragility: Why it's so hard for White people to talk about racism* by Robin DiAngelo
- *White Privilege: The myth of a post-racial society* by Kalwant Bhopal
- *Pedagogy of the Oppressed* by Paulo Freire
- *Teaching to Transgress: Education as the practice of freedom* by Bell Hooks
- *You Wouldn't Understand: White teachers in multiethnic classrooms* by Sarah Pearce
- *Natives: Race and class in the ruins of empire* by Akala
- *Black and British: A forgotten history* by David Olusoga
- *Women, Race and Class* by Angela Y. Davis
- *Representation Matters: Becoming an anti-racist educator* by Aisha Thomas
- *Brit(ish): On race, identity and belonging* by Afua Hirsch
- *Intersectionality in Education: Toward more equitable policy, research, and practice* by Alfredo J. Artiles, Sonia Neito, Wendy Cavendish and Jennifer F. Samson
- *The New Age of Empire: How racism and colonialism still rule the world* by Kehinde Andrews
- *British Queer History: New approaches and perspectives* by Brian Lewis
- *Black British Lives Matter* by Lenny Henry and Marcus Ryder
- *The Feminism Book* by DK
- *Pupil Book Study: An evidence-informed guide to help quality assure the curriculum* by Alex Bedford
- *When the Adults Change, Everything Changes* by Paul Dix
- *Will It Make the Boat Go Faster?* by Harriet Beveridge and Ben Hunt-Davis
- *Atomic Habits* by James Clear

Websites

Black history

- www.ourmigrationstory.org.uk/oms/roman-britain-the-ivory-bangle-lady

Disability

- www.historicengland.org.uk/research/inclusive-heritage/disability-history
- www.worldofinclusion.com

LGBT

- www.stonewall.org.uk/system/files/lgbt_history_home_learning_pack_-_primary.pdf

Geography

Must sees!

- 'Man' – YouTube video made by Steve Cuts (www.youtube.com/watch?v=WfGMYdalCIU)
- *Planet Earth* – BBC David Attenborough series
- *Blue Planet* – BBC David Attenborough series

Best publishers of maps for the classroom

Atlases

- Collins
- Oxford University Press
- Phillips

Display maps

- TTS
- MaxiMap
- Hope Education

Further reading

- 'Critical multicultural geography: Moving beyond the "Four Fs" of fairs, festivals, food and folktales' by Joe Usher and Lesley Burnett (2022, *Primary Geography*, Issue 107, pp. 18–20)
- 'Teaching map skills to inspire a sense of place and adventure' by Dr Paula Owens (https://digimapforschools.edina.ac.uk/files/resource-hub/downloads/pupils%20planning%20document-low%20ink%20version_2.pdf)
- Geography Expert Subject Advisory Group, www.geognc.wordpress.com

Art

- A collection of diverse artists: www.padlet.com/teachingartatschool/2fbe6fmljvfd357a
- LGBT art stories: www.tate.org.uk/kids/explore/kids-view/5-lgbtq-art-stories
- Queer artist stories: www.tate.org.uk/art/five-stories-queer-artists
- The amazing art of disabled artists: www.webdesignerdepot.com/2010/03/the-amazing-art-of-disabled-artists

Some great websites to check out for diverse book stalls are:

- www.thisisbooklove.com: BookLove is an independent, grassroots UK-based multicultural travelling book carnival and online shop, highlighting and celebrating inclusive, anti-racist and multicultural books for children. They also sell bilingual books!
- http://knightsof.media: Making books for every child, starting with who's behind the scenes (UK-wide).
- www.mirrormewrite.com: Indie bookseller bringing relatable, diverse and inclusive literature for children and young adults into homes and schools across the UK (Manchester-based).

Bibliography

BBC Newsround (2019), 'Stonewall: LGBT charity marks 30 years fighting for equality'. Available at: www.bbc.co.uk/newsround/48393481

BBC Newsround (2022), 'London Pride parade: History of gay rights in the UK'. Available at: https://www.bbc.co.uk/newsround/40459213

Blood, I., Lomas, M. and Robinson, M. (2016), 'Every child: Equality and diversity in arts and culture with, by and for children and young people'. Arts Council England. Available at: www.artscouncil.org.uk/sites/default/files/download-file/FINAL%20report%20web%20ready.pdf

British Science Association (2020), 'The state of the sector: Diversity and representation in STEM industries in the UK'. APPG on Diversity and Inclusion in STEM. Available at: www.britishscienceassociation.org/Handlers/Download.ashx?IDMF=d7899dce-22d5-4880-bbcf-669c0c35bda6

Campbell-Stephens, R. (2020), 'Global majority: Decolonising the language and reframing the conversation about race'. Available at: www.leedsbeckett.ac.uk/-/media/files/schools/school-of-education/final-leeds-beckett-1102-global-majority.pdf

Camerini, V. (2019), *Greta's Story: The schoolgirl who went on strike to save the planet*. Simon & Schuster Children's UK.

Carlone, H. B. and Johnson, A. (2007), 'Understanding the science experiences of successful women of color: Science identity as an analytic lens'. *Journal of Research in Science Teaching*, 44, (8), 1187–1218.

Chipperton, J., Georgiou, G., Seymour, O. and Wright, K. (2018), 'Self-evaluation/audit questions (primary)'. The Church of England Education Office. Available at: https://api.warwickshire.gov.uk/documents/WCCC-1075664550-1089

City Arts (2013), 'Art works: Using the arts to promote emotional health and wellbeing in schools'. Available at: https://city-arts.org.uk/wp-content/uploads/2013/03/Art-Works.pdf

de la Cretaz, B. (2022), 'The fat-positive potential of sports'. Global Sports Matters. Available at: https://globalsportmatters.com/culture/2022/02/22/creating-positive-spaces-fat-athletes

Department for Education (DfE) (2013a), 'History programmes of study: Key Stages 1 and 2'. Available at: https://assets.publishing.service.gov.uk/government/uploads/system/uploads/attachment_data/file/239035/PRIMARY_national_curriculum_-_History.pdf

Department for Education (DfE) (2013b), 'National Curriculum in England: Geography programmes of study'. Available at: www.gov.uk/government/publications/natio

Department for Education (DfE) (2013c), 'Art and design programmes of study: Key Stages 1 and 2'. Available at: https://assets.publishing.service.gov.uk/government/uploads/system/uploads/attachment_data/file/239018/PRIMARY_national_curriculum_-_Art_and_design.pdf

Department for Education (DfE) (2013d), 'Music programmes of study: Key Stages 1 and 2'. Available at: https://assets.publishing.service.gov.uk/government/uploads/system/uploads/attachment_data/file/239037/PRIMARY_national_curriculum_-_Music.pdf

Department for Education (DfE) (2013e), 'Science programmes of study: Key Stages 1 and 2'. Available at: https://assets.publishing.service.gov.uk/government/uploads/system/uploads/attachment_data/file/425618/PRIMARY_national_curriculum_-_Science.pdf

Department for Education (DfE) (2013f), 'National Curriculum in England: Computing programmes of study'. Available at: www.gov.uk/government/publications/national-curriculum-in-england-computing-programmes-of-study/national-curriculum-in-england-computing-programmes-of-study

Department for Education (DfE) (2013g), 'Design and technology programmes of study: Key Stages 1 and 2'. Available at: https://assets.publishing.service.gov.uk/government/uploads/system/uploads/attachment_data/file/239041/PRIMARY_national_curriculum_-_Design_and_technology.pdf

Department for Education (DfE) (2013h), 'National Curriculum in England: Physical education programmes of study'. Available at: www.gov.uk/government/publications/national-curriculum-in-england-physical-education-programmes-of-study/national-curriculum-in-england-physical-education-programmes-of-study

Department for Education (DfE) (2014a), 'National Curriculum in England: English programmes of study'. Available at: www.gov.uk/government/publications/national-curriculum-in-england-english-programmes-of-study/national-curriculum-in-england-english-programmes-of-study

Department for Education (DfE) (2014b), 'The Equality Act 2010 and schools: Departmental advice for school leaders, school staff, governing bodies and local authorities'. Available at: https://assets.publishing.service.gov.uk/government/uploads/system/uploads/attachment_data/file/315587/Equality_Act_Advice_Final.pdf

Department for Education (DfE) (2019), 'Relationships education, relationships and sex education (RSE) and health education: Statutory guidance for governing bodies, proprietors, head teachers, principals, senior leadership teams, teachers'. Available at: https://assets.publishing.service.gov.uk/government/uploads/system/uploads/

attachment_data/file/1019542/Relationships_Education__Relationships_and_Sex_Education__RSE__and_Health_Education.pdf

Department for Education (DfE) (2021), 'National Curriculum in England: Mathematics programmes of study'. Available at: www.gov.uk/government/publications/national-curriculum-in-england-mathematics-programmes-of-study/national-curriculum-in-england-mathematics-programmes-of-study

Doull, K. (2021), 'Women and space: Reaching for the stars'. Historical Association. Available at: www.history.org.uk/publications/resource/10290/women-and-space-reaching-for-the-stars

Elliot, V., Nelson-Addy, A., Chantiluke, R. and Courtney, M. (2020), 'Lit In colour: Diversity in literature in English schools'. Penguin. Available at: https://litincolour.penguin.co.uk

Fowler, K. (2021), 'LGBT+ and gender: Auditing your school curriculum'. Headteacher Update. Available at: www.headteacher-update.com/best-practice-article/lgbt-and-gender-auditing-your-schools-curriculum-diversity-teaching-learning/240317

Geographical Association (2018), 'Investigating weather through story'. Available at: www.geography.org.uk/write/MediaUploads/teaching%20resources/Weather_story_list_download.pdf

Guardian (2009), 'World maps'. Available at: www.theguardian.com/global/gallery/2009/apr/17/world-maps-mercator-goode-robinson-peters-hammer

Halo Collective (2020), 'Loc it up! Adopt the Halo Code'. Available at: www.halocollective.co.uk/halo-code-school

Hashim, T. (2020), 'The extraordinary life of Azeem Rafiq'. Wisden. Available at: www.wisden.com/stories/interviews/the-extraordinary-life-of-azeem-rafiq

HM Government (2011), 'Prevent Strategy'. Available at: https://assets.publishing.service.gov.uk/government/uploads/system/uploads/attachment_data/file/97976/prevent-strategy-review.pdf

Hobson, N LF (2017) 'Six Ways Mathematics Instructors Can Support Diversity and Inclusion'. Available at: https://blogs.ams.org/matheducation/2017/03/06/six-ways-mathematics-instructors-can-support-diversity-and-inclusion/

Howard, T. (2020), 'Racial literacy: A call to action for teachers', HMH. Available at: www.hmhco.com/blog/racial-literacy-a-call-to-action-for-teachers

Joseph-Salisbury, R. (2020), 'Race and racism in English secondary schools'. Runnymede Perspectives. Available at: https://assets.website-files.com/61488f992b58e687f1108c7c/61bcc0cc2a023368396c03d4_Runnymede%20Secondary%20Schools%20report%20FINAL.pdf

Lewis, P (2021), 'Black History Month: Racism in football'. House of Lords Library. Available at: https://lordslibrary.parliament.uk/black-history-month-racism-in-football/

London Mathematical Society (2013), 'Advancing women in mathematics: Good practice in university departments'. Available at: www.lms.ac.uk/sites/default/files/LMS-BTL-17Report_0.pdf

Marian, V. and Shook, A. (2012), 'The cognitive benefits of being bilingual'. *Cerebrum (Dana Foundation)*. Available at: www.dana.org/article/the-cognitive-benefits-of-being-bilingual

Maxwell, L. (2019), 'Pop-up inclusive children's bookshop asks you #readtheonepercent'. Book Riot. Available at: www.bookriot.com/inclusive-childrens-bookshop

Menzel, T, Braumüller, B Hartmann-Tews, I (2019) The Relevance of Sexual Orientation and Gender Identity In Sport in Europe. Available at: https://equalityinsport.org/docs/The%20Relevance%20of%20Sexual%20Orientation%20and%20Gender%20Identity%20in%20Sport%20in%20Europe%20-%20Findings%20from%20the%20Outsport%20Survey%202019.pdf

McIntyre, N., Parveen, N. and Thomas, T. (2021), 'Exclusion rates five times higher for black Caribbean pupils in parts of England'. *Guardian*. Available at: www.theguardian.com/education/2021/mar/24/exclusion-rates-black-caribbean-pupils-england

Moffat, A. (2019), 'Diversity: What is No Outsiders?' No Outsiders. Available at: www.no-outsiders.com/about-us

National Education Union (NEU) (2021), 'Framework for developing an anti-racist approach'. Available at: https://neu.org.uk/media/11236/view#:~:text=The%20framework%20is%20designed%20to,concept%20of%20'decolonising%20education

National Foundation for Educational Research (NFER) (2022), 'Racial equality in the teacher workforce: An analysis of representation and progression opportunities from initial teacher training to headship'. Available at: www.nfer.ac.uk/media/4921/racial_equality_in_the_teacher_workforce_summary_report.pdf

Office for National Statistics (ONS) (2021), 'The lasting impact of violence against women and girls'. Available at: www.ons.gov.uk/peoplepopulationandcommunity/crimeandjustice/articles/thelastingimpactofviolenceagainstwomenandgirls/2021-11-24#:~:text=In%20the%20year%20ending%20March,7%25%20of%20the%20female%20population

Ofsted (2018), 'An investigation into how to assess the quality of education through curriculum intent, implementation and impact'. Available at: https://assets.publishing.service.gov.uk/government/uploads/system/uploads/attachment_data/file/936097/Curriculum_research_How_to_assess_intent_and_implementation_of_curriculum_191218.pdf

Ofsted (2019), 'School inspection handbook'. Available at: www.gov.uk/government/publications/school-inspection-handbook-eif/school-inspection-handbook

Olusoga, D. (2017) *Black and British: A forgotten history*, Pan Macmillan.

Out on the Fields (2020), '50 years of research: Girls still avoid sport due to lesbian stigma'. Available at: https://outonthefields.com/female-sport-participation

Oxfam (2015a), 'Education for global citizenship: A guide for schools'. Available at: https://oxfamilibrary.openrepository.com/bitstream/handle/10546/620105/edu-global-citizenship-schools-guide-091115-en.pdf?sequence=11&isAllowed=y

Oxfam (2015b), 'Global citizenship in the classroom: A guide for teachers'. Available at: https://oxfamilibrary.openrepository.com/bitstream/handle/10546/620105/edu-global-citizenship-teacher-guide-091115-en.pdf?sequence=9&isAllowed=y

Oxford Learner's Dictionaries (2022), 'Search Oxford Advanced Learner's Dictionary'. Available at: www.oxfordlearnersdictionaries.com/definition/english

Pearson (2021), 'Power of maths: Stat-shot series: Perceptions, diversity and inclusion in maths'. Available at: www.pearson.com/content/dam/one-dot-com/one-dot-com/uk/documents/subjects/mathematics/B0478-PofM-StatShot-Diversity-Maths-Learning.pdf

Rashid, N. and Tikly, L. (2010), 'Guidelines for inclusion and diversity in schools'. British Council. Available at: www.britishcouncil.es/sites/default/files/british-council-guidelines-for-inclusion-and-diversity-in-schools.pdf

Rees, P (2014) 'We got off the coach and the National Front was there ... People spat at us', *Guardian*. Available at: www.theguardian.com/football/2014/jul/25/west-brom-three-degrees-book-extract

Rollins, M. (2020), 'Diversity in STEM: What is it, why does it matter and how do we increase it?' Sea Grant, California. Available at: https://caseagrant.ucsd.edu/news/diversity-stem-what-it-why-does-it-matter-and-how-do-we-increase-it

Sharples, J., Albers, B., Fraser, S. and Kime, S. (2019), 'Putting evidence to work: A school's guide to implementation'. Education Endowment Foundation. Available at: https://d2tic4wvo1iusb.cloudfront.net/eef-guidance-reports/implementation/EEF_Implementation_Guidance_Report_2019.pdf?v=1635355218

Shaw, B., Bernardes, E., Trethewey, A. and Menzies, L. (2016), 'Special educational needs and their links to poverty'. Joseph Rowntree Foundation. Available at: www.jrf.org.uk/report/special-educational-needs-and-their-links-poverty

Skybadger (2022), 'Ivarr the Boneless'. Available at: www.skybadger.co.uk/schools-carers/sky-badger-schools/ivarr-boneless

Sport England (2016), 'Mapping disability: The facts: A statistical review of disabled people in England'. Available at: https://sportengland-production-files.s3.eu-west-2.amazonaws.com/s3fs-public/mapping-disability-the-facts.pdf

Stonewall (2017), 'School report: The experiences of lesbian, gay, bi and trans young people in Britain's schools in 2017'. Available at: www.stonewall.org.uk/system/files/the_school_report_2017.pdf

Stonewall (2019), 'LGBTQ-inclusive education: Everything you need to know'. Available at: stonewall.org.uk/lgbtq-inclusive-education-everything-you-need-know

Stonewall (2019) 'Creating an LGBTQ+ inclusive primary curriculum'. Available at: www.stonewall.org.uk/system/files/stw_pearson_creating_an_inclusive_primary_curriculum_2022_1_-_march.pdf

The Black Curriculum (2021), 'KS2 learning activities: The history of John Blanke'. Available at: https://static1.squarespace.com/static/5f5507a237cea057c5f57741/t/5f8912355af00f1b3c723158/1602818625113/John+Blanke+KS2.pdf

The Key (2020), 'Anti-racism: how to review and re-frame your curriculum'. Available at: https://schoolleaders.thekeysupport.com/curriculum-and-learning/curriculum-guidance-all-phases/structuring-curriculum/anti-racism-how-review-and-re-frame-your-curriculum

The Key (2021), 'Curriculum audit: Gender and LGBTQ+ inclusivity'. Available at: https://schoolleaders.thekeysupport.com/curriculum-and-learning/curriculum-guidance-all-phases/structuring-curriculum/curriculum-audit-gender-and-lgbtq-inclusivity

The P4C Co-operative (n.d.), 'About P4C: What is it and how is it done?' Available at: https://p4c.com/about-p4c

Todd, J. and Lewis, C. (n.d.), 'Bringing the untold stories of Black Tudors into the classroom'. Available at: www.history.org.uk/files/download/21044/1558524345/SSJT4__Jason_Todd__Chris_Lewis__Bringing_the_untold_stories_of_black_Tudors_into_the_classroom.pdf

Unicef (n.d.), 'Rights Respecting Schools'. Available at: www.unicef.org.uk/rights-respecting-schools

United Nations (UN) (n.d.), 'Do you know all 17 SDGs?' Available at: https://sdgs.un.org/goals

United Nations (n.d.) Sustainable Development Goals. Available at: https://www.un.org/sustainabledevelopment/ The content of this publication has not been approved by the United Nations and does not reflect the views of the United Nations or its officials or Member States.

United Nations (UN) (1990) The United Nations Convention on the Rights of the Child. Available at: www.unicef.org.uk/what-we-do/un-convention-child-rights

Myers, V. (2014), 'How to overcome our biases? Walk boldly towards them'. TEDxBeacon Street. Available at: www.ted.com/talks/verna_myers_how_to_overcome_our_biases_walk_boldly_toward_them

Wordlaw, S. (2019), 'Diversity and Inclusion in the Primary Classroom'. HWRK Magazine. Available at: www.hwrkmagazine.co.uk/coming-out-of-the-closet-diversity-and-inclusion-in-the-primary-classroom

Wordlaw, S. (2022), 'Writing your own global curriculum'. UKEDChat. Available at: www.ukedchat.com/2022/03/29/uked-magazine-issue-57/4

World Health Organization (WHO) (2020), 'WHO guidelines on physical activity and sedentary behaviour: At a glance'. Available at: www.who.int/publications/i/item/9789240014886

YMCA (2020), 'Young and Black: The young Black experience of institutional racism in the UK'. Available at: www.ymca.org.uk/research/young-and-black

YouGov (2021), 'Racism in football'. Available at: https://docs.cdn.yougov.com/jn30na1za8/YouGov%20-%20European%20football%20fans,%20racism%20in%20football.pdf

Young, S. (2014), 'Inspiration porn and the objectification of disability: Stella Young at TEDxSydney 2014'. Available at: www.youtube.com/watch?v=SxrS7-I_sMQ

Youth Sport Trust (nd) '10 Top Tips to Adapt Activities for Young People', National School Sport Week.

Zick, W. (2008), 'John Blanke (16th century)'. Black Past. Available at: www.blackpast.org/global-african-history/blanke-john-16th-century

Index

A
Abbess Hilda of Whitby 65
Aderin-Pocock, Maggie 134
African instruments projects 133
African music 110
Agnodice of Athens 74
ancient civilisations, strong women in 72
Ancient Greeks, with disabilities 74
Anderson, Hurbin 101
Anglo-Saxons 65–6
animal ambassadors 89
anti-racism, in auditing current curriculum 4, 11, 66
    Black History Month 9
    decolonising education and 8–9
    practising 8
    questions in 7
    reviewing in 6–7
APPG on Diversity and Inclusion in STEM, The 119
Arrival, The (Tan) 50
arts curriculum
    aim of 97–101
    art environment, creating 101–2
    and fieldtrips 95–6
    importance of 96–7
    need for 95–6
    teacher recruitment for 97
Asakawa, Chieko 133
Asian music 111
assemblies 105–8, 152, 162
auditing curriculum 3–16
    anti-racism and 6–9
    cross-curricular approach in 5
    diverse groups in 5
    LGBTQ+ inclusive teaching and 9–11
    neuro and physical diversity inclusive teaching 11–13
    religious education (RE) and 13–15
    resources of 5, 7
    steps to 4
    time allotment for 4
Azuma, Makoto 101

B
BAME 6, 7, 23
Barnaby Bear toy 83
Batson, Brendon 143
Beachy Head Lady 64–5
Bedwei, Farida 123
Billinghurst, Rosa May 60
Black and British: A Forgotten History 50, 55
Black and British: A short, essential history (Olusoga) 50, 55
Black Curriculum, The (website) 32, 55, 69
Black Girl Hike @UKBgh 147–8
Black History Month 7
Blanke, John 69
Bonetta, Sarah Forbes 61
books, choosing and stocking 33, 36, 39
    book lists 47–52
    budget and fundraising 53–4
Bowling, Frank 100
Braille, Louis 61
Braun, Ralph 133
breadmaking projects 133
Bristol Bus Boycott of 1963, The 59
Britain
    history beyond 1066 66–72
    settlement by Anglo-Saxons and Scots 65
    from the stone age to iron age, changes in 63
British history theme 66–72
British Science Association 124
British science week 124
British values 34, 45, 153–4
Brown, Marie Van Brittan 130
Brunel, Isambard Kingdom 61

C

Cahun, Claude 99
Carri, Caterina Delli 52
cerebral palsy (CP) 140
Challenge Partners 197
Chang, Angel 52
children, conversations with 33–4, 43–6, 114, 197
Chinese inventions projects 133
Chipperton, J. 13
Chronically Sick and Disabled Persons Act (1970) 59
clay freeze-frames 115
Cleopatra (queen of Egypt) 73
colonialism 7
computing in STEM 128–9
    diversity enhancement 130
    role models 130–1
    teaching and learning in 129
    tools 129–30
corridor displays 162
creativity competition 162
cross-curricular approach 5
curriculum
    implementation of 191–3
    intent of 193–4
curriculum monitoring
    evaluation of 195–6
    findings in 198–9
    impact of 194–5
    ways to 196–8

D

Davison, Emily 60
decolonisation, of education 6, 8, 9, 22
Definition of a Miracle (Bedwei) 123
design and technology (DT) in STEM
    teaching and learning 131–2
    project ideas 132–5
Disability Matters (website) 33
disability-inclusive teacher training 33
diverse curriculum 9, 24–6
Doull, Karen 68
Down's syndrome 139–40
drama curriculum *see also* literacy curriculum
    diversity through drama 116–18
    objectives of 114
    spoken language in 114
    teaching 115–16
Duncan, Kate 95
Durand, Aurelia 50

E

EAL students, strategies for teaching 35–6
earliest civilizations, achievements of 72–4
Education Endowment Foundation (EEF) 191
Elliott, Rebecca 52
equal rights, campaigns for 66
Equality Act (2010) 6, 189
European music 111

F

Fanque, Pablo 71
female migration to Australia, history of 68
fieldtrips 90, 91–2, 95–6, 152, 153
Fillis, Mary 71
First Page Friday 38
flashback/flash-forward 116
'Focus on frozen worlds' 85
Football Spectators Act (1989) 144
football, racism in 144–5
'Framework for developing an anti-racist approach' 21, 245
Francis, Jacques 69
Fransman, Karrie 51
freeze-frames 115
Fry, Elizabeth 60
Fu Hao (Shang dynasty) 73–4

G

Galton, Mary Anne 61
gay rights in UK, history of 67–8
gender stereotypes books 50–1
Gender Swapped Fairy Tales (Fransman) 51
Geographical Association 86
geography curriculum
    aim of 79–80

challenging bias 80–1
maps in 78–9
national curriculum and linked projects 81–94
need for 77–8
skills and fieldwork 90–1
global citizenship education 20–2
global food projects 132
global majority 6
Global Sport Matters 138
Go bananas: Discover where food comes from project 89–90
Go Fund Me 53
Gooding, Louise 52

H

Hadid, Zaha 100
Halo Code, The 189
Hannah, Marc Regis 130
Harrison, Vashti 49
heritage sites 96
history curriculum
  international history 57
  local history 56, 62, 66
  national curriculum history 57–75
  national history 56–7
Hockney, David 100
homes around world projects 133
homophobia 43–4, 46
Hookey, Cathy 52
human rights, exploring through song 112–13
Hunter, Clementine 99

I

Ibn Battuta the Explorer 58, 61, 173
inclusive curriculum mapping/designing
  knowledge organisers, creating 174
  lesson plans 174
  medium-term plans 174
  planning documents storage 179
  progression of skills documents preparation 172
  publishing on websites 179–80
  subject, long-term plan for 173–4
  whole-school themes, planning 171–2
  year group long-term plans 174
inclusive recruitment 22–4
International Women's Day 89
inventors list 133
Islamic art 128
Islamic civilisation 75
Ivar the Boneless 65–6
Ivory Bangle Lady 64
Iwai, Melissa 52

J

Jemison, Mae 122
Jewell, Tiffany 50
Johnson, Katherine 123
Julian, Percy Lavon 122
Just Ask: Be different, be brave, be you (Sotomayor and López) 52
Just Like Me: 40 neurologically and physically diverse people who broke stereotypes (Gooding) 52

K

K'abel, Lady 75
Kahlo, Frida 99, 100
kalimba 133
Kao, Charles 122
Kapoor, Sir Anish 100
Kebede, Daniel 22
Keller, Helen 61
Key, The 7, 10, 159
Khan, Hena 50
Kick it Out @kickitout 147
Kusama, Yayoi 100

L

Land for life (WWF) 88
language, role in literacy curriculum 33, 34, 35–6, 40, 45
Latin American music 111–13
learning environment
  dress code 188
  Halo Code 189
  indoor 181–5
  outdoor 185–8

learning walks 197
lesson plans 5, 174, 196
Lewis, Chris 71
LGBT books 50–1
LGBT/LGBT+ History Month 9, 40, 44, 99
LGBT/LGBTQ+-inclusive teaching 9–11, 39–46
   DfE guidance for 42
   ethos and culture review 11
   parent guide for 43–6
   parent's prejudice in 39–42
   resources for 32
   RSE policy in 42
libraries 181–2
literacy curriculum
   books in, stocking 47–54
   diverse images in 34
   for English as additional language (EAL) students 35–36
   importance of 30–2
   LGBT+ inclusive teaching 39
   modelling writing 35
   reading profile in 36–9
   staff CPD 32
   teaching of 33–4
   writing, genre of 29–30, 35
'Lit in colour' 31
living memory changes, history of
   days of life 59
   food 57–9
   and Morris, Lord Alf 59
   music 59
local community relationship 8, 19, 24, 25, 56, 59, 96, 148, 152
local history 56, 62, 66
Longstaff, Peter 101
López, Rafael 52
Lovelace, Ada 123, 130

M

maps, usage in geography curriculum 78–9, 81–2, 90–1
maths, teaching in STEM 125
   inclusive maths practice 125–6
   learning environment 126
   mathematical games 128
   Maths4Girls 127
   reasoning and investigative tasks 127–8
McLaren, Dame Anne 123
Mercator map 78, 79
minority ethnic people 6
Morgan, Garrett 134
Morris, Lord Alf 59
Moss, Marlow 99
music curriculum 103
   aim of 103–4
   education in communities through 109–10
   genres of 104–5
   history through 109
   map 106–7
   singing assemblies 105–8
   teaching 108–14
   world music, role of 110–12

N

Naidoo, Beverley 50
national and global events, history of 59
national and international achievers' history 60–1
national curriculum history
   Key Stage 1 57–62
   Key Stage 2 62–75
national days, history on 59
National Education Union (NEU) 7, 21
national geography curriculum 81–94
   locational knowledge 81–2
   place knowledge 83–4
   human and physical geography 85–90
   geographical skills 90–1
   fieldwork 91–2
Nefertiti (Egyptian queen) 72
neuro and physical diversity inclusive teaching 11–13
newsletters 162
Nightingale, Florence 123
Nyong'o, Lupita 49

O

Olusoga, David 50, 55
O'Malley, Grace 61

Other Side of Truth, The (Naidoo) 50
Our changing world project (PlanBee) 85–6
Our planet: Biomes (WWF) 88

P

Palacio, R.J. 52
Papworth, Sarah 51
Paralympics 66
parent guide, for LGBT/ LGBTQ+-inclusive teaching
   different families' relationships 44–5, 46
   homophobia, tackling 43–4
   talking with children, importance of 43, 46
   values in 45
Park, Jessy 100
people with disabilities, books on 52
Perey, Marguerite 124
Perry, Grayson 101
personal favourites books 49–50
Philosophy4Children (P4C) 117–18, 152
phone calls activity 116
physical education (PE)
   for children with amputations or limb difference 140
   for children with cerebral palsy (CP) 140
   for children with Down's syndrome 139–40
   for learners with different needs 139
physical education (PE) curriculum
   importance of language usage in 142
   initiatives 147
   kit 149
   LGBTQ+ inclusive teaching 142–3
   need for 137–8
   project ideas 144–6
   racism in sport 143–4
   social media 148
   teaching and learning 139–40
   young people training 141–2
Plackett, Jonathan 51
posters 126, 144, 162
Prager, Sarah 48, 49, 51

Pride: The Story of Harvey Milk and the Rainbow Flag (Sanders) 50
PSHE (personal, social, health and economic education) 9, 10, 20, 34, 88, 89, 90, 131, 152, 162
Public Order Act (1986) 144
pupil data 197
pupil surveys 197
pupil voice 39, 197
Putting evidence to work: A school's guide to implementation' 191

R

Race Relations Act (1965) 59
'Racial equality in the teacher workforce' (NEFR report) 22
racial literacy 6, 32
racism in sports 144–5
Rafiq, Azeem 143
Rainbow Revolutionaries: 50 LGBT people who made history (Prager) 51
raised gloved fists, protests in sports 145
Rajendran, Kusala 122
reading profile in literacy curriculum 36–9
   author of week, highlighting 36
   book fairs, conducting 36
   First Page Friday 38
   pupil voice, involving 39
real-life people, photos of 126
recruitment process, inclusiveness in 23–4
Red Lady of Paviland, The 63–4
relationships and sex education (RSE) 9, 42, 153
religious education (RE) 13, 152, 153
   human and social sciences (living) of 15
   philosophy (thinking) of 14–15
   in practice 15
   theology (belief) of 13–14
Ride, Sally 68
Rights Respecting Schools Awards (RRSA) 154–7
Roberts, David 51
role plays 115
Roman empire, and its impact on Britain 64

Rotich, Juliana 130
Royal Geographical Society 91
Ruby's Reads 36–7
Runnymede 31
Rustin, Bayard 61

S

Sainbury 141
Salerno, Steven 50
Salmon, Keith 100
Sanders, Rob 50
school
    development plan 198–9
    values of 18, 45, 152
    vision of 4
school community books 47
scientists as role model 122–3
Seacole, Mary 61
Shaping our future: The climate challenge (WWF) 87
Sightsavers charity, The 33
Singh, Princess Sophia Duleep 60
SMSC (spiritual, moral, social and cultural development)
    British values, teaching 153–4
    celebration, planning 158–62
    and cultural development 153
    global citizenship education 166–8
    and moral development 152
    Rights Respecting Schools 154–7
    role of 151
    and social development 152–3
    and spiritual development 151–2
    whole-school practices 158
Sometimes (Elliott) 52
song, exploring human rights through 112–13
Sotomayor, Sonialand 52
soundscapes 116
spices, history of 68
Sport England 138
staff CPD
    disability-inclusive teacher training 33
    LGBT-inclusive teacher training 32
    racial literacy teacher training 32

Stand with refugees project 90
STEM (science, maths and technology)
    computing 128–9
    design and technology (DT) 131
    maths, teaching 125–8
    research opinion on 119–21
    science, teaching 121–4
    women in 123–4
Stonewall Rainbow Laces Campaign 143
Stonewall 10, 32, 137
story, weather exploration through 86
subject action plans 198–9
Suffragettes: The battle for equality (Roberts) 51
Sulwe (Nyong'o) 49
Sustainable Development Goals (SDG) 21, 79–80, 81, 83, 85, 86
symbols 15, 34, 35, 91, 125
symbol-supported resources 34, 35

T

taking the knee, protest in sport 145
Tan, Shaun 50
Tereshkova, Ludmila 68
theatres visit 96
This Book Is Anti-Racist (Jewell) 50
This Girl Can @thisgirlcanUK 148
thoughts, diversity of 5, 15, 22
Todd, Jason 71
Tudors, history of 69
Tull, Walter, and World War I 61
Turing, Alan 68

U

Under My Hijab (Khan) 50
United Nations
    Convention on the Rights of the Child 154
    Sustainable Development Goals (SDG) 21, 79–80, 81, 83, 85, 86
Universal Declaration of Human Rights 6

V

Victorians 71
Vikings 65–6
visual supports in literacy curriculum 34, 35

W

Warhol, Andy 100
water fight (Water Aid website) 87–8
weather exploration, through story 86
Wharton, Arthur 72
whole-school calendar 158
whole-school curriculum map 56, 57, 58, 171
whole-school intent for new curriculum
  curriculum statement for 18
  diverse curriculum designing, research on 24–6
  educational principles of 17–18
  global citizenship and 20–2
  inclusive recruitment, importance of 22–4
  local community networks and 18
  purpose of 17
  schemes of work and long-term planning in 19
  Sustainable Development Goals (SDG) and 21
whole-school map for genres of music 105
whole-school themes 56, 99, 105, 109, 171, 172
Wiltshire, Stephen 101
women and space, history of 68
Wonder (Palacio) 52
world music 110–12
writing, genre of literacy curriculum 29–30, 35

Y

Yiadom-Boatye, Lynette 101
Youth Sport Trust 139, 141
Youyou, Tu 124

Z

Zubayda Bint Ja'far Al-Mansur 75